Plants for the Future

A Gardener's Wishbook

Plants for the Future

A Gardener's Wishbook

JEROME MALITZ

*To Lois & Frank,
Remember crops forever!
Jerry*

Timber Press
Portland, Oregon

ISBN 0-88192-349-4

Printed in Hong Kong

TIMBER PRESS, INC.
The Haseltine Building
133 S.W. Second Avenue, Suite 450
Portland, Oregon 97204, U.S.A.

Library of Congress Cataloging-in-Publication Data

Malitz, Jerome, 1936–
    Plants for the future : a gardener's wishbook / by Jerome Malitz.
        p.   cm.
    Includes bibliographical references and index.
    ISBN 0-88192-349-4
    1. Plants, Ornamental—Breeding. 2. Plant introduction. 3. Plants,
Ornamental—Varieties. I. Title
SB406.8.M34   1996
635.9′1523—dc20   95-37113
                                                              CIP

To Suzy, Seth, and Jed

Contents

Color plates follow page 128

Preface

Although occasionally some wonderful new plant of garden merit is found in the wild, the golden age of plant discovery is now surely behind us. Today, most of our new plants are hybrids and chance mutations of old garden favorites. In the future, it is likely that more and more of our garden ornamentals will come into existence by way of the knowledge and techniques discovered in the laboratory, and not by exploration in the field. And we can be certain that many of the new plants will be radically different than any seen so far.

Wondrous processes to bring about the revolution are already in place, and new ones arise year after year. Some of these, like cell culture techniques, manipulate bits and pieces of plants. Other strategies, such as gene transfer, sculpt new organisms at the molecular level, altering the very genetic code itself. Although there is no doubt that the traditional pollen-to-stigma approach will continue to be the major tool in the development of new plants, the older methods will be enhanced and facilitated by newer ones, presenting all sorts of exciting possibilities.

This book is intended to encourage the quest for new plants, to present worthwhile objectives, and to describe strategies likely to achieve them. How can we improve upon the many garden plants that we currently know and love to grow? How can we circumvent their faults? Would it be possible to create new plants that possess the spectacular ornamental qualities of some tropical species, but which are hardy enough to be grown in non-tropical gardens? And new colors, shapes, and sizes are always appreciated by garden enthusiasts.

The first part of the book presents brief, elementary surveys of several topics that are of fundamental importance to the development of new plants: genetic relatedness, as illustrated by plant classification; advances in biotechnology that are now ready to serve ornamental horticulture; and universal goals in plant development and the strategies that can be used to pursue them.

The second part of the book discusses the potential contributions of forty-five plant families. Some of the families are little known and under appreciated; others are garden favorites of long standing, with much more yet to offer. I discuss the merits and shortcomings of various members of each family, and emphasize the need to introduce new plants that will improve the offering.

Throughout, suggestions are made for bringing desired new plants into being. Some of the strategies involve only traditional methods, others require more modern techniques, and still others suggest a blend of the two approaches. Some of the goals will be easy to obtain, some difficult, and some impossible. But whatever the method, the promise is there: a garden of new plants, plants of unimagined beauty and adaptability—plants that garden dreams are made of.

Acknowledgments

In preparing the manuscript, I was most fortunate in obtaining comments and suggestions from several people. I wish to express my gratitude and thanks to the following, who gave of their time and knowledge so graciously and patiently.

Professor Lois Abbott, of the University of Colorado Biology Department, made several useful recommendations regarding the presentation of the material on taxonomy and genetics. Horticulturists Tim Mahony, of Sturtz and Copeland Nursery, and Pamela Perry, Elinor Wilshop, and Kelly Grummons from the Paulino Gardens nursery, generously shared their wealth of horticultural information with me. Dr. Jeffrey Haemer, of Canary Software, explained several of the more complicated techniques of plant biotechnology to me. Professor Richard Holley, from the University of Colorado Mathematics Department, prepared the figures that accompany the text. Professor Thomas Ranker, of the University of Colorado Biology Department, clarified various methodologies used in taxonomy. Professor Warren Wickelgren, neurophysiologist at the University of Colorado Medical Center, read the manuscript and made several useful comments that helped clarify the chapter on genetics. My son Seth was of great assistance, and contributed several of the photographs.

And I owe special thanks to my long-suffering wife Susan, who proofread the manuscript and provided encouragement throughout the project.

PART I

Creating the Plants
of the Future

CHAPTER 1

Introduction

All gardeners are pie-in-the-sky visionaries—sanguine optimists who see in every winter storm the moisture to prime a flower-filled spring. They imagine their gardens bursting with more plants than their tract has in square inches, and each plant is seen as a specimen of perfect form and beauty far beyond its genetic endowment.

Every garden catalog plays to this blind optimism, irresistibly tempting the Nebraskan with cotton-candy rhododendrons, the Floridian with plant jewels from the highest and driest regions on the planet, and the Arizonan with ever-thirsty primulas and other lovely swamp things. In the dim light of winter, the gardener can see these as dominant features of the landscape, full grown and grown to full perfection. With imagination so kindled, the gardener goes on to envision all sorts of other plants, each of which would make an enormous contribution to the landscape if only they existed and could survive there.

On the other hand, who but the dreamer could have foreseen today's German bearded iris cultivars in their species precursors? Who but the visionary could have imagined azaleas bred in Minnesota for bud hardiness to −35°F (−37°C)? What about evergreen hollies of the English type pushing their luck into zone 4? These are but a few examples of what foresight, patience, and knowledge can accomplish. Although a plant development program may go on for years and involve the work of many people, there are many examples of great successes realized by single individuals in a relatively short time.

Plant breeding is a popular hobby, and many of us have been tempted to set anther to stigma either to satisfy idle curiosity or for some more purposeful end. All sorts of clubs and societies foster the pursuit of new plants: there is a *Hemerocallis* society for daylily enthusiasts, a *Penstemon* society, a *Hosta* society, a *Primula* society, a gentian society, infinitely many rose societies, and societies for Siberian iris, for remontant iris, for Pacific Coast iris, for Louisiana iris, and who knows what other iris. For many, the game is simply to add more frills and ruffles. Do we really need yet another peach-colored German bearded iris, even if it does have blue beards? Will this year see another thousand daylilies registered? I suppose so, if the breeders continue to enjoy the game. And, no doubt, there will be scores of new rhododendrons and roses to add to the list, many of them barely distinguishable from already existing ones.

Yet, although many of these "new" plants may not seem to be of particular consequence, the possibilities for creating radically different plants seem endless. The desire certainly is there and the need may be also. There is no shortage of past horticultural accomplishments to inspire further pursuits, and science and technology offer support as never before. Of course, the new plants will be derived from existing plants, exploiting their virtues and avoiding their shortcomings. In the chapters that follow, I will describe various strategies that promise to yield radically new plants.

What can we imagine? Why not zone 3 hardy maples in all the sizes, shapes, and colors of the Japanese maples? How about flowering cherries with the indomitable constitution of the sour cherries and the drought-tolerant, cold-tolerant bush cherries? Let us have flowering dogwoods of the *Cornus florida* type that can tolerate miserable soils, fierce winds, and late-spring frosts. How about a full pallet of *Ceanothus* for those of us who know the real meaning of winter? Let us have shrubby oaks of *Quercus gambelii* hardiness with the huge exotic leaf of *Quercus macrocarpa*. Can we combine the fluorescent colors of the summer-flowering long-season Mexican phlox with those of the neater, hardier, spring-flowering moss phlox? And those of more timid imagination can look to the wizardry of the orchidists—black magicians—who create quadrageneric hybrids unlike anything seen before. Part II of this book is devoted to specific goals as applied to particular plants: Why are they needed, and how might they be achieved?

In order to appreciate the potential of the modern biotechnological methods that are now available for the creation of new plants, one must have a basic understanding of the biology of plant reproduction, Mendelian genetics, taxonomy, and the advances in plant hybridizing and cloning techniques—each a fascinating topic in its own right. Chapters two through five present brief introductions to these topics that will make the strategies for the development of new plants discussed in Part II of the book more understandable and plausible.

CHAPTER 2

What's in a Name?

The tomato and the potato belong to the family Solanaceae, although the first is a member of the genus *Solanum* and the second is a member of the genus *Lycopersicon*. Although the similarities between the two plants may not be obvious to the layperson, they are significant to the taxonomist and the decision to place them in the same family is on the mark since the two have been successfully hybridized.

Similarly, there is little in the outward appearance of barberries (*Berberis*) and grapehollies (*Mahonia*) that would suggest the two plants are close relatives, but both are members of the Berberidaceae and several intergeneric crosses between them have been made. It may surprise some that the humble bearberry (*Arctostaphylos uva-ursi*) is in the *Rhododendron* family (Ericaceae), the apple (*Malus*) is in the rose family (Rosaceae), and the crape myrtle (*Lagerstroemia*) is in the *Lythrum* family (Lythraceae), but these are all good taxonomic assignments.

What makes taxonomic relationships so interesting to the breeder is that they tend to reflect genetic similarity: two species of the same genus are more likely to be similar in their genetic makeup than two species of different genera, and the difference is expected to be even greater if the two come from different families. A good classification system, therefore, provides an approximate measure of genetic compatibility and the likelihood of hybridizing various species.

Judged by the vast number of hybrids on record, contemporary classification systems appear to have succeeded quite well. Crosses between different species of the same genus are quite common and often show a high degree of fertility; crosses between different genera of the same family are less common and often show low levels of fertility; and crosses between different families are almost unheard of. So, what's in a name? Plenty, as far as the hybridizer is concerned.

By the same token, if two species are able to cross and produce fertile progeny, one has to assume some degree of genetic similarity. In this way plant breeding experiments influence taxonomy—a neat symbiosis.

Defining the Taxonomic Hierarchy

The classification of plants and animals is hierarchical—defined groups are combined into larger, more broadly defined groups: species are collected into genera, genera are grouped into families, families are gathered in orders, orders into classes, and classes into divisions (phyla). Each such group, large or small, is called a taxon (plural, taxa). The classification scheme creates a branching, treelike structure of implied relatedness among the taxa. Figure 2-1 illustrates the stratified character of plant classification as it follows a few familiar plants down the taxonomic tree.

Exactly what defines these taxa? How is a classification scheme decided upon? These fundamental questions of taxonomy do not have clearcut answers. It is a matter of science and observation, insight and experience, with a good measure of judgment and persuasion.

The classification of plants is in a constant state of refinement; revision follows revision as new evidence is brought to bear on the relatedness between groups. Even style plays a role, and taxonomists have classified themselves into two taxa—the "lumpers" and the "splitters." Taxa such as Liliaceae have been split into several separate families by some taxonomists, only to be reunited by others. The same is true of the family Leguminosae. Some give the hydrangeas their own family, Hydrangeaceae, whereas other taxonomists accord the hydrangeas genus status within the family Saxifragaceae. Confusing? It can be, but each revision suggests

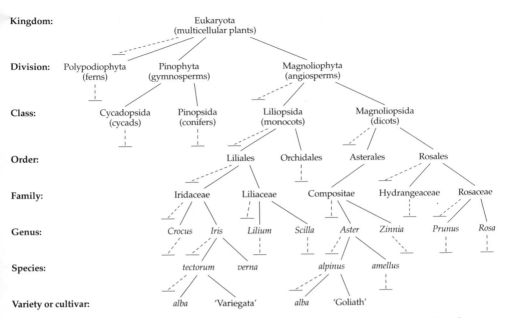

Figure 2-1. A fragment of a classification tree showing the hierarchical nature of taxonomy. Note that because different organisms evolve at different rates, the distance between the levels of the tree do not correspond to equal time intervals. The dashed lines indicate truncations of the tree where taxa are omitted. For example, the family Liliaceae contains nearly 300 genera but only two appear in the example. Nor does the example show all partition levels—subdivisions can refine divisions, subclasses can divide classes, and so on.

new possibilities for hybridization, just as it suggests moderating expectations of others.

Sources of Data

What sort of information is used in arguing for a certain classification system? Evidence is drawn from a wide variety of sources involving, with time, more and more scientific and technical sophistication. The raw data are from three different sources: (1) from the individual organism; (2) from interactions between organisms; and (3) from the interactions of the organisms with the environment.

The first category includes the following considerations: physical features (morphology); microscopic features of internal anatomy; cell structure features (cytology), such as number, shape, and size of chromosomes (karyotype); molecular evidence derived from techniques such as DNA sequencing; and chemical analyses. To date, macroscopic morphology has been the most frequently used factor in the classification of higher plants. The second source of data includes things like pollinator specificity and, most important for our interests, hybridization data. The last category of data is taken from studies of geographical distribution patterns and analyses of habitats.

So it is not for want of data that arguments arise and taxonomic relocations occur. It is a question of how one is to make sense out of all this information and decide upon a single classification system on the basis of all the data. The answer does not come easily, nor does it come without considerable controversy.

The Traditional Approach: The Relative Primacy of Traits

Traditionally, there was near universal agreement that certain plant characteristics were more fundamental to classification than others. For example, the configuration of the reproductive organs was deemed more basic than leaf shape. It was thought that classifying plants by according greater importance to the more fundamental characteristics would result in a classification tree that represented the actual evolutionary tree. Taxonomy was to mirror phylogeny.

Unfortunately, the history of plant evolution cannot be viewed directly. Some hints are found in the fossil record, but the record for plants is even skimpier than it is for animals and there are enormous gaps. Hence, attempting to classify plants according to phylogeny and evolutionary history leaves too many unanswered questions, and relatedness has to be deduced from the shared traits of existing plants.

But the question remains: How does one measure the relative primacy of traits? What degree of similarity between two plants determines that they belong to the same class, or the same family, or the same genus?

The Modern Approach:
Computers and Mathematical Formulae

Some systematists believe that the traditional methodology allows such judgments to be made on grounds that are too subjective and hence unscientific. Alternative methods have been proposed that advocate presenting the data in a more mathematical way and then analyzing it by some clustering algorithm, a mathematically explicit method of grouping data according to some precisely defined criteria. The algorithm will assign individuals to groups and then cluster groups into successively larger groups, resulting in a hierarchical classification scheme.

These approaches have several clearcut advantages over traditional methods. There is a greater degree of objectivity as the clustering is done according to the strict mathematical rules of the algorithm. The possibility of using high-speed computers to implement the clustering algorithm can be a great advantage when analyzing large amounts of data, and it can improve the rigor and clarity of the presentation of data as well.

Although a more mathematical approach has clarified many problems, subjectivity still remains. Even here one must decide which traits to analyze, how to weigh them, and which of the many clustering algorithms to use. As before, one has to decide when a cluster is called a genus, a family, a class, or some other taxon. It is doubtful whether any of these issues will ever be settled to the satisfaction of all taxonomists, and subjectivity will inevitably remain a feature of the discipline. Taxonomy will continue to be part science and part art.

In spite of the unending revisions, and in spite of all the theoretical and methodological disputes, the classifications in use have been remarkably effective in predicting the likelihood of successfully crossing various plants. The serious plant breeder has to regard taxonomy as much more than an art for art's sake—it is an inexhaustible source of ideas and information and the very best predictor we have for the success of a proposed cross.

CHAPTER 3

The Inheritance of Traits

A grain of pollen, a mere speck to the naked eye, finds its way to the stigma of a flower. There it grows a tube the length of the pistil through which it delivers half the genetic material needed to make a new organism. Waiting in the ovary are the ovules, one of which receives this haploid ration of genetic material and adds it to its own haploid supply (Figure 3-1). This creates a zygote, a fertilized cell, with a full diploid complement of genetic material that carries the complete code for the making of a new organism. The zygote divides and becomes an embryo, is encapsulated as a seed, and if the seed germinates in a hospitable situation, the embryo differentiates and grows into a complete plant. The plant displays features encoded in its genome, and if the genetic material is from two different plants, the plant will exhibit some traits of each parent and some traits that are a mixture of the two. Here, in these processes of cell reproduction and development, are the secrets of inheritance, and only by understanding some of the basic aspects of these processes can one get a sense of what can be achieved in developing new plants and what means can be used. That is the point of this chapter: to present a simplified overview of plant reproduction and inheritance, providing information that will be of use to the hybridizer.

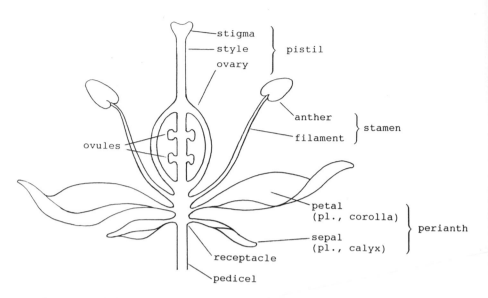

Figure 3-1. Schematic representation of the cross section of a flower.

Cells and Cell Structure

In plants as in animals, the basic building block of anatomical structure is the cell, and present in almost every cell is a copy of the organism's complete genetic blueprint. In the higher plants, the cell is enclosed in a membrane pressed against a wall composed mostly of cellulose. Inside the cell is the nucleus, and within the nucleus is a copy of the plant's genetic code. Important structures called organelles are found in the fluid (cytoplasm) that is contained between the cell and nuclear membranes. Two types of organelles, the mitochondria and the chloroplasts, contain genetic material that is also of interest to the plant breeder. Figure 3-2 presents a schematic picture of a plant cell.

Genes and Chromosomes

The genetic blueprint of an organism is laid out on the chromosomes. The chromosomes are present in pairs, called homologous pairs. In the simplest situation, one member (homologue) in each pair is the contribution of one parent, and the other is the contribution of the other parent, as in the example diagrammed in

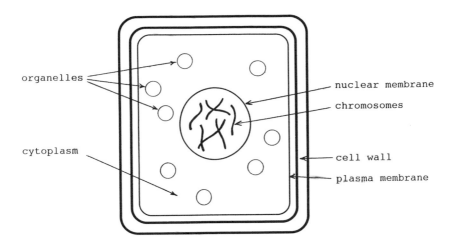

Figure 3-2. A highly simplified and schematic representation of a plant cell, showing the nucleus containing the chromosomes and the organelles found in the cytoplasm outside of the nucleus. Among the organelles are the chloroplasts, which house the mechanism of photosynthesis, and the mitochondria, which act as "energy brokers," storing and transferring energy within the cell.

Figure 3-3. The number of pairs varies from organism to organism. In most animals and plants the number is constant for the species—the human cell has twenty-three pairs, for example. In many plants, however, there can be redundant copies of homologous pairs.

The genetic information governing traits is carried by genes, each of which is a segment of some chromosome. There may be several different versions (alleles) of a gene for a given trait. For example, in the garden pea (*Pisum sativum*), which Gregor Mendel employed to such great purpose in discovering the basic laws of inheritance, flower color is governed by a gene with two alleles, one allele that determines red flowers in the plant and another that determines white flowers; we will label these alleles R and r, respectively. A plant that receives an R from at least one parent will have red flowers; if it receives an r from both it will be white. In this sense R is said to be dominant over r, and r is said to be recessive with respect to R. Similarly, there is a dominant-recessive pair of alleles for seed coat texture—W for wrinkled and w for smooth. The complete catalog of an organism's alleles is its genotype. The

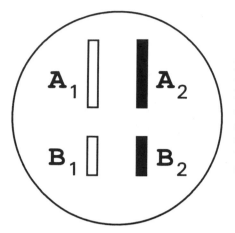

Figure 3-3. A simplified view of the nucleus of a cell of a species having four chromosomes. A_1 and B_1 come from one parent, and A_2 and B_2 come from the other parent. A_1 and A_2 constitute a homologous pair, as do B_1 and B_2.

resulting physical makeup of the organism—macroscopic, microscopic, and chemical—is its phenotype. Table 3-1 illustrates the various possibilities for the two genes in this example.

Mitosis and Differentiation

The process by which a cell duplicates itself, the process underlying an organism's growth, is called mitosis. Figure 3-4 presents a simplified version of the process, but it diagrams the essential result: a cell splits into two daughter cells, each having the complete genetic blueprint of the original cell. In this process each chromosomal homologue is duplicated, and then the cell divides into two daughter cells, each of which receives exactly one copy of each homologue from the original cell. In this way an organism grows and increases its mass, each cell retaining a copy of each of its parent's genetic makeup.

The process by which an organism is sculpted in accordance with its genetic blueprint into an intricate entity of many diverse organs is in many ways a mystery: How can simple cell duplication give rise to a wide diversity of interacting organs? If mitosis produces identical cells, how can the process yield the different cell types that distinguish tissues in the root, the stem, the leaf, and other parts of the organism? The position of cells with respect to light, gravity, and to other cells is known to be responsible for turning certain genes on and others off, thereby inducing differentiation at the cellular level. But there is still much mystery in the

Genotype	RR WW	RR Ww	Rr WW	Rr Ww	RR ww	Rr ww	rr WW	rr Ww	rr ww
Phenotype	color		red		red		white		white
	texture		wrinkled		smooth		wrinkled		smooth

Table 3-1. Given two genes, each with two alleles in a simple dominant-recessive relationship, there are nine possible genotypes and four possible phenotypes. Here the gene for flower color has the alleles R (red) and r (white), with the first dominant over the second; the gene for seed coat texture has the alleles W (wrinkled) and w (smooth), and again, the first is dominant.

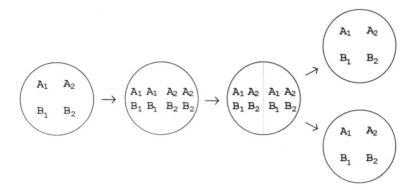

Figure 3-4. A schematic diagram of a cell with four chromosomes—A_1 and B_1 from one parent, A_2 and B_2 from the other—undergoing mitosis. The result is two cells of the same genotype as the original cell.

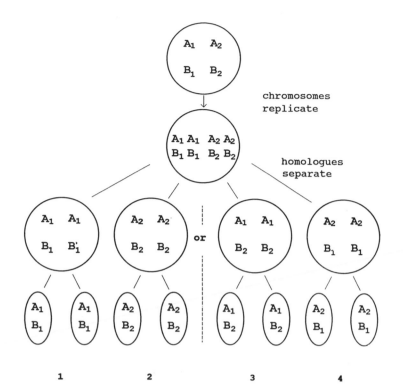

Figure 3-5. In the formation of gametes through meiosis, diploid cells divide twice, the second division resulting in haploid cells, or cells containing half the original number of chromosomes. Each of the haploid gametes receives a copy of only one member of each homologous pair of chromosomes. The allocation of homologues is independent from pair to pair, as illustrated. This simplified diagram omits several intermediate steps, but it does show the four genotypes that occur with equal probability when two homologous pairs are involved. For three homologous pairs there would be eight $(2 \times 2 \times 2)$ possible gamete genotypes.

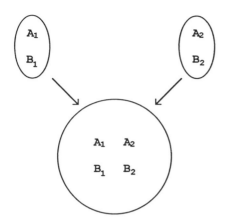

Figure 3-6. The union of two haploid gametes during fertilization produces a diploid cell in which the chromosomes are present in homologous pairs.

process, and much more research needs to be done before we can claim to have an adequate understanding of differentiation.

Meiosis

Another type of cell division serves an entirely different end. It is called meiosis and is the process by which the sex cells are produced. Sex cells, the male and female gametes, are haploid—they have only half the number of chromosomes of a somatic (vegetative or body) cell, one homologue selected at random from each homologous pair. So, when a male and female gamete unite in fertilization the result is an embryo with a full diploid number of chromosomes, again present in homologous pairs. Meiosis is illustrated in Figure 3-5, and fertilization in Figure 3-6. These diagrams for meiosis and fertilization, although greatly simplified, illustrate the crucial steps of plant development: haploid cells are produced by meiosis, and two haploid cells unite through fertilization to form a diploid zygote ready to undergo mitosis and differentiation on its way to becoming a full-fledged plant.

Generation F_2: Where Recessive Traits are Expressed

Consider a cross between individuals 1 and 2, where 1 has RR and WW as part of its genotype and 2 has rr and ww as part of its genotype. We say that 1 is homozygous for R and for W, and that 2 is homozygous for r and for w. Since 1 can only produce gametes of the type *RW* and 2 can only produce gametes of the type *rw*, it follows that the offspring all have *Rr Ww* in their genotype; that is, all offspring are heterozygous for these two genes.

The first generation of such a cross is called the F_1 generation; crossing two members of the F_1 generation produces the F_2 generation. As is demonstrated in the example above, when two homozygous individuals cross and produce a heterozygous F_1 offspring with the genotype *Rr Ww*, the F_1 generation will display only the dominant traits of *R* and *W*. If, however, as in the case of this F_1 generation, *W* and *w* are alleles of a gene situated on one chromosome and *R* and *r* are alleles of a gene situated on another chromosome, then the F_2 generation can display the full variety of genotypes and, thus, phenotypes illustrated in Table 3-1. No new genotypes will be found in successive generations, at least no new genotypes created by simple independent assortment of chromosomes of the type illustrated. Other mechanisms, however, such as "crossing over," can yield different combinations of genes and, thus, more variations of phenotype. Crossing over and other such mechanisms for variation are discussed later in this chapter.

The following coin-tossing experiment provides a convenient model for the breeding experiment described above. Suppose player 1 tosses two coins, a quarter and a nickel; and suppose that player 2 does the same. An *R* is recorded if heads comes up when player 1 tosses the quarter, and an *r* is recorded if it is tails; a *W* is recorded if heads comes up when player 1 tosses the nickel, and if tails comes up a *w* is recorded. The same is done for player 2. For example, if player 1 tosses the quarter and it comes up tails and the nickel comes up heads, while player 2 comes up with a heads with the quarter and a tails with the nickel, it would be recorded

Player	1	2
Quarter	*r*	*R*
Nickel	*W*	*r*

As is shown in Table 3-2, there are sixteen possible outcomes in this scenario, all equally likely. Hence, the probability that any particular one of these outcomes occurs is 1/16. One of the basic laws of nature, formalized and deduced as the law of large numbers in probability theory, dictates that as the experiment is repeated over and over, it becomes more and more likely that the

Player	1	2	1	2	1	2	1	2	1	2	1	2	1	2	1	2
Quarter	R	R	R	R	R	R	R	R	R	r	R	r	R	r	R	r
Nickel	W	W	W	w	w	W	w	w	W	W	W	w	w	W	w	w
Player	1	2	1	2	1	2	1	2	**1**	**2**	**1**	**2**	**1**	**2**	1	2
Quarter	r	R	r	R	r	R	r	R	**r**	**r**	**r**	**r**	**r**	**r**	r	r
Nickel	W	W	W	w	w	W	w	w	**W**	**W**	**W**	**w**	**w**	**W**	w	w

Table 3-2. The sixteen possible outcomes of the coin-tossing experiment.

ratio of tosses that result in any one of the sixteen possible genotypes will be close to 1/16.

Relating the sixteen possibilities of the model to the genotypes in the breeding experiment discussed above, and assuming that R is dominant over r and that W is dominant over w, what is the expected ratio for the phenotype white-wrinkled? Since such a phenotype can be obtained only from the three genotypes in boldface in Table 3-2, the expected frequency is $3 \times (1/16) = 3/16$. The expected frequency for the phenotype red-smooth is also 3/16, for red-wrinkled it is 9/16, for white-smooth it is 1/16, and so on.

Of course, if player 1 is using a two-headed quarter and an ordinary nickel with one head and one tail, then one can say that player 1 is homozygous for R but heterozygous for W; that is, player 1 has genotype $RR \, Ww$. In the case of three gene sites, each on a different chromosome, in the corresponding coin-tossing model each player would toss three different coins, and so on as more and more gene sites are considered.

The special cases discussed here illustrate the importance of carrying a breeding experiment into the second generation, particularly if some new mixture of several traits is desired and there is a suspicion that the genes that code for these traits lie on different chromosomes. For example, if plants of genotype other than $RR \, WW$, $rr \, ww$, or $Rr \, Ww$ are desired, but only individuals of genotype $RR \, WW$ and $rr \, ww$ are available, one has to wait for the F_2 generation in order to reach that goal.

Meiosis and the independent assortment of chromosomes to the zygote during fertilization have been the primary tools in the creation of new plants. Several other mechanisms—such as chromosome crossovers, mutations, and the delivery of traits carried on organelles outside of the nucleus—allow for an even greater range of possibilities.

Chromosomal Crossovers

As pictured in Figure 3-5, there is a stage in the process of meiosis during which the chromosomes are duplicated—each homologue is replaced by two copies of itself, called chromatids. During this duplication process chromatids arising from different homologues can exchange corresponding segments, and this can produce different gametes; this is illustrated in Figure 3-7 using one chromosome pair. In this example of chromosomal crossover, a total of four gametes are produced.

The frequency of crossover is more or less proportional to the distance between the gene sites—the greater the distance, the more likely is a crossover between these sites. By noting the relative frequency of crossover between various pairs of genes, one can deduce their relative positions on the chromosome. For example, if the frequency of crossover between site x and site y is less than that between site x and site z, and the frequency of crossover between site y and site z is also less than the frequency of crossover between site x and site z, then y is between x and z. In this way, crossover frequency has been a useful tool in the construction of gene maps for various organisms, from the fruit fly to the human.

Gene Mutations

Genes are long molecular segments, each made up of an enormous number of subunits called bases (nucleotides) of which there are only four different kinds. Add a base pair, or delete a base pair, or exchange one base pair for another, and part of the code carried by the gene is altered. Such changes are called gene mutations, and often this can disable the gene entirely, usually with lethal consequences to the organism. But sometimes a mutation creates a new allele that codes for a variant of the trait, a variant that may be useful to the plant or interesting to the breeder.

Mutations arise naturally, and astute gardeners are always on

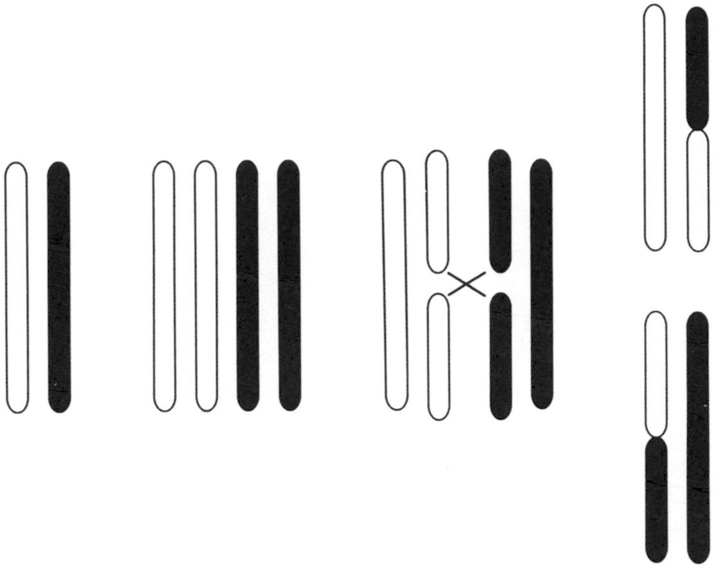

Figure 3-7. During meiosis, two chromatids, each from a different homologue, may break at the same location and exchange segments. Two new kinds of gametes will be produced with this crossing over, those with segments from the two different chromatids.

the lookout for new variants with traits such as different flower color or double flowers, increased or decreased height, better fruiting properties, interesting leaf patterns or colors or forms, disease resistance, greater pH tolerance, and increased hardiness. Such plants can be propagated vegetatively or bred to fix the trait. And if the new variant is meritorious enough, or at least different enough, the plant will eventually find its way to the gardening public.

Somatic Mutations

Another kind of mutation other than gene mutation can bring about new variants of a plant. Occasionally, a mutation will occur in a somatic cell, a cell not involved in the production of gametes. Such a cell may grow into a stem or a branch complete with leaves and maybe flowers. This "branch sport" can be cloned, or it can even be used in breeding if the trait is transmitted through the chromosomes rather than cytoplasmically. Some of the most popular garden plants originated in this way. Many variegated forms of maples (*Acer*), *Ajuga*, *Daphne*, *Hydrangea*, and ivy (*Hedera*), as well as many dwarf conifers, arose this way; some of the double-flowered cherries (*Prunus*) and crabapples (*Malus*) originated as branch sports; and there are many more examples of popular plants developed from somatic mutations.

Cytoplasmic Inheritance

With the process of cytoplasmic inheritance the development of an organism is more influenced by the female gamete than by the male gamete. A male gamete carries little more than the haploid complement of the nuclear genome—one homologue of each homologous pair of chromosomes. The female gamete is huge by comparison; in addition to a haploid complement of chromosomes, the female gamete carries a quantity of cytoplasm containing various other components, among which are factors that inhibit the expression of certain genes and factors that facilitate the expression of others.

The cytoplasm of the female gamete also contains several types of complex inclusions (separate bodies contained within the cytoplasm) that perform specific functions. In some sense they are analogous to organs, but these organelles, as they are called, are subcellular. Two types are of particular interest to us here: mitochondria, which store and distribute energy for the cell; and chloroplasts, which contain the chlorophyll that enables plants to turn the energy of sunlight into glucose. What makes these organelles so interesting to plant breeders is that they contain genes—not many, but some of importance—and these genes determine traits that are not passed on according to the scheme followed by the nuclear genes.

Since the male gamete lacks cytoplasm, and since the female gamete is rich in cytoplasm, the cytoplasmic genetic factors are solely the contribution of the female gamete. This is why the careful plant breeder will make a cross in both directions—transferring pollen from each member of the cross to the stigma of the other—keeping careful records of the results for each direction.

In some sense, the organelles lead a life of their own, replicating on a time schedule independent of that followed by the nuclear genetic material. The population of a certain organelle may increase in response to the chemical and physical environment of the cell. For example, yeast cells are resistant to certain antibiotics when they have enough mitochondria of a certain type. In the presence of the antibiotic, those cells having sufficient numbers of this type of mitochondrion have a distinct survival advantage. This creates a sort of Darwinian microcosm in which the organelles carry on a kind of struggle of the fittest, except if the fittest do not survive in sufficient numbers the cell itself will die.

Mutation, branch sports, chromosome crossover, cytoplasmic inheritance—all these processes and phenomena hold enormous promise for the creation of new plants, and some have been creatively employed by plant aficionados for centuries. Yet, there are limits. Some desirable plants are sterile. Some show such high variability when grown from seed that they need to be vegetatively cloned—a procedure that if done in the traditional way might be prohibitively slow and expensive. And one can entertain all sorts of crosses that seem promising but cannot be realized by the traditional method of applying the pollen of one species onto the stigma of another.

In the latter half of the twentieth century a whole new battery of techniques has been developed—techniques that are revolutionizing the creation of new plants and techniques with seemingly limitless potential. This new technology has been called genetic engineering and it deals with ways of altering the genetic code of an organism directly and creating new codes. Add to this new methods of hybridization, cloning, and propagation and we have what promises to be an explosion in the creation of novel plants in the years to come.

CHAPTER 4

Engineering New Plants

The early 1970s witnessed a worldwide explosion of horticultural research that opened the door to theretofore unimaginable advances in the development of new plants—advances that in some ways still seem closer to science fiction than to science. This enormously exciting and imaginative science is building the foundation of a new technology devoted to the creation and production of novel plants. To date, most of the technology has been at the service of agronomy since that is where the greatest economic incentive lies, but already there have been many applications to ornamental horticulture. Crucial to the implementation of many of the techniques is the ability to grow cells into complete organisms *in vitro*, outside of the living organism itself.

Tissue Culture and Other Cloning Devices

The seemingly magical process of taking a tiny piece from a mature plant and growing from it an entirely new, complete plant is a practice that has been employed for a long time and is the preferred way in which some root crops are propagated. Potatoes, in particular, are usually grown this way since contemporary agricultural varieties are such a complex mix that they do not come true from seed. There are limits to the usefulness of the technique, however. Cut too small a piece and it is unlikely to survive being planted out—desiccation, bacteria, and fungi take their toll. Take too large a piece and there may not be enough material to plant to make this method of propagation economical.

These problems became a major consideration in 1955, when it seemed that Ireland was about to suffer another potato blight. Blight-resistant strains were available, however, and the French government gave Professor Georges Morel the task of quickly finding an effective method of cloning these virus-free potatoes by the millions. He struck upon the idea of culturing *in vitro* undifferentiated tissue found in the growing tips of roots and stems. He found that under the right conditions the undifferentiated meristem tissue would reproduce in the test tube and form a larger and larger mass without differentiating. The mass could be separated into small pieces containing only a few cells, and each of these pieces could then be used to produce large masses of undifferentiated cells. Then, when the conditions of cultivation were changed appropriately, the masses would differentiate and grow to become entire plants.

The potato blight never materialized, and the practical aspect of Professor Morel's research in this regard was never put to the test. But Morel grew orchids as a hobby and he tried meristematic propagation of some of his plants. The technique worked beautifully! Many of the prized orchid cultivars are complex hybrids, sometimes involving dozens of crosses. Such plants cannot be expected to come true from seed, and waiting for a *Cattleya* or *Laelia* orchid to produce its one or two annual offsets will test one's patience and one's wallet. Orchids that fetched thousands of dollars in the 1920s could now be produced in quantity meristematically and sold at very affordable prices. The techniques revolutionized the orchid growing industry and revitalized the orchid hobby the world over.

Now all sorts of ornamentals are propagated by tissue culture—hostas, daylilies, roses, azaleas and rhododendrons, mountain laurels, maples, and planetrees, to name a few—and no doubt the list will grow at an even faster rate in the future. The technique's importance is not only due to its efficacy in propagating existing clones, however. At least as much promise is held by its usefulness in producing radically new plants. It is only by cell culture and tissue culture that we can exploit the latest techniques of cell fusion, *in vitro* fertilization, induced mutation, anther and ovule culture, and embryo culture.

Cell Fusion

In the seemingly futuristic process of cell fusion a single diploid somatic cell from one organism is united with one from another organism to get a single viable replicating cell that has the genetic information of both. It has been done, and it is being done more and more frequently. In fact, these wizards in white lab coats have succeeded in fusing a mouse cell and a human cell. The fused cell divides, and repeated division leads to a colony that can survive through many generations. The experiment is not merely a technical flourish—it has practical and purely scientific implications as well. As the colony grows, the cells gradually shed the human chromosomes until only one or two remain. Microscopic examination of a cell can identify which human chromosomes are present. An assay of the gene products within the cell will reveal what human gene products are present. Combine the two bits of information, and one discovers which chromosome contains the gene that codes for each product. A human gene map—a linearly ordered assignment of specific genes to specific chromosomes—can then be assembled by examining chromosome crossover events.

Although, fortunately or unfortunately, the human-mouse cell does not develop into a full-blown organism and there is no indication that any creature will develop from the fusion of cells or from tissues taken from higher animals, the situation for plants is quite different. There are many instances where cell fusion between plants of different species, even different genera, has resulted in totipotent cells, cells that have the capacity to produce entire plants—organisms completely new to the planet. For example, poplar (*Populus*) cells have been fused with beech tree (*Fagus*) cells, and poplar cells have been fused with cells from the empress tree (*Paulownia*), and entire plants were regenerated. Sometimes the cell culture shows extreme instability, shedding chromosomes haphazardly from this parent or that, resulting in an enormous variety of new creations from a single cross. Sometimes, more rarely, the cross is stable and the organism retains the complete genetic code of each parent. Either way the result is something new—very new.

Unlike animal cells, plant cells are surrounded by a cellulose-based wall, and this must be removed before fusion can take place.

Several chemical agents have been found to dissolve the wall, but usually the wall is digested enzymatically. In either case, the result is a protoplast, a naked cell with its outer cell membrane intact but no cell wall. The protoplasts tend to repel each other by a common electrical charge, but in the right medium this is avoided and some protoplasts are able to come together and fuse.

Often this fusion is partial, resulting in a cell with two nuclei and combined cytoplasm. If this cell splits, the result is usually two cells, one with the intact nucleus of one parent, the other with the intact nucleus of the other parent. One might think that little has been accomplished in this case, but often there is some exchange of cytoplasmic organelles, such as mitochondria, chloroplasts, and other plasmids. The code carried by these organelles is expressed in the new cells and in the ensuing organism if the cell divides and a plant develops. Such fusions that introduce new cytoplasmic organelles but no nuclear genes are called *cybrids*.

In other situations, cells may combine in a more complete fashion in such a way that the nuclear contents of both are present within a single nuclear membrane. Such a cell is referred to as a *somatic hybrid*.

Whether the fusion resulted in a cybrid or in a somatic hybrid, unions have been created between species that could not be hybridized in the standard way. Tomato cells and potato cells have been fused, for example, and the resulting fused cell was totipotent. Although the lack of totipotency of fused cells has been a major problem in such efforts, advances are being made and the potential for creating new ornamental plants by cell fusion is enormous.

Hunting the Chimera

The Chimera of Greek mythology was a fire-breathing monster with the foreparts of a lion, the midsection of a goat, and the hindquarters of a serpent. We do not see such creatures in real life, but in plants we occasionally find organisms composed of cells of two distinct genotypes. Such plants are called chimeras.

A chimera is not a hybrid in the usual sense, nor is it the result of cell fusion. To form a hybrid, gametes from two different taxa unite to produce a single fertilized cell—an organism in which all the somatic cells are of the same genotype as the zygote. Cell fusion, if the fused cell is totipotent, also gives rise to an organism whose somatic cells are of one genotype. In a chimera, however, the somatic cells are of two different types, each derived from a different plant. For example, *Crataegus* and *Mespilus* have been joined to produce the chimera +*Crataegomespilus*, *Laburnum* and *Cytisus* to produce the chimera +*Laburnocytisus*, and *Cydonia* and *Pyrus* to produce the chimera +*Pyrocydonia*. In each case, the resulting plant has two different cell types. +*Pyrocydonia* plants, for example, are comprised of both pear and quince cells.

Although chimeras arising from the union of different species or even different genera most pique the imagination, it is those that arise from the union of two varieties of the same species that have given us the greatest number of garden-worthy plants. The most common manifestation is a variegated leaf pattern, as in many chimeras of hostas, grasses, ivies, and pelargoniums. *Daphne* ×*burkwoodii* 'Carol Mackie', *Hydrangea macrophylla* 'Variegata', the Norway maple cultivar *Acer platanoides* 'Drummondii', and all sorts of variegated junipers and chamaecyparises are only a few of the other examples of garden plants resulting from chimeras.

The phenomenon of variegation may appear as a pattern on flowers: the picotee pattern on some gesneriads, azaleas, and petunias are examples. Flowers may show a striped, stippled, or blotched pattern as in certain carnations and roses. Or the flower form may be affected in chimeras, as in the "apetalous" form of certain erigerons, erigerons that lack typical ray florets.

Fruit can also show chimera effects, as in the classic example *Citrus* 'Bizzarria', a chimera combining citron (*Citrus medica*) and a sour orange (*C. aurantium*). Here, almost every fruit is partitioned into two parts, an orange part and a citron part. Some of our commercial apples, lemons, and pears are chimeras. Agronomists are experimenting with chimeric peaches, plums, and other fruits as well. Why? Because chimeras open the door to customized fruit. For example, the fruit can derive its flesh from the tastiest varieties and the skin from the smoothest, most colorful, and maybe sturdiest varieties.

Chimeras can arise in several different ways. A somatic cell can mutate and the clone of cells derived from it will also bear the mutation. Grafting one plant onto another plant has given rise to chimeras, as in the case of +*Laburnocytisus*, *Citrus* 'Bizzarria', and

+*Crataegomespilus*, as well as many newer examples. The most recent and promising technique involves tissue culture of two different taxa in the same test tube—with prodding, the two clones can grow together and form a complete plant.

Once you have a chimera, how do you propagate the beast? Certainly these plants cannot be propagated by seed, since the gametes will be of one parent or the other. Vegetative propagation can work quite well, whether by leaf or stem cuttings or meristem tissue culture. So, whether or not you fancy variegatas, picotees, and other chimeric manifestations, the variety and availability of these creations are bound to increase.

Variations Through Mutations

Occasionally, as discussed in Chapter 3, the genetic code in a cell will change. After all, the code is written on the genes and a gene is a very long sequence of base pairs made even more complicated by its intricate, three-dimensional folding pattern. A stray bit of radiation, a sharp temperature transition, the presence of certain chemicals, or an electrical charge can alter the structure of a gene and transform it into an unreadable strip of nonsense (by far the most common result) or into a new piece of code. In either case, the changed molecular makeup of the gene can be lethal to the cell and even to the entire organism, or in certain scenarios, it can have inconsequential and unnoticeable effects. Another possibility, and the one of greatest interest to agronomists and horticulturists, is that the mutated gene structure can result in significant morphological changes in the cell and consequently in the entire plant.

In addition to mutations that affect individual genes, there are those that act on the chromosomes. One example of this kind of chromosomal mutation occurs when an entire set of chromosomes undergoes replication but the cell fails to divide, causing a doubling of the cell's chromosome number. This phenomenon of multiple copies of the entire genome is called polyploidy, and polyploid plants often have attributes that make them highly desirable. Foliage is often more robust; the plant can be more floriferous and more fruitful; the blossoms are often larger, more substantial in texture, and more intensely colored; and in some instances the number of petals is doubled.

Mutation has long been a key player in the quest for new ornamental plants. We have always valued the unusual variety, and in the past it was often pure luck that brought a new and unusual variety to our gardens. We waited and watched and hoped—a chance chimera, a witch's broom branch sport, a color break, a doubling of petals—the mutations occurred, slowly, in their own time. Many modern daylilies and German bearded iris cultivars are tetraploids (have twice the diploid number of chromosomes of the species), and this accounts for much of their flamboyance and vigor. Some of the double-flowered cherries and azaleas are polyploids, and there are many other examples of plant varieties resulting from this kind of genetic mutation.

Several techniques have been developed that can vastly increase the rate of mutation. Electrical charge, x-radiation, and heat and cold treatment may be mutagenic, and many chemical agents have been found to encourage mutation *in vitro*. Current methods of tissue culture, cell culture, and other cloning techniques tend to yield a large number of mutations. Polyploidy can be routinely induced by irradiation or treatment with the chemical colchicine (an extract from the autumn crocus, *Colchicum autumnale*), and we are likely to see more and more polyploids in the future, although many feel that polyploids have sacrificed elegance and naturalness for their sturdiness and flamboyance.

The ease with which mutations can be encouraged in plants is the boon and bane of commercial growers—providing on the one hand new plants of potential value while destroying the genetic uniformity of the plant being cloned. The plant might be an improvement on some prize-winning daylily, but if it is not what the customer ordered there might be complaints. Nevertheless, professionals and amateurs alike, wittingly and unwittingly, have been using methods to accelerate mutation for many decades.

In Vitro Fertilization

Another technique used in the development of new plants, more familiar to us and much less astonishing than somatic cell fusion, is *in vitro* fertilization. This is the process involved in creating test-tube babies: a male sex cell is joined to a female sex cell in a test tube to create a single fertilized cell, a zygote with the full diploid chromosome complement. The zygote is then placed in a womb

where it is nurtured to full term. The procedure has been successfully used in animal husbandry for decades, and more recently in
human reproduction as a means of overcoming sterility.

In ornamental horticulture this technique augurs a bonanza
of new crosses previously impossible to make because of physical
or chemical barriers that prevent the male gamete from traveling
to or uniting with the female gamete. After fertilization the zygote
can be cultured *in vitro*, and with a bit of luck, will yield an entire
plant.

Again, we should remember that embryo culture and tissue
culture seem to encourage mutation and wide variation—a nuisance to those using the technique for the purpose of propagating
a clone but an exciting phenomenon that can multiply the possibilities for the plant breeder.

Embryo Rescue Operations

Sometimes a cross between two widely different taxa can be
made in the usual way, transferring the pollen of one plant onto
the stigma of the other. Often in such traditional crosses, however,
the zygote fails to develop. In a rapidly growing number of such
cases, the embryo can be rescued by excising it from the plant and
growing it *in vitro* to become a full-fledged plant. The naked embryo itself can be cultured, as can the ovary containing the
embryo—there are several techniques, each boasting its particular
successes. In ornamental horticulture, the technique has been used
to create the lily cultivars 'Black Beauty' and 'Eureka', crosses that
were unsuccessful without the aid of embryo rescue techniques.
No doubt we will see this device used more and more frequently,
and it is expected to become a major tool for the production of
radically new hybrids.

Haploidy from Anther, Ovary, and Ovule Culture

Organ differentiation and other variations can often be at-
tained from *in vitro* cultures of male and female gametes—the
male gamete contained in the pollen of the anther and the female
gamete, or ovule, contained in the ovary (see Figures 3-1 and 3-5).
From *in vitro* cultures, the unfertilized gametes can ultimately
grow to mature gamete-producing plants. These plants are all

haploid, and the gametes they produce are identical to the one that gave rise to them. The technique has been successfully applied to several common plants, including apple (*Malus*), buckeye (*Aesculus*), *Camellia*, *Citrus*, *Euphorbia*, grape (*Vitis*), and poplar (*Populus*).

What end is served by creating haploid plants from anther or ovary cultures? In these haploid plants you have what you see and nothing more; there is no hidden code in the sense that some recessive allele is masked by a dominant partner. These pure-bred plants are as pure as pure can be. The gametes from these haploids can be united to create new diploid plants whose genetic makeup is completely determined.

Gene Transfer Strategies

All the procedures described so far affect the number and types of chromosomes, the karyotype of the cell, but the genetic structure within chromosomes is not altered. Techniques have been developed that can introduce new genes into a chromosome, extending the genetic information.

Genes that render immunity from certain herbicides, genes that confer resistance to certain diseases, genes that alter flower color, and many other genes have been successfully transferred from one plant to another. This fine tuning of the genome avoids long and complicated breeding programs—in fact, such programs may not even be possible because of a lack of compatible partners.

How is the transfer accomplished? The most obvious way is to inject the desired gene through a microhypodermic needle, piercing the cell wall, the cell membrane, and the nuclear membrane to deposit the gene within the nucleus, where, it is hoped, it will be taken up by some chromosome. Unfortunately, this direct method is tedious and has a low incidence of success. Another procedure involves transporting the gene to the nucleus of the host cell by a benign virus or bacterium. A third method is to fuse the cell to a cell fragment that has the desired gene. In yet another method, microscopic metal fragments or pellets are coated with copies of the gene, and the pellets are loaded into a gunpowder-charged cartridge and fired into a petri dish containing the cells—the target of this small-bore shotgun shell. Some of the pellets will have just enough momentum to carry them into the interior of the nuclei of

some of the cells, where the alien gene will have a chance of link-
ing onto a host's chromosome. It all seems like magic; but success
has followed success, and though I have yet to hear of any applications to ornamental plants that have reached the public, it is
hard to see many limitations.

Past, Present, and Future

Each of the procedures described above has infinite potential
for creating new plants. Of course, there is no reason to consider
them in isolation—the various methods can be linked in a plant
development program in a variety of ways. A wide cross might be
planned and two haploid parents chosen for uniformity, the parents themselves the product of anther culture and ovule culture.
The cross might be accomplished *in vitro* or in the field, and then
the embryo might be rescued and raised *in vitro*. If the hybrid has
the desired traits, it can then be cloned by tissue culture or cell culture. This is the ornamental side of the "Great Green Revolution,"
and how lucky we are to be able to reap the benefits of it.

Ever since our species first began cultivating plants, natural
variability and selective breeding have been the basis for the development of new varieties, and these processes will continue to
play a major roll. Even the most traditional of horticulturists must
admit, however, that the new techniques of tissue culture, cell fusion, induced mutation and polyploidy, embryo rescue, *in vitro*
fertilization, gene transport, and other methods are certain to revolutionize plant breeding in agriculture as well as ornamental horticulture. There is more than a hint that new techniques will cause
plant engineering to take on features of engineering in other
areas—genotypes tweaked and customized, plants made to order.
Laboratory synthesis of specific genes, transfer of genes by plasmids, insertion of genes by viruses, and all sorts of other techniques are now closer to fact than fiction. But even with what is
currently at hand, the possibility for creating wildly new and desirable plants is real—excitingly real and eminently plausible.

For the time being, most of the techniques mentioned here are
in the domain of professional horticulturists and botanists work-
ing in well-equipped laboratories. Amateurs will most likely continue to develop new plants by the patient selection of distinctive
sports, close crosses, and line breeding; but even now many ama-

teurs employ tissue culture and colchicine-induced polyploidy in their breeding programs. There is no doubt that more and more of the techniques discussed in this chapter will become commonly used tools for amateurs, enabling the layperson to create plants that could only have been dreamed of before these innovations.

It is the beginning of a new era in ornamental plant development, and both amateur and professional will play a crucial role. With the new and the old techniques in mind and with past accomplishments for encouragement, we can imagine great possibilities for exciting new plants for the future and have some confidence that some of these plants can actually be created.

CHAPTER 5

Plant Traits of Universal Merit

Many plant attributes have nearly universal desirability, traits that contribute to the worth of the plant as a garden ornamental. Can one say that a plant has too much hardiness? Can it have too much disease resistance or insect resistance? Does it make sense to reduce drought tolerance, heat tolerance, or pH tolerance? Can we have too much genetic variability—will a plant have less ornamental value if it offers too many sizes, shapes, flower forms, and colors?

It is exactly in the pursuit of such broadly desirable qualities that the new technologies available in plant breeding and cultivation promise to make the greatest impact. Later, in Part II, we consider specific examples of pursuing such goals and suggest ways of attaining them for specific plants. Here our focus is broader, as we consider some general methods for bringing desirable traits to new and different plants.

Genetic Variability

Perhaps the most important objective in breeding ornamental plants is to increase variability; a rich gene pool provides the basis for all other breeding goals, such as those mentioned above. Some species come endowed with enormous variability; others with only a bit. There are hundreds of distinctive varieties of the Japanese maple *Acer palmatum*, for example, but relatively few of "the other Japanese maple," *A. japonicum*.

One of the most effective ways of introducing genetic variability is by crossing different plants. To exploit all the variability contained in the combined genome of a hybrid, the hybrid has to be fertile. This restriction, however, places limitations on the distance of the crosses possible; in general, although the wider crosses foster greater variability, the wider the cross the more likely it is that the hybrid will be sterile. The superb roses, mock-oranges, crabapples, magnolias, tulips and other bulb plants, and daylilies in many of today's gardens are mostly hybrids of complex ancestry, sometimes involving more than a dozen species. What led to the continued success of these lines was the retention of fertility in the crosses—the breeding could go on and on.

Up through the middle of the twentieth century successful crosses were largely the result of patience and luck coupled with restraint in choosing the distance of the cross. Now, with the advent of the new technologies, the situation has changed dramatically and we can look forward to genetic combinations previously undreamed of. Physical barriers that tend to prevent certain crosses can now be avoided by *in vitro* fertilization. The tendency of a plant to abort can be countered by embryo culture. Cell fusion and the creation of cybrids, somatic hybrids, and chimeras widely expand the notion of hybrid. The technique of gene transfer has even allowed traits of an organism from one phylum to be transferred to an organism of a different phylum. Bacteria now make human insulin, and a certain patented tomato carries a mouse gene that marks the presence of another gene that delays the onset of fruit senescence. It is truly the dawn of the golden age of horticulture.

Hybrid Vigor

In addition to broadening the gene pool, hybrids are often endowed with another benefit: vigor greater than that of either parent. Vigor can be manifest in stature, in flowering propensity and flower size, and in general hardiness. The London planetree (*Platanus ×acerifolia*), for example, is a hybrid of *P. orientalis* and *P. occidentalis* that is more vigorous and hardier than either of its parents. Hybrid vigor is a phenomenon that has been well known for more than a century, but even today it is not completely understood.

In a sense, outcrossing, which brings together in the offspring the genetic variability from different parents, is an antidote for the loss of vitality so often encountered in inbreeding and vegetative propagation and even in plants produced by tissue culture. In many breeding lines an occasional outcross is warranted to maintain the vigor of the hybrid. If the line happens to be sterile, the new strategies may work where the old ones could not.

Cold Tolerance, Heat Tolerance

Since the number of plant species drops precipitously as one moves farther and farther away from the tropical zone, the need to increase cold hardiness of ornamentals is a top priority for many gardeners. It is a goal that has been pursued for many years, pursued in the customary way by judicious selection in the field and by line breeding. Success by these methods has given us hardier azaleas, crape myrtles, dogwoods, lilacs, magnolias, redbuds, rhododendrons, roses, and all sorts of other blessings, bringing the plants into the realm of millions of gardeners who previously could not have enjoyed them.

The traditional methods are enormously time consuming and laborious, however. Observing and selecting the stock, making the crosses and gathering the seed, and planting generation after generation of seedlings can be a long and frustrating process. The new technologies promise results much more quickly.

Cells have been cultured in suspension, that is scattered throughout a growth medium *in vitro*. When the vessel is subjected to cold some cells will die, and the survivors can then grow to become mature plants. This has been done with English ivy (*Hedera helix*) and spruce (*Picea*), among others. In these cases, not only do the adult plants that are derived directly from the cell culture show an increase in cold tolerance but so do their offspring. The implications for agronomy and ornamental horticulture are profound.

Heat tolerance is another desirable trait for many gardeners and plant breeders, although there has been no work done along these lines to date. The cell culture techniques might be useful in advancing this goal as well.

Salt Tolerance

Salt-tolerant cells can similarly be selected by the method of *in vitro* cultures, and these cells sometimes can be induced to form entire salt-tolerant plants. This method has found success with the carrot (*Daucus carota*), tobacco (*Nicotiana tabacum*), rice (*Oryza sativa*), purple fountain grass (*Pennisetum purpureum*), and several others. In each of these examples, fertile plants were recovered that showed tolerance to sodium chloride. This holds great promise for gardeners who live along seaboard regions and other areas where this salt is a problem.

Moreover, these examples suggest that the technique of cell culture might be used to produce strains that are resistent to other chemicals, or maybe to high pH or low pH. Any progress toward improvement in pH tolerance, say with heaths, heathers, mountain laurels, rhododendrons, and other ericaceous plants with narrow pH tolerance, would be a boon to many millions of people. As yet, however, there seems to be no work in this direction.

Resistance to Disease

Cell culture has also been used to develop disease-resistant strains. In this case, a pathogen is added to the culture medium and some of the plant cells that survive continue growing to become mature plants. These plants and their offspring have greater resistance to the pathogen. Success has been obtained in this area with many species, including rape (*Brassica napus*), pink (*Dianthus caryophyllus*), sugarcane (*Saccharum officinarum*), eggplant (*Solanum melongena*), and potato (*Solanum tuberosum*). Most of the examples are food crops, but more application to ornamentals cannot be far off.

Resistance to Specific Insecticides, Fungicides, and Herbicides

The desirability of selecting for resistance to insecticides and fungicides is fairly obvious—if an insecticide or fungicide has to be sprayed on a crop, it is essential that the crop itself not be damaged in the process. Crop resistance to specific herbicides is also desirable because it facilitates the management of weeds that can cause a significant reduction (as much as 70%) in crop yield if left unchecked. These traits, too, have been selected for by cell culture methods. The number of successes is growing annually and, in the area of herbicide resistance, now includes tobacco (*Nicotiana tabacum*), tomato (*Lycopersicon esculentum*), and maize (*Zea mays*), where regenerated plants have shown resistance to several herbicides.

Success in this area has also been achieved by gene transfer methods, where a small number of genes that confer the desired trait are inserted directly into the host's nucleus. Tomato, soybean (*Glycine max*), cotton (*Gossypium*), oilseed rape (*Brassica napus*), and others have been successfully cultivated to have tolerance to the broad-spectrum systemic herbicide Roundup (active ingredient, glyphosate). The potential of these techniques is immeasurable, and the progress to date has been astounding.

Blocking Flower Senescence

Work with a variety of plants, particularly chrysanthemums, has increased our understanding of the biochemistry of flower aging. It is known that ethylene plays a major role in flower senescence, and its synthesis within the plant is known to be mediated by several specific enzymes. Blocking a gene that codes for even one of these enzymes by a mutation that renders the gene inoperative, for example, should do much to reduce the rate at which a flower ages.

The question of flower aging is being explored worldwide because of its potential importance to the cut-flower trade. But what gardener, amateur or professional, would not like to extend the floral display of some favorite plant, both in the ground and in the vase? This research promises a method for doing just that.

Another method of postponing senescence is to induce sterility; flowers of plants that cannot produce embryos usually have a greatly extended life. In the past, the propagation of such plants would have to be done vegetatively by cutting or division. Now tissue culture propagation methods can be much more efficient.

Another concern, perhaps related to flower senescence, that seems not to have been studied at all but that may be exploitable by advances in plant development techniques, is the matter of the shedding of a plant's spent blooms. Some plants, such as elderberries (*Sambucus*), shed their spent bloom in a discrete and timely fashion; others, such as the blackberry lily (*Belamcanda chinensis*), work them into a piece of sculpture and then dispose of them neatly. Certain plants, however, refuse to let go—they cling to their spent blossoms until the plant becomes a sad and shabby mess. Daylilies, rhododendrons, lilacs, and many other garden favorites have this unappealing characteristic, but their other attributes are so desirable that we suffer the nuisance and endure the dead-heading chores. Can we modify these plants so that they drop their blossoms when they are past their prime? If so, it would save endless hours of drudgery and go far to enhance the utility and desirability of many otherwise wonderful plants.

Exploiting Infertility

In the past, infertility meant the end of the road to the breeder who wanted to pursue a certain line. Now, with the new methods such as embryo culture and cell fusion, even infertility arising out of wide crosses can be overcome. Furthermore, tissue culture has reduced the necessity of propagating through seed, though seed is still the most economical method in most cases.

There are, however, reasons to seek infertility in certain plants. As previously mentioned, there is some evidence that sterility increases flower life, maybe even the length of the flowering period and possibly the life span of the plant itself. In addition, some plants reseed themselves to the point of weed status; in others, fruit drop is a major nuisance. If one is not interested in eating them, who needs the mess and stench of ginkgo fruit? Who needs the hazards and clutter of horse chestnuts, or the mess of fallen crabapples, or the litter of honeylocust pods? In such cases, a little plant parenthood planning may be called for, and the insertion of infertility can be a blessing. Cottonless cottonwoods are now available, as are male ginkgos and podless, thornless honeylocusts.

In addition to employing wide crosses to induce sterility, plants subjected to mutagenic agents also show a high frequency of infertility. There are well-understood cytoplasmic factors that impart male sterility, and sterile male clones can be propagated by tissue or anther culture. Clearly, several techniques can be used to obtain sterile plants where desired.

Wide Crosses, Diverse Traits—Some General Questions

Some genera consist of both trees and shrubs; others may contain trees, shrubs, and vines; and still others will contain shrubs and perennials—*Prunus, Euonymus,* and *Potentilla* are such examples. But most often a genus will not contain both woody and nonwoody plants. Many families, on the other hand, contain both woody and nonwoody genera. Bignoniaceae, for example, includes woody members such as *Catalpa* and nonwoody members such as hardy gloxinia (*Incarvillea*); Leguminosae contains the woody *Acacia* and nonwoody *Lupinus;* and Lythraceae contains crape myrtle (*Lagerstroemia*), a woody plant, and loosestrife (*Lythrum*), a nonwoody perennial. One important question for the curious breeder is whether there are any general rules regarding the woodiness of the progeny in a cross between a woody and a nonwoody plant. Is woodiness the effect of many genes? Will it be all or nothing in the first generation, or will there be a stepped gradation in the second generation?

The same kinds of questions can be raised in considering many wide crosses, such as those between vines and trees or between vines and herbaceous plants. Any general principles regarding such crosses might be useful to the hybridizer. What happens when an early-blooming plant is crossed with a late-blooming plant? Is flowering time of the progeny extended to span those of the parents; or do the progeny tend to show two flowering periods; or one or the other? Are all the possibilities present in the F_1 generation, or do we have to wait for the F_2 generation?

What if a perennial is crossed with an annual? Will we get a short-lived perennial, or can we do better than that—at least in the F_2 generation? Will the flowering proclivity of the annual be passed on to its successors?

What about the distribution of height? Are there any general principles determining the distribution of cold hardiness, drought tolerance, heat tolerance, and pH tolerance in complex hybrids? What about the distribution of leaf shape, color, and size? What about flower shape, color, and size? Wide crosses may well yield some general principles relating to these many concerns, and such general principles would likely motivate a new round of wide crosses.

Joining Forces

For those of us who look forward to new and better plants for the garden, it could not be a more exciting time. We are witnesses to the beginning of a revolution in the development of new plants. It is a revolution led by biochemists, geneticists, molecular biologists, taxonomists, and horticulturists. Basic knowledge is being gathered from so many diverse camps that it will take a great deal of time to access and assess it all, more time to translate it into practice, and still more time to put it into the service of ornamental horticulture. But it should prove to be well worth the time and effort.

The creation of new plants will surely not remain the purview of professional scientists and technicians forever. Regardless of how the goals are pursued—by the old methods or the new—amateurs will play an increasingly active and important role; but how might this participation be encouraged?

Specialty clubs clearly have fostered tremendous advances in the groups of plants they represent. The American Rose Society, the Canadian Rose Society, the Royal National Society (England), and many others are devoted to the cultivation and improvement of roses; the Australian, British, and South African fuchsia societies, among others, cater to the lovers of fuchsias; the British Cactus and Succulent Society, the Cactus and Succulent Society of America, and the Aloe, Cactus, and Succulent Society of Zimbabwe serve those with dryer tastes; and the list goes on and on. If it is classified as a plant, there is probably at least one club somewhere dedicated to its promotion. Chapters of such clubs exist in almost every major city, and they sponsor shows, award prizes for outstanding new varieties, and publish newsletters describing the newest developments in their area of interest. Perhaps the most important function of these societies is to keep the members in touch with one another, and this social contact, a reward in itself, fuels enthusiasm in the development of new plants.

The American Hemerocallis Society registers hundreds of new varieties each year—this in addition to the more than 20,000 already on the books—and the American Iris Society is not far behind in its development of new plants. Other clubs, such as the American Rhododendron Society and the American Rose Society, lag somewhat behind, but they nevertheless bring about an impressive amount of new herbage each year. In addition, there are specialty clubs devoted to primulas and peonies, penstemons and poppies, and who knows how many more just beginning with the letter p. Leaving aside the social considerations, one wonders if the benefits to gardening of all this effort and activity is as significant as it might be.

So what am I proposing as an improvement?—that's right, another club. I propose a society dedicated specifically to fostering the creation of new plants—radically new plants, not reworkings of old themes and embellishments of old patterns. Perhaps the members of such a club could exchange seed and pollen. Perhaps they could share seedlings and test them under different growing conditions worldwide, or perhaps they could evaluate their new creations and make the better ones available to the gardening public. Perhaps they could discuss larger goals and plan strategies for expanding upon existing methods and approaches, as well as considering entirely new ones.

Such a society could support a seed bank for ornamental plants, organized and run like those devoted to plants of agricultural importance. Seeds of rare ornamentals would be stored and planted out periodically to retain viability. *The Index of Plant Chromosome Numbers* is updated periodically; perhaps it could be supplemented to keep track of which genes are located on which chromosomes, and maybe keep track of crossover frequency between genes. Perhaps a club could simply keep a record of successful crosses—now that would be a help to taxonomists as well as plant breeders.

Most of all, perhaps such a club would encourage breeders in the pursuit of significantly different ornamental plants and offer the social environment to recognize and reward meritorious achievement. Anything can be accomplished under such auspices, and there is no better way to take part in the revolution occurring in ornamental horticulture.

PART II

A Wishlist

Introduction to Wishlist

There has been an explosion of knowledge in the fields of biology and biotechnology in the last century. With a better understanding of soil chemistry, genetics, and plant physiology have come remarkable advances in the management and development of crop plants. Hydroponic culture, systemic fungicides and insecticides, biological pest control, tissue culture, and all sorts of other technological advances have furthered the introduction of new plants for agriculture. The main avenues for the development of new ornamental plants, however, have been based on experience, patience, and trial and error. For the most part, low-tech rather than high-tech approaches have ruled the game, and plant breeding has proceeded, as usual, in its slow, methodical, and rather canonical way, largely oblivious to the great advances taking place in biotechnology.

This is understandable since many of the most promising innovations in biotechnology did not begin until the 1960s, and the full range of applications is still only hinted at. There is little doubt, however, that what is currently known and available has the power to revolutionize ornamental horticulture.

Tissue culture, colchicine-induced polyploidy, and induced mutation have been in use for years, even by amateurs. The effect that these techniques have had on the development and availability of such plants as hostas, iris, lilies, mountain laurels, orchids, rhododendrons, and many others has been astounding. The more recent techniques of protoplast fusion, *in vitro* fertilization, embryo culture, and gene transfer promise a much greater explosion in the number of radically new plants for the garden. The range of application of these techniques is already expanding at an astonishing rate. In the early 1980s, obtaining viable plants from protoplast fusion was a rarity, tissue culture of evergreens was generally unsuccessful, and haploid trees from tissue culture seemed a pipe dream—but within just a few years all that had changed. These biotechnological innovations began to be utilized by more and more people and with greater and greater success. Today, the possibilities are indeed limitless, but it may take some time for this potential to filter down to ornamental horticulture in the pursuit of new plants.

The wishlist that follows was assembled to encourage this endeavor and to spark further interest in the creation of new plant varieties. The entries in the list are arranged alphabetically by family name. The vernacular family name follows its scientific name, and that in turn is followed by the number of genera in the family and the number of species (here I used David Mabberley's *The Plant-Book* as the source). Under each family heading I list the genera discussed in the wishlist and others of horticultural importance. In each entry of the wishlist, the merits and demerits of some of the more important garden plants in the family are discussed. I also argue the desirability of creating new plants within the family and suggest ways of bringing them about.

In some cases, it is expected that the time-tested techniques of careful selection, close crosses, and line breeding will succeed; but in others, it is likely that newer technologies will have to be used. Not only can one expect that the new technologies will allow crosses of unprecedented width, but even crosses between related taxa with overlapping distributions that are distinct because of incompatible breeding systems. So when I suggest a cross between two taxa with incompatible breeding systems, or far enough apart to raise a skeptical brow, one must have in mind using the more modern techniques to bring it about.

The list is not intended to be a comprehensive assay of attainable breeding goals for ornamental plants, but rather, it focuses on those that we find of particular interest. Some of the projects proposed are clearly more likely to succeed than others, and some will require more time to complete. In addition, some of the goals that I propose are obviously more important than others. Many projects of considerable potential have undoubtedly been overlooked, but the hope is that plant lovers and gardeners will find enough suggestions here to encourage them to pursue the creation of radically new ornamental plants for future gardens. The prospects are great enough to set the visionary gardener dreaming, and maybe the dreams will be vivid enough to lead some to bring them to life.

ACERACEAE

Maple family   2 genera, 113 species

GENUS DISCUSSED   *Acer*

The family Aceraceae consists of only two genera, and only one of these is of established garden merit. But what a grand variety of superb plants this genus contains.

Acer Maple   PLATES 1–5

Our planet is blessed with 111 species of maples (*Acer*), most of which are native to the northern hemisphere, and this blessing is magnified by a rich assortment of hybrids and cultivars. Long considered to be among the choicest trees and shrubs, maples grace gardens of every style from zone 2 to zone 8. Some members of the genus are treasured for the shape and color of their leaves. Many are prized for their autumn tints, and others for the color, texture, or pattern of their bark. Some maples are cultivated for their habit, and some are planted for more utilitarian reasons: for shade, for fine wood, or for the sugary sap used to make maple syrup and other sweet treats.

This extraordinary variety not only exists between the many species of *Acer* but within many of the species as well. The Japanese maple (*Acer palmatum*) is a prime example, with hundreds of cultivars treasured worldwide. There are cultivars with red leaves, purple leaves, yellow leaves, and of course, green leaves. Size varies from 2-ft (0.6-m) shrubs to 25-ft (7.5-m) trees. Habit among Japanese maple varieties ranges from weeping to fastigiate, including everything in between.

Interspecific hybrids point the way to even more variety within this vast genus. Some interesting crosses that have been achieved include the Shantung maple (*Acer truncatum*) with the Norway maple (*A. platanoides*), to give such cultivars as 'Norwegian Sunset' and 'Pacific Sunset', and the sugar maple (*A. saccharum*) has been crossed with the black maple (*A. nigrum*) to produce the hybrid 'Green Mountain'.

Unfortunately, over a vast region of North America the choice of dependable maples is frustratingly narrow. The silver maple (*Acer saccharinum*) is the most ubiquitous of the North American maples. Although it is often snubbed for being weak limbed and prone to break up in snowstorms, the silver maple is a fast-growing, cold-hardy tree that is tolerant of miserable soils, shows a lovely buttery yellow fall color, and offers a variety of leaf shapes. The Norway maple (*A. platanoides*) may be the next most common maple, and it, too, shows great diversity of leaf shapes, leaf colors, and form. Overall, however, it is a rather coarse tree and a magnet for aphids. The third most commonly grown maple in harsh climates is probably the Amur maple (*A. ginnala*). It can play the role of a shrub or a small tree, and it often has a spectacular fall display. The Amur maple is hardy to zone 2 and flourishes on all types of soils, from acid to sweet and from moist to dry. It tolerates considerable shade, yet thrives in full sun. However, this maple is prone to snow damage.

In addition to these three species, several other maples are able to adapt well to difficult sites, but they are much less frequently encountered. The bigtooth maple (*Acer grandidentatum*) and the Rocky Mountain maple (*A. glabrum*) are native to the Rocky Mountain region of North America and tend to grow as shrubs. The hedge maple (*A. campestre*) and the Shantung maple (*A. truncatum*) show some promise, but they are seldom used. As yet, the assortment of maples being grown inland is only a small fraction of those being grown near the coasts.

So the need is clear, and the capabilities for satisfying that need seem to be right at hand. With a little science and creativity, the diversity of form, color, and habit of the Japanese maple could be combined with the hardiness and adaptability of the Amur, hedge, bigtooth, silver, mountain, or Norway maples—hybridize the Japanese maple with the others and the possibilities and the benefits to gardeners would be substantial.

Many other crosses have similarly exciting potential. Consider crossing the zone 5 bigleaf maple (*Acer macrophyllum*) with one of the hardier and more adaptable maples—maybe with a dwarf Amur maple, or better yet, with one of the small globe-shaped clones of the Norway, red, or sugar maple. Might this yield a tree or shrub of modest size with extremely bold and beautiful leaves? Would the full moon maple (*A. japonicum*) or the vine maple (*A. circinatum*) impart their eleven-pointed leaf and blazing fall color to hardier partners in a cross? No genus holds as much promise as *Acer* for satisfying the need for more small, hardy shade trees of four-season interest.

ARACEAE

Arum family 106 genera, 2950 species

GENERA DISCUSSED *Alocasia* • *Anthurium* • *Arisaema* • *Arum* •
Lysichiton • *Philodendron* • *Zantedeschia*

OTHER ORNAMENTAL GENERA *Aglaonema* • *Caladium* •
Dieffenbachia • *Monstera* • *Spathiphyllum* • *Syngonium*

The arum family contains some of the most ornamental foliage plants. We decorate our homes and offices with them, coddle them in greenhouses, and grow them in aquaria. A few are occasionally planted in our gardens, but how pleasant it would be to have more Araceae available for outdoor use in temperate zone landscapes.

Alocasia, Anthurium PLATES 6, 7

Among all the plants in the vast arum family, none have more strikingly beautiful foliage than the alocasias and anthuriums. Atop 18-in (46-cm) stalks, the 16-in (41-cm) long, dark velvety green, arrow-shaped leaves of the green velvet alocasia (*Alocasia micholitziana*) show off a bold yet simple venation pattern in brilliant white. *Alocasia sanderiana* and *A.* ×*amazonica* (a hybrid of *A. lowii* × *A. sanderiana*) have somewhat larger leaves on slightly shorter stalks. They are less velvety and more leathery, but they have the same sort of vein pattern as the leaves of *A. micholitziana*. *Alocasia cuprea* is smaller and has oval, slightly convex, dark, shimmering leaves 12 in (30 cm) long; the veins are so deeply set that the leaves appear corrugated.

Many people are familiar with only one species of anthurium, the florist's flamingo flower (*Anthurium andraeanum*), with its big, brash, veiny spathes in white, pink, or scarlet. They are crass, but they might be used to impart a bit of flamboyance to more modest members of the family, so keep them in mind.

Anthurium clarinervium and *A. crystallinum* have broad, heart-shaped, velvety green leaves with a superb venation pattern in crystalline white. *Anthurium clarinervium* is shorter at 8 in (20 cm), with leaf blades to 7 in (18 cm); *A. crystallinum* grows to 20 in (51 cm) and has 12-in (30-cm) leaves. *Anthurium warocqueanum* has leaves of the same pattern as these other two anthuriums, but *A. warocqueanum*'s are much longer (to 3 ft (0.9 m)) and narrower. The leaves of *Anthurium veitchii* are the same size and shape as those of *Anthurium warocqueanum*, but they are embossed like the leaves of *Alocasia cuprea*. These last two anthuriums are more vine-like than the others.

Many of these alocasias would make fine designs for cere-monial shields, and the anthuriums could inspire ritual pennants. Several of these plants from each genus are more adaptable than previously believed, and some hybrids and cultivars now on the market can be grown as houseplants, although they do require some shade and perfect drainage.

Arisaema Jack-in-the-pulpit   PLATE 8
Arisaema americanus is our most familiar Jack-in-the-pulpit. Simultaneously stately, strange, and beautiful, this zone 3 plant grows to 2 ft (0.6 m) in height. The tripartite leaves, the greenish spathes, and the cluster of scarlet berries are all both interesting and ornamental. Even more exotic-looking species, such as the zone 5 *A. sikokianum*, are highly coveted and quite expensive. A few interspecific crosses of arisaemas have been made, and these seem to exhibit some hybrid vigor.

Arum
The Italian arum (*Arum italicum*), particularly in the cream-spotted cultivar 'Pictum', is a striking plant, with its arrow-shaped leaves, its large whitish spathe, and its stalked cluster of red berries. The leaves of *A. italicum* come up in late autumn and last until flowering time in the spring. It grows to 18 in (46 cm) and is hardy to zone 6 (and maybe to zone 5 if well sited).

Lysichiton Skunk Cabbage
The western version of skunk cabbage (*Lysichiton americanus*) is a prized ornamental. Its 2-ft (0.6-m) leaves and 2-ft (0.6-m) yel-low spadices emerge from a crown to form a bold feature that is perfectly suited to a waterside garden. Not as malodorous as its eastern relative (*L. camtschatcensis*) and far more ornamental, this distinctive plant is hardy in zone 4.

Philodendron
Philodendron is another genus in the family Araceae whose members are noted for their remarkably beautiful and distinctive leaves. Some philodendrons, such as *Philodendron verrucosum* with

its heart-shaped leaf blades to 2 ft (0.6 m), shiny as satin and intri-
cately patterned with veins of a lighter green, have such exacting
requirements that they are best grown in the greenhouse. Others
are adaptable enough to be commonly grown for indoor decora-
tion, and *P. selloum*—that most familiar philodendron with its
short, stout trunk and its 3-ft (0.9-m) long, deeply lobed leathery
leaves—can be grown outdoors throughout the year in zones 9
and 10.

Other favorites include the birdnest philodendron (*Philodendron wendlandii*) and the quilted birdnest philodendron (*P. wendlandii* 'Lynette', a hybrid of *P. wendlandii* and *P. elaphoglossoides*).
The plants have elliptical, shiny leaves growing in a rosette from
a stout crown. *Philodendron wendlandii* grows to 2.5 ft (0.75 m), and
the quilted form grows to only 2 ft (0.6 m) but its leaves are trans-
versely corrugated to add to its interest.

Zantedeschia Calla Lily

In zones 8 through 10, calla lilies (*Zantedeschia* spp.) are grown
as garden plants, often near the water's edge. Decorative arrow-
shaped leaves, some flecked with translucent silvery spots,
emerge from rhizomes on plants 1 to 3 ft (0.3 to 0.9 m) in height.
But it is their inflorescence that brings the calla lilies their fame:
long-stemmed chalices (spathes), as much as 10 in (25 cm) long in
white, pink, or yellow, some with a purple blotch at the base, sur-
round a yellow spadix. The simple elegance of the inflorescence
gives the calla lily a noble solemnity that has made it a choice
flower for funeral arrangements. This, it should be said, in no way
blunts the appeal of the plant's singular beauty. Unfortunately,
not many of us can enjoy calla lilies in a garden setting.

But why should temperate zone gardeners care about these
tropical and subtropical aroids, like the calla lilies, philodendrons,
alocasias, and anthuriums? In their world this family is nearly in-
visible. Only the caladium (*Caladium bicolor*) is commonly grown,
and then only as a summer plant—the tuber to be lifted and stored
in autumn. Other members of the family Araceae, however, such
as the Italian arum, Jack-in-the-pulpit, and skunk cabbage, have
garden merit in temperate zones.

What contrasts one finds in this single family! *Arisaema* and
Lysichiton are rugged and hardy woodlanders adapted to heavy

moist soils; *Alocasia, Anthurium,* and *Philodendron* are tropicals that require perfect drainage; and the calla lilies are subtropical bog plants.

Suppose *Arisaema* and *Lysichiton* could be made to join forces with the other more decorative Araceae found in tropical regions: Would that foster an entirely new race of stunning foliage plants for temperate gardens, plants whose patterns, colors, and textures would outshine many of those we now cherish? Maybe so, provided we can take full advantage of the growing opportunities being presented in the breeding of ornamental plants.

BERBERIDACEAE

Barberry family   15 genera, 570 species

GENERA DISCUSSED   *Berberis* • *Mahonia* • ×*Mahoberberis* • *Nandina*

OTHER ORNAMENTAL GENERA   *Epimedium* • *Podophyllum* •
Vancouveria

The Berberidaceae are a family of very useful, if not overused, plants. Most have excellent foliage, a few have appealing flowers, at least one is a superb groundcover, and some are renowned for their elegant structure. Fall color is a hallmark of the barberry family, and the palette includes purples, oranges, and the most fiery reds. Hardy members abound in this family, although many are pushing their luck when they venture into regions colder than zone 6.

Berberis Barberry
Barberries are noted for their rugged constitution, though they vary in their tolerance of cold. The zone 4 Japanese barberry (*Berberis thunbergii*) is most commonly grown as a hedge plant, but cultivars ranging in height from 2 to 6 ft (0.6 to 1.8 m), with purple, red, yellow, and variegated leaves, are sometimes grown as specimens. Even the green-leaved forms are spectacular when they take on their fiery fall colors. The Korean barberry (*B. koreana*) is zone 3 hardy and has attractive 3-in (7.5-cm) pendant racemes of yellow flowers in the spring, but its fall color is no match for the Japanese barberry.

The evergreen barberries, such as Darwin's barberry (*Berberis darwinii*), and those renowned for their floral display, such as the rosemary barberry (*B.* ×*stenophylla*, a *B. darwinii* × *B. empetrifolia* hybrid), are less hardy—*B. darwinii* to zone 8, and *B.* ×*stenophylla* to zone 7. Crossing these less-hardy barberries with the hardier ones could bring evergreen and flowering barberries into entirely new regions. Since there are many hybrid barberries already on record, such as the Chenault barberry (*B.* ×*chenaultii* = *B. gagnepainii* × *B. verruculosa*), Frikart's barberry (*B.* ×*frikartii* = *B. candidula* × *B. verruculosa*), and Mentor barberry (*B.* ×*mentorensis* = *B. julianae* × *B. thunbergii*), such a plan for developing new hybrids seems quite reasonable.

Mahonia Grapeholly

Creeping grapeholly (*Mahonia repens*) is one of my favorite groundcovers. Certain populations of this hardy mahonia are zone 4 hardy, and some stalwarts nudge into zone 3. In fact, it is one of the very few broadleaved evergreens adapted to dry heat, alkaline soil, and cold. Depending on the plant, this stoloniferous shrub can grow to between 1 and 3 ft (0.3 and 0.9 m). In autumn, the matte, hollylike leaflets of *M. repens* turn a startling bronze, red, or purple hue in some clones but remain green in others. Over a long period in late spring, creeping grapeholly bears clusters of brilliant yellow flowers, and these in turn give way to purple-blue fruits that remain decorative for a long time.

What more can one ask of this plant? Since the species shows considerable variability, selections should be made for height and fall color, as well as for flower color, quality, and abundance. Why not make a very useful shrub even more so?

In addition to the creeping grapeholly, several other mahonias are garden-worthy plants, including the Oregon grapeholly (*Mahonia aquifolium*), the leatherleaf mahonia (*M. bealei*), and *M. lomariifolia*. The Oregon grapeholly is hardy, with some protection, to zone 4, and it has varieties that grow to only 2 ft (0.6 m) and others that grow to as much as 7 ft (2 m). The leaves and flower clusters are similar to those of *M. repens*, but the leaflets are much glossier. *Mahonia bealei* and *M. lomariifolia* are hardy only to zones 7 and 9, respectively. These two species have larger leaves clustered at the ends of upright stems, and this "legginess" gives them a striking architectural character akin to some palms and sumacs. The flower clusters are also different than those of other common mahonias—longer, drooping clusters, somewhat like those of a giant yellow-flowering *Pieris* of the family Ericaceae.

What would we get if we crossed *Mahonia repens* with one of these more bold and upright species? Any approximation to the latter would be greatly appreciated and also quite useful. Furthermore, if the flower display could be transferred, there would certainly be no complaints.

×*Mahoberberis*

×*Mahoberberis*, a cross between *Mahonia* and *Berberis*, is an example of the willingness of members from different genera within the barberry family to hybridize. What did this cross yield? As far as I have seen, not much; but maybe an F_2 generation is worth pursuing, especially in a cross between the more tender mahonias and the more hardy barberries. Maybe we could capture some of the grace of *Mahonia* and combine it with some of the hardiness of *Berberis*. It is worth a try, and ×*Mahoberberis* is evidence of the potential for hybridizing within the family Berberidaceae.

Nandina Heavenly Bamboo

Heavenly bamboo is the common name for *Nandina domestica*, the only species in its genus, and the name is well taken—the plant is heavenly in its elegance and has the look of true bamboo. Unlike bamboo, however, the flowers of *N. domestica* give way to clusters of red berries, and autumn paints the foliage in incandescent reds. Cultivars vary in the size and placement of their leaflets. There are forms that are dense and forms that are open, forms that are bold (but never coarse) and forms that are airy and light. Some of the cultivars barely reach a height of 1 ft (0.3 m) but others top 6 ft (1.8 m). There are even some miniatures that mature at 4 in (10 cm) with stems seemingly devoid of leaves, giving the plant a hairlike fineness, and some of these miniatures are colored red throughout the year.

Clearly, there is much to choose from among the many forms of heavenly bamboo; unfortunately, this assortment is restricted to zone 6 and above. In zones colder than zone 6 the only substitute for *Nandina* that I know of is the false spiraea (*Sorbaria sorbifolia*, in the family Rosaceae), but it is second best at best.

Since *Berberis* and *Mahonia* are willing to mate across genus lines, why not encourage *Nandina* to join the game? Each of the three genera is so highly individualistic that it may be necessary to carry the adventure into the F_2 generation in order to properly assess its worth. Should the experiment succeed, however, we may get a taste of heaven in zone 4 gardens with a plant that has the grace of heavenly bamboo and the ruggedness of barberry.

BETULACEAE

Birch family   6 genera, 150 species

GENUS DISCUSSED   *Betula*

OTHER ORNAMENTAL GENERA   *Alnus* • *Carpinus* • *Corylus* • *Ostrya*

Included among the Betulaceae are some extremely popular, overused trees and some little-known, underused trees of considerable promise. Hop hornbeam (*Ostrya virginiana*) and American hornbeam or ironwood (*Carpinus caroliniana*) fall into the latter group, and they need only a little publicity to get the attention they deserve. Birch trees, on the other hand, have some major problems.

Betula Birch   PLATE 9
    Queen-of-the-forest: an apt title for either the European white birch (*Betula pendula*) or the paper birch (*B. papyrifera*). Both species of birch are lithely built, with a fairly open crown of ovate leaves (about 3 in (7.5 cm) long) that turn lovely shades of yellow to golden brown in the fall. Both have papery, brilliantly white bark, a singularly striking feature in the landscape throughout the year. Add to this a hardiness range of zone 2 to zone 6, and it is easy to justify the worldwide popularity of these trees.
    Unfortunately, these birches and most other members of the genus have problems—major problems. The very beauty of the bark—its purity of color, its thin and delicate texture, and its obvious vulnerability—is for many an open invitation to peel it, slash it, and engrave it with inane love sonnets. Both the European white birch and the paper birch are also susceptible to numerous diseases and insect pests. Some of these pests, like the birch leaf miner, disfigure the tree, and others, like the bronze birch borer, threaten its very life. Effective control of some of the most serious pests is often difficult; legal control of the human pests, the thoughtless vandals, is impossible. Of the two trees, the paper birch appears to be significantly more resistant to both the bronze birch borer and the birch leaf miner, and this tree is considered the best of the birches by Donald Wyman, renowned former horticulturist at the Arnold Arboretum.
    What can be done to make the necessary improvements in

these trees? I do not see a quick fix, and this is more of a plea for attention to the problem than a proposed solution. However, a cross between the 'Whitespire' cultivar of the Japanese birch (*Betula platyphylla* var. *japonica* 'Whitespire') and either *B. pendula* or *B. papyrifera* might hold promise. 'Whitespire' is somewhat resistant to the bronze birch borer, it will take some drought, and it is very tolerant to both heat and cold. Although it is white, the bark of 'Whitespire' is a chalkier white than the silky white color of the bark of the other birches, and it does not exfoliate. 'Whitespire' may be the closest one can come to a substitute for the European white birch or the paper birch, but it is not the real thing. We will have to see whether a cross can preserve the grace and beauty of the European or paper birch while giving it the greater hardiness of 'Whitespire'.

In climates with a marked winter, only the quaking aspen (*Populus tremuloides*, in the family Salicaceae) rivals the white-barked birches in graceful habit and in the white linear pattern that the trunks impart to a landscape, but the aspen, too, is beset by all sorts of pests and diseases. Unfortunately, there is no satisfying substitute for the European white birch and the paper birch for their contribution to a landscape's design, and so I believe that of all the goals set forth in this book, none is more important to ornamental horticulture than the improvement of these two birch trees.

BIGNONIACEAE

Trumpet-creeper family   112 genera, 725 species

GENERA DISCUSSED   *Campsis • Catalpa • Incarvillea • Jacaranda •*
Tabebuia

Only a few members of the family Bignoniaceae hold wide acceptance as garden ornamentals, but what few there are offer some exciting possibilities. Not only does this family include a couple of the most outrageously flamboyant tropical trees, but it also has several thoroughly hardy members that are scene stealers in their own right. Herein lies the promise.

Campsis Trumpet Creeper, Trumpet Vine   PLATE 10
The trumpet vine (*Campsis radicans*) is—as its name suggests—a vine with large (3 in (7.5 cm) long and 1.5 in (4 cm) wide), trumpet-shaped blossoms in yellow, orange, or red. The vine can scramble upward to 40 ft (12 m) and forms a stout trunk. The 15-in (38-cm) pinnate leaves densely clothe the vine, giving it a somewhat coarse appearance, but in bloom, with its foxglovelike flowers, the plant is undeniably showy. The trumpet vine will bloom from early July to late August. It is zone 4 hardy and an undemanding, rampant grower.

Catalpa   PLATES 11, 12
I personally love the hardy catalpas—particularly *Catalpa bignonioides* and *C. speciosa* and their cultivars—but I would never plant one in my yard. They are too big (*C. bignonioides* to 40 ft (12 m), and *C. speciosa* to 60 ft (18 m) or more), too coarse, too ungainly, and too messy, littering the ground with faded blossoms, 18-in (46-cm) pods, and 12-in (30-cm) leaves. But when they have the stage to themselves, what a show they put on. These hardy catalpas flower in early summer when most flowering trees are out of the limelight, and the 10-in (25-cm) panicles of bloom, as well as the individual frilled, trumpet-shaped, 2-in (5-cm) white blossoms, create a spectacular display. The huge, heart-shaped leaves are as bold as any found in regions colder than zone 8, yet these trees have no problem coping in zone 4, and they thrive in drought, miserable soils, and high winds.

Incarvillea Hardy Gloxinia

Hardy gloxinia (*Incarvillea delavayi*) is a herbaceous perennial. The 2-in (5-cm) flowers, clustered at the top of stems as much as 3 ft (0.9 m) tall, come in a variety of pinks from near white to near red. It has the appearance of a tropical but is actually quite hardy, at least to zone 5.

Jacaranda

The leaves of *Jacaranda mimosifolia* are twice compound, delicate, and graceful, not at all like those of the catalpas; it is not until one examines the flowers and fruit that the similarities between these two plants become apparent. The blue-violet, foxglovelike 2-in (5-cm) flowers of the jacaranda are born in impressive 8-in (20-cm) panicles in the spring, and the beauty of the tree is unsurpassed at that time. It grows to 50 ft (15 m) and is fairly soil tolerant, given good drainage. Unfortunately, this magnificent tree is reliable only to zone 9 or 10.

Tabebuia Golden Trumpet Tree

The fabulous golden trumpet tree (*Tabebuia chrysotricha*) is another zone 10 treasure. Blooming on leafless branches in the spring, the massive clusters of 4-in (10-cm), trumpet-shaped yellow blooms on this 50-ft (15-m) tree are unforgettable. With its shiny, oblong, 4-in (10-cm) leaves and a pleasing form, the golden trumpet tree is a landscape asset in every season—at least in those zones that have no true seasons.

Even limiting the discussion of the Bignoniaceae to the few plants mentioned here, one can imagine some exciting hybridizing prospects. Crossing the trumpet vine with a catalpa could produce a tree of moderate size with colorful blossoms borne throughout the summer. Crossing a catalpa with either the jacaranda or the golden trumpet tree might usher the tropics into the temperate zone. And if a cross between hardy gloxinia and any of the others can be realized, it could lead to all sorts of exceedingly showy novelties, from subshrubs to shrubs and small trees.

CAPRIFOLIACEAE

Honeysuckle family   16 genera, 365 species

GENERA DISCUSSED   *Diervilla* • *Kolkwitzia* • *Lonicera* • *Sambucus* •
Viburnum • *Weigela*

OTHER ORNAMENTAL GENERA   *Abelia* • *Symphoricarpos*

The Caprifoliaceae are a diverse family containing several of the most useful shrubs (and some overused ones) and several underutilized shrubs of considerable promise.

Diervilla Bush Honeysuckle
Although the bush honeysuckles (*Diervilla lonicera, D. sessilifolia*, and others) will not steal the scene at any time of the year, they are attractive throughout the growing season. Attaining a very usable height of 3 to 5 ft (0.9 to 1.5 m), these mildly stoloniferous plants leaf out in a coppery hue that seems to confuse spring with autumn. Set against these new leaves are small, long-lasting clusters of small, yellow blossoms—not a spectacular display, but pleasing nevertheless. The leaf colors return in late summer and last for months. Unlike the true honeysuckles of the genus *Lonicera*, these bush honeysuckles are not magnets for mildew and aphids. Diervillas are conservatively rated as hardy in zone 4. They take full sun or partial shade, and tolerate gravelly soil, moderate levels of acidity or alkalinity, drought, and moisture.

Kolkwitzia Beauty Bush
The beauty bush (*Kolkwitzia amabilis*) is well named—at least when it is covered with 3-in (7.5-cm) corymbs of 0.5-in (1.5-cm), tubular pink blossoms this shrub is a beauty. In flower, it could pass as a somewhat scraggly azalea, but this plant needs no pampering—indeed, it resents it. Happiest on lean, fast-draining soil, indifferent to pH and wind, completely hardy in zone 4, and very drought tolerant, *K. amabilis* needs little more than a place in the sun. Taken out of flower, however, it is a lanky, disheveled mediocrity in or out of leaf. Cultivars are available, but the selections were based on flowering proclivity and not on habit or foliage effect. Clearly, there remains room for improvement for this beauty.

nicera Honeysuckle

Lonicera, a genus of popular and serviceable plants, includes some of the most fragrant garden shrubs and vines. Plants such as the 10-ft (3-m), zone 4 winter honeysuckle (*Lonicera fragrantissima*) are grown primarily for the exceptionally intense and pleasing fragrance of their small blossoms. Others like the 5-ft (1.5-m), zone 5 boxleaf honeysuckle (*L. nitida*) are grown for their thick, glossy, evergreen foliage, similar to that of the boxwood (*Buxus*). Several cultivars of the zone 5, deciduous European fly honeysuckle (*L. xylosteum*), such as the 5-ft (1.5-m) 'Claveyi' and the 3-ft (0.9-m) 'Emerald Mound', are grown for their attractive mounding habit. Still other honeysuckles, like the irredeemably shabby but popular 10-ft (3-m) tall, zone 4 Tatarian honeysuckle (*L. tatarica*), are grown for reasons beyond my comprehension. Although spring flowers come in white, pink, and red, and are followed by red berries, *L. tatarica* grows and seeds itself like a weed.

Some of the honeysuckles, including the Hall honeysuckle (*Lonicera japonica* 'Halliana') and the trumpet honeysuckle (*L. sempervirens*), are vines. The Hall honeysuckle is hardy to zone 4, has highly fragrant white blossoms, and can ramble rampantly to 30 ft (9 m) or more. The trumpet honeysuckle vine is hardy to zone 5, grows to about 30 ft (9 m), and has varieties with red, orange, and yellow blossoms.

As a group, loniceras take some drought, some heat, a fair degree of cold, miserable soil, and both sunlight and shade. So where do the possibilities for improvement lie? Most of these plants are bug-ridden, none will vie with the azaleas in flower, and few are notable in leaf. I see no great hope for a startling breakthrough by staying within the genus, but crosses with beauty bush (*Kolkwitzia amabilis*) or one of the species of bush honeysuckle might yield something quite special. A cross of a *Lonicera* with *Diervilla* might improve habit, texture, and leaf color in the true honeysuckles; the beauty bush might contribute floriferousness and a good pink flower color to a genus that already has many whites, reds, and yellows. And all the crosses might be adaptable, hardy to zone 4, and less buggy than the honeysuckles. Not a big prize, but it is worth a try.

Sambucus Elder   PLATES 13, 14

The elders (*Sambucus*) are mostly big (10 to 15 ft (3 to 4.5 m) tall), bold-leaved shrubs, best used in informal areas of the garden. They bear 10-in (25-cm) flat cymes of four-petaled, 0.25-in (0.5-cm) white blossoms, and these give way to clusters of blue-black or red berries. The golden elders (*Sambucus canadensis* 'Aurea' and *S. nigra* 'Aurea') are among the few yellow-flowered shrubs that I can tolerate in my own garden—their spring garishness modulates to a pleasant yellow-green that can brighten those somber corners without overwhelming them. The cutleaf elder (*S. canadensis* 'Acutiloba') and the cutleaf golden elder (*S. racemosa* 'Plumosa Aurea') have a finer texture than others in the genus. I do not know why the cutleaf golden elder is not seen more often—it is superb.

Perhaps we can cross a bush honeysuckle with an elder. That might give shrubs of intermediate size, with relatively large plates of flowers, maybe showing some yellow, and abundant fruit, but with finer and more interesting foliage than the elders.

Viburnum   PLATE 15

Of all the genera in the family Caprifoliaceae, none promises more nor has delivered more than *Viburnum*, a collection of premier shrubs with diverse appeal over many seasons. Some are renowned for the fragrance of their blossoms—the 5-ft (1.5-m), zone 4 Korean spice viburnum (*Viburnum carlesii*) and the 6-ft (1.8-m), zone 4 Burkwood viburnum (*V.* ×*burkwoodii*) have particularly pleasing fragrances—while others have blossoms that smell like unwashed gym socks. But even if some have to be viewed at a distance, most viburnums are grand in flower.

Some people may find the ball-like inflorescence found on the Japanese snowball (*Viburnum plicatum*) a bit too gaudy for their own gardens; the flattish cymes of the 20-ft (6-m), zone 2 nannyberry (*V. lentago*), the 20-ft (6-m), zone 3 arrow wood (*V. dentatum*), or the 15-ft (4.5-m), zone 4 wayfaring bush (*V. lantana*), may be more palatable. My favorite is the lacecap inflorescence—a circle of sterile flowers to 1.5 in (4 cm) surrounding a disk of beadlike fertile flowers—that is found on the 12-ft (3.7-m), zone 3 European cranberry bush (*V. opulus*), the 12-ft (3.7-m), zone 2 American cranberry bush (*V. trilobum*), and the 10-ft (3-m), zone 5 or 6 doublefile viburnum (*V. plicatum* var. *tomentosum*) cultivars. This last viburnum is my favorite among favorites, with its cymes held above drooping foliage on horizontal branches, rank upon rank, as though the shrub was layered by snow.

The linden viburnum (*Viburnum dilatatum*) is renowned for its long-lasting display of fruit—huge clusters of berries ripening to a brilliant scarlet, although in some cultivars the fruit may be yellow or orange. The berries of linden viburnum ripen to raisin blackness, and then they are quite palatable. The nannyberry and arrow wood are only slightly less spectacular in fruit, and the cranberry bush and doublefile viburnum have a still more modest display but are quite attractive nevertheless.

Many of the deciduous viburnums mount an autumn foliage color show that cannot be outdone: arrow wood, nannyberry, and the cranberry bushes are among the best for brilliant reds, and doublefile viburnum and its cultivars lean more toward purple. Most of the species of *Viburnum* that show no color keep their leaves and provide an excellent foliage mass throughout the year. The 4-ft (1.2-m), zone 8 David viburnum (*V. davidii*), the 15-ft (4.5-m), zone 5 leatherleaf viburnum (*V. rhytidophyllum*), and the 10-ft (3-m), zone 7 laurustinus (*V. tinus*) are among the best evergreens.

Certain species of viburnum mature to 20 ft (6 m), such as the zone 4 *Viburnum sieboldii*, and some barely make it to 3 ft (0.9 m), like *V. opulus* 'Nanum', and there are all sizes in between. Plant habit among viburnums ranges from upright to horizontally spreading.

With all this diversity of traits to work with, plant breeders have developed many new forms of *Viburnum*, enhancing flower size, fruit production, compactness, and disease resistance. Most of the improvements have been found in cultivars of species, although several notable interspecific hybrids have been achieved: *Viburnum* ×*burkwoodii* = *V. carlesii* × *V. utile*; *V.* ×*carlcephalum* = *V. carlesii* × *V. macrocephalum*; and *V.* ×*juddii* = *V. bitchiuense* × *V. carlesii*, to name just a few.

Is this all that one could hope for? Not by a longshot. For starters, many of our finest viburnums could use a little boost in hardiness. Some of the best plants for flowers, like the doublefile viburnum, turn up their roots at −20°F (−28°C) (although the splendid cultivar 'Shasta' may be a bit hardier). Some of the best for fruit, such as the linden viburnum, will not put up with true zone 4 conditions either, and most of the evergreens are risky in the colder parts of zone 6.

What to do? Select for hardiness in the species, surely, but what about interspecific hybridization? The arrow wood viburnum and the American cranberry bush are hardy in zone 2, and each has several ornamental attributes to contribute to a union as well. In particular, the American cranberry bush has cymes in the lacecap pattern, maplelike leaves, excellent fall color, and a fair abundance of fruit, all of which would be welcome additions in such a cross.

Many of the outstanding viburnums are too large for today's smaller gardens. Perhaps selecting smaller clones, or breeding to smaller ones—like the compact versions of the American or European cranberry bush—would produce more space-saving varieties. The petit *Viburnum opulus* 'Nanum' is superb but unfortunately seldom flowers. Maybe a bit of magic in the test tube or cell fusion efforts would bring about a more floriferous, yet small hybrid. Just imagine a hardy viburnum of the doublefile type, but only 3 ft (0.9 m) tall.

Some gardeners may see a need for more flower color in their viburnums. For the most part, one has a choice between white and white. True, some plants have pink buds and some have flowers that age to pink, but for the most part it is white, white, and more white. Of course, we can sit around and hope for a fortuitous mutation, and there is always prayer. But the impatient infidel might want to try something different, something more promising—say a cross with a different genus, a genus that is replete with red-flowered cultivars, a genus like *Weigela*.

Weigela

Spectacular in flower, the smaller weigelas, such as *Weigela florida* 'Minuet', might pass as azaleas, particularly among envious nearsighted gardeners in zone 4. The tubular flowers, born in shameless abundance in spring and then again sparingly until fall in some cultivars, can be red, pink, white, or near purple, often with contrasting colors here and there, like yellow in the throat and purple on the petals. Out of flower, confusing one of the larger weigelas with an azalea is quite unlikely, since the former are decidedly untidy in habit. The smaller weigelas are not bad, however, and these easily satisfied plants will tolerate harsh soil, some shade, and even a bit of drought.

At the moment, hybridization is proceeding apace. Agricultural Canada has released a whole series of interesting crosses, including some interspecific ones. Crosses have produced zone 4 dwarfs with good foliage, good form, and a proclivity toward repeat blooming; crosses with names like 'Polka', 'Samba', 'Rumba', and 'Tango'—I can hardly wait for the 'Lambada'.

If the trend continues, we may yet have everblooming weigelas that rival southern azaleas in flower power but take temperatures and soils that would send an azalea to "the great garden in the sky." As far as creating a significantly different plant, it may be better to think of the weigelas as donors of genetic material, rather than as recipients. Could they be used to deliver a shot of pink and red to the viburnums? It sounds like a grand reach, but if successful, if something like a doublefile viburnum with deep pink or red flowers could be created, it might be a real winner.

CISTACEAE

Rockrose family   7 genera, 175 species

GENERA DISCUSSED   *Cistus* • *Helianthemum*

Cistus Rockrose
Unfortunately, the rockroses (most notably *Cistus ladanifer, C. laurifolius*, and various hybrids) have a narrow distribution in gardens. Zone 8 (maybe 7 for some) is the low hardiness limit, and rockroses seem to prefer lean, droughty soils and full sun, although their garden distribution in Europe seems to suggest some greater tolerance. Although often disheveled and a bit leggy, these evergreens are magnificent shrubs nevertheless, ranging in height from 3 to 6 ft (0.9 to 1.8 m), depending on the variety. When in bloom, rockroses reign supreme, sporting a profusion of flowers to 4 in (10 cm) wide reminiscent of hollyhock (*Alcea*). Flowers come in a wide range of whites and pinks, some with a contrasting eye. There are several species and many hybrids between them, and that is promising for further endeavors.

Helianthemum Sunrose
Helianthemum nummularium, sunrose to those of us who are easily tongue-tied, is a garden favorite across the United States. Often listed as hardy from zone 6 to zone 7, *H. nummularium* does have cultivars that are perfectly happy in zone 4, and even a few that flirt with zone 3. These plants ask only for good drainage and some sun. In return, these tidy, semievergreen to evergreen shrublets, 1 to 2 ft (0.3 to 0.6 m) high, cover themselves with flowers for weeks in early summer. Cultivars are available with single flowers or with double flowers, and colors include white, yellow, orange, pink, and red, as well as many bicolored types. The plants are cherished wherever they are grown, and are prized additions to rock gardens and xeriscapes.
What might happen were one to cross a sunrose to a rockrose? Could the neatness and hardiness of the sunrose be incorporated with the floriferousness and flower size of the rockrose? Would this yield a whole new collection of drought-tolerant shrubs in a continuum of sizes, from ankle-high to shoulder-high and more? Not many shrubs flower spectacularly in midsummer, and such crosses could fill this gap perfectly.

COMPOSITAE

Daisy family   1314 genera, 21,000 species

GENERA DISCUSSED   *Achillea* • *Anaphalis* • *Antennaria* • *Arnica* •
Aster • *Bellis* • *Bellium* • *Catananche* • *Chrysanthemum* •
Cichorium • *Coreopsis* • *Cosmos* • *Cotula* • *Dahlia* • *Echinacea* •
Echinops • *Erigeron* • *Gaillardia* • *Gazania* • *Gerbera* • *Helenium* •
Helianthus • *Helichrysum* • *Heliopsis* • *Hymenoxys* •
Leontopodium • *Melampodium* • *Raoulia* • *Rudbeckia* • *Senecio* •
Venidium • *Wyethia* • *Zinnia*

OTHER ORNAMENTAL GENERA   *Ageratum* • *Anacyclus* • *Anthemis* •
Artemisia • *Centaurea* • *Chamaemelum* • *Chrysogonum* •
Doronicum • *Liatris* • *Ligularia* • *Petasites* • *Santolina* • *Solidago* •
Stokesia • *Tagetes*

A vast family, rivaling the Orchidaceae in number of species, Compositae (also known as Asteraceae) reflects its size and its worldwide distribution by the great number of plants it has contributed to our gardens. While this abundance provides boundless opportunities for creating new plants, it does make the prospect of *radically* new creations somewhat unlikely as so much variation is already available within this family. Therefore I will limit our discussion to only a few examples involving some personal favorites.

Achillea Yarrow   PLATE 16

Yarrows (*Achillea*) have been enjoying a recent surge in popularity. Feeding this demand is a gallery of new colors that includes everything but blues and greens. Most of these new yarrows are the taller forms in the 2 to 3 ft (0.6 to 0.9 m) range, such as the 'Summer Pastel' series, with corymbs to 5 in (13 cm) across. Unfortunately, they do not stand up well to wind and rain—a little summer storm and they get floppy, look sloppy, and are best picked for the vase as soon as possible.

Yet yarrow species such as Greek yarrow (*Achillea ageratifolia*) and woolly yarrow (*A. tomentosa*) grow to less than 4 in (10 cm) in height. *Achillea ageratifolia* has loose panicles of 0.25-in (0.5-cm) white flowers above silvery gray foliage. Woolly yarrow has corymbs of yellow flowers above finely cut foliage. Both species flower for many weeks, from spring into summer.

What is lacking is a selection of achilleas in the 10 to 18 in (25 to 46 cm) range that are sturdy enough to stand in rain and wind and have a range of flower colors and forms that includes all those mentioned. We can expect to at least fill, if not someday surpass, these needs with a judicious cross between the taller and shorter species.

In another direction, one might entertain crossing an *Achillea* cultivar, perhaps 'Coronation Gold' (*A. filipendulina* × *A. clypeolata*) or one of the 'Galaxy' series (hybrids of *A. taygetea* and *A. millefolium*), with a shrubby sage, like *Artemisia*. In such a case, one would not expect a reduction in height but rather woodier and stiffer self-supporting stems, silvery silky foliage, and the transference of new colors—all of which would further fuel the demand for new yarrows.

Anaphalis Pearly Everlasting, *Antennaria* Pussytoes,
Echinops Globe Thistle, *Leontopodium* Edelweiss   PLATES 17, 18
The four genera discussed here—*Anaphalis, Antennaria, Echinops,* and *Leontopodium*—are being considered together because they all have a similar type of inflorescence. The inflorescence of these members of Compositae is not daisylike at all but rather a globular cluster of many tiny flowers perched atop a stem. Edelweiss (*Leontopodium alpinum*) embellishes this theme with a collar of silvery bracts subtending the flower cluster.

Anaphalis margaritacea is my favorite pearly everlasting. It is a mountain dweller, hardier (to zone 3) and more drought tolerant than the others. The flowers are like clusters of pearls atop leafy, silvery stems that can grow to 3 ft (0.9 m) but are usually much shorter.

Pussytoes (*Antennaria*) are becoming very popular xeriscape groundcovers. These highlanders are free-spreading stoloniferous plants, with silvery, ground-hugging rosettes of leaves, and flower stems to 3 in (7.5 cm) bearing white or pink clusters of blossoms. They take zone 2 or zone 3 cold, heat, drought, and wretched soil, but they do need reasonable drainage.

I see no compelling reason to consider a hybrid involving any two of these three genera, but on the other hand, a cross of *Leontopodium* or *Anaphalis* or *Antennaria* with globe thistle might prove to be very interesting. Globe thistle (*Echinops ritro*) is the only popular garden ornamental among these four genera. Its popularity, no doubt, rests on its blue flowers, clustered in 2-in (5-cm) diameter spheres rising to 4 ft (1.2 m) on leafy stems. Unfortunately, the stems are tall enough that they require staking. The coarse leaves are thistlelike, but they are curled, rolled, and puckered as though thoroughly infested with plant lice—not a pretty picture, and there is too much of it in relation to the beautiful and fascinating inflorescence. I like thistlelike leaves, but I much prefer to see them on *Eryngium* species or *Carlina acaulis* rather than on *Echinops*. Globe thistle is also not as tough as it appears; although hardy into zone 3, it does need its fair share of water.

Not many garden plants offer a blue lollypop inflorescence, so why not try to modify the globe thistle to improve some of its shortcomings—reduce its height, moderate its coarse habit and foliage, and make it even more adaptable? A cross with any of the other three genera mentioned might accomplish this. Pearly everlasting and pussytoes might be good choices for enhancing foliage; edelweiss might be the choice to yield novel floral structure. Any of these crosses might achieve the shape and color of globe thistle's inflorescence in a neater package.

Arnica, Echinacea, Helianthus Sunflower, *Heliopsis, Hymenoxys, Venidium, Wyethia* Mule Ears

Plants in the following genera sport big, bold blossoms that deserve the name "sunflower," although the color of some might argue against it.

Heliopsis helianthoides is a zone 4 perennial, forming clumps of stems to 4 ft (1.2 m), with semidouble or double flowers to 3 in (7.5 cm) in a range of colors from yellows to near orange. The 'Golden Greenheart' cultivar is a fully double yellow with a green center. These are superb plants, but maybe something new can be developed in conjunction with some of the other Compositae.

The annual sunflower (*Helianthus annuus*) has varieties from 2 to 10 ft (0.6 to 3 m) tall, with flowers ranging from a mere 4 in (10 cm) to a plate-sized 14 in (36 cm) across. Besides sunflower's usual yellows, the cultivar 'Italian White' provides striking black-centered white flowers and 'Sunburst' has some rich red-browns and patterned forms. *Venidium* is another annual, similar to the sunflower in flower and plant form, but it is shorter at 2 ft (0.6 m) and has flowers to 4 in (10 cm) across. It, too, has a superb black-centered white-flowered cultivar, 'Zulu Prince'.

White-flowered Compositae in the 2 to 3 ft (0.6 to 0.9 m) range are not very common. Two of the finest are *Echinacea purpurea* 'White Swan' and white mule ears (*Wyethia helenioides*). The 'White Swan' cultivar usually grows to about 3 ft (0.9 m) in height; *W. helenioides* is closer to 2 ft (0.6 m). The flowers of both forms are in the 3 to 4 in (7.5 to 10 cm) range. 'White Swan' will take some drought, whereas white mule ears needs a bit more moisture. Both are hardy to zone 3. Richard Shaw, in his book *Plants of Yellowstone and Grand Teton National Park*, calls white mule ears the most striking white-flowered Compositae—however I have yet to see it offered for sale.

We might ask for shorter forms of these white-flowered plants, or maybe taller forms. Maybe the best use for *Echinacea purpurea* 'White Swan' and *Wyethia helenioides*, along with *Helianthus annuus* 'Italian White' and *Venidium* 'Zulu Prince', would be as breeding partners for heliopsis in order to produce perennial, hardy plants with sunflowerlike blossoms in white and pastel yellows, blooming over a long period in summer.

Several alpine genera, such as *Arnica* and *Hymenoxys*, have relatively huge (to 3 in (7.5 cm)) sunflowerlike blossoms atop diminutive plants 2 to 10 in (5 to 25 cm) tall. Their sun tolerance and hardiness (to zone 2) is unquestioned. Some species, however, like *Arnica montana*, need moist, peaty soil and are not overjoyed at being cultivated at lower altitudes; others, such as *A. sachalinensis*, respond to the easy life of the lowlands with near-weedy fecundity.

If *Arnica* or *Hymenoxys* will cross with *Echinacea*, *Helianthus*, *Heliopsis*, *Venidium*, or *Wyethia*, we could get an entirely new race of sunflowerlike ornamentals—huge flowers on dwarf plants, maybe in white or cream with dark centers. For those of us who like bold daisies, these new plants would be most welcome additions to the plant world.

ster

Asters are among the most popular perennials. Particularly valued for their late-summer and fall bloom, asters come in several wonderful spring-flowering kinds as well. One of the most highly touted of all asters is *Aster ×frikartii* 'Monch', a 3-ft (0.9-m) plant with a profusion of 2.5-in (6.5-cm), yellow-centered pale blue flowers lasting from summer into fall. It is a superb plant, even though its habit might be considered unkempt or even downright sloppy by some, and it is hardy only to zone 5 (zone 6 is a safer bet). Several asters, however, are hardier and much tidier in habit than *A. ×frikartii* 'Monch'. The zone 3 alpine aster (*A. alpinus*) is just such an example. It is available in various sizes from 6 to 12 in (15 to 30 cm) tall, with yellow-centered flowers in white, blue, and violet that appear in spring over a long period. Maybe a cross will yield neater 'Monch'-like asters with an even longer flowering period.

Bellis English Daisy, *Helichrysum* Strawflower

The English daisy (*Bellis perennis*), hardy in zones 3 to 11, is a perennial for some, but for others it is an annual or biennial. This plant objects to high summer heat and prefers a bit of shade, but it is a popular plant no matter how it is grown. English daisies have single, semidouble, or double blossoms to 3 in (7.5 cm) in white, pink, or red, above 4- to 8-in (10- to 20-cm) plants. The doubles sacrifice much of the grace of the species for blowzy bluster, but the plant is an attraction in all its varieties.

Strawflowers (*Helichrysum*) are primarily grown as summer annuals. Some species and hybrids have flowers to 3 in (7.5 cm) across in white, pink, and near red. The flowers are exceedingly long-lasting, and they dry well enough to deserve being called "everlasting."

A number of zone 4 perennial species and hybrids of strawflowers have been introduced, including *Helichrysum aroanum*, *H. thianschanicum* 'Golden Baby', and *H. trilineatum*. These new varieties are gaining popularity not only for their cymes of small yellow flowers but also for the beauty of their foliage—often fine-textured and silvery gray atop plants 6 to 12 in (15 to 30 cm) in height. *Helichrysum bellum* is different than the other strawflowers, but it is a gem. Its black-eyed, double white flowers are 1 in (2.5 cm) across atop 4-in (10-cm) plants, with spatulate leaves 1 in by 2 in (2.5 cm by 5 cm). All these species require full sun, fast-draining soil, and very little water, although *H. bellum* appreciates a bit more moisture than the others.

The flowers of many of the strawflowers, such as *Helichrysum bellum*, resemble those of double English daisies, and this suggests the possibility of crossing the two genera. After all, the English daisy is zone 3 hardy and fairly tolerant of shade and moist soil, while many of the showiest strawflowers are annuals and abhor moisture and shade. The English daisy flowers in the spring; the strawflowers blossom throughout most of the summer. The result of such a cross could be an extraordinarily long-flowering perennial, showy in bloom and foliage effect, quite hardy, and tolerant of a wide diversity of soils and climates.

Yarrows such as *Achillea ageratifolia* or *A. tomentosa* might also be crossed with some strawflower or English daisy. From such a cross one would expect hardy, adaptable, compact, silver-leaved plants with relatively large and long-lasting flowers. Of course, involving other yarrows and other strawflowers could introduce an even wider selection of flower colors.

Bellium

Bellium minutum is one of the smallest daisies on record. This delightful miniature forms a stoloniferous mat, barely 2 in (5 cm) high, of tiny orbicular leaves over which hover 5-in (13-cm) white daisies. It is hardy to zone 5, tolerates some shade, and is not fussy as to soil conditions.

Dwarf plants are enjoying a surge in popularity that is likely to continue as private gardens become smaller and smaller. *Bellium minutum* seems to be a likely vehicle for the creation of a whole new race of miniatures. One might try crossing it with some of the asters, coreopsis, chrysanthemums, chicory, or any of the other Compositae mentioned here, and hope for great things in little packages.

Catananche Cupid's Dart

Catananche is a plant that offers something different—very different and very appealing. The silvery green, linear, basal leaves of the catananche grow to about 10 in (25 cm), and the wiry, branched 2-ft (0.6-m) stems support 1.5-in (4-cm) flowers of various shades of blue and a superb silvery white. The flowers' two concentric disks of petals are wedge-shaped and pink at the tips. The plant flowers in summer for many weeks, is zone 4 hardy, drought tolerant, and indifferent to soil as long as it is well drained. Some say that cupid's dart is short-lived, but in this regard the available cultivars provide tremendous variation. Some varieties that I have grown have persisted for years, forming larger and more floriferous clumps each year.

Clearly, selecting for the longer-lived catananches is a primary concern. Beyond this objective, shorter plants might prove popular, something that might be obtained by selection or by crossing cupid's dart to a miniature *Erigeron* like the blue *Erigeron pinnatisectus* or the white *E. melanocephalus*. But please, try to retain the pearly buds and distinctive flowers of cupid's dart.

Chrysanthemum PLATE 19

Dwarf, giant, formal, informal, quill, button, spider, spoon—all these and every other imaginable flower-shape that has radial symmetry has already been obtained in a chrysanthemum. What we want is more attention paid to plants like *Chrysanthemum weyrichii*, a zone 4 hardy species with single 2-in (5-cm) flowers colored pink or white on evergreen plants. There is a great deal of variation here that can be exploited. Cultivars like 'White Bomb' and 'Pink Bomb' barely reach 10 in (25 cm) in height and have stiff, 12-in (30-cm) tall flower stems. Others can scramble to a rank 18 in (46 cm), with floppy flower stems 2 ft (0.6 m) long. Flowering begins in mid or late summer, depending on the cultivar, and plants remain in bloom for a month or more. *Chrysanthemum weyrichii* is vigorously stoloniferous and makes a superb groundcover in its shorter forms.

The groundcover potential of these chrysanthemums should be exploited by breeding for shorter and denser forms, while keeping the evergreen leaves, the hardiness and adaptability, and the delightfully simple flowers. Maybe *Bellium minutum* or a small *Erigeron* can be enlisted for the project.

Partridge feather (*Chrysanthemum haradjanii*, syn. *Tanacetum densum* var. *amanum*) is grown for its silvery gray, finely cut leaves, similar to the best *Artemisia*. It is sun and drought tolerant, but surprisingly, this plant tolerates a great deal of shade. Partridge feather spreads stoloniferously to form a dense 8-in (20-cm) high groundcover. The flowers are secondary but not unappealing—0.25-in (0.5-cm), button-shaped yellow blooms are held in flat corymbs late in the season, so late that they may never materialize in zone 5. One could cross this plant with a small erigeron, or *Bellis minutum*, or a cotula to reduce its size and also to encourage flowering at an earlier time.

Chrysanthemum pacificum, too, has great groundcover potential. Its lovely lobed leaves are edged with silver, creating a striking and distinctive effect, but at 12 in (30 cm) this plant is too tall for most groundcover demands. It also does not produce flowers in the northern part of its range, and its zone 5 rating is a bit overly optimistic. A cross with dwarf forms of *C. weyrichii* might remedy these deficiencies, or maybe employing an erigeron in the cross would work.

The popular painted daisy or pyrethrum (*Chrysanthemum coccineum*) should be considered as a possible donor for red coloring. Since it flowers in the spring, it could also be considered as a partner to extend the flowering time of the fall chrysanthemums. Painted daisy has yellow-centered red, pink, or white flowers to 3 in (7.5 cm), borne 3 ft (0.9 m) above mounds of ferny foliage—spectacular, but loose and sloppy after flowering, and the stems are weak. A cross between painted daisy and *C. weyrichii* 'Pink Bomb' or *Bellium minutum* or a dwarf *Erigeron* might yield long-flowering, short, sturdy plants with tight habit and interesting foliage, as well as stunning flowers in a wide range of colors.

Cichorium Chickweed, Chicory

Chicory (*Cichorium intybus*) is a plebeian plant, an irrepressible interloper common along roadsides throughout the United States. It is zone 4 tough, indifferent to soil conditions, and extremely drought tolerant. Yet, it is extraordinarily beautiful, with pale blue yellow-centered asterlike flowers 1.5 in (4 cm) across. The flowers are born aloft on wiry branching stems well above the foliage in a profuse display from early July through mid-September. The flowers do not droop and the stems do not flop—the bearing is always jauntily upright. The spent blossoms are unnoticeable, and the inflorescence always looks neat.

Chicory is, however, a rambunctious weed, too eager to colonize, and most have the damnable trait of closing their flowers by noontime. But this is a variable species—variable in height from 3 to 5 ft (0.9 to 1.5 m) and variable in flower color from midblue to white. There is even some variability in the curtain time of the daily flower show, some forms holding the stage until as late as three in the afternoon.

Selecting and breeding this plant for stature, duration of flowering, and color are obvious and worthwhile projects. One is tempted to entertain crosses with other Compositae—like the asters, for example. Would crossing the chicory plant tame its rampant nature? Would the weedy plant impart its sprightly bearing to the often untidy habit of the asters? Would it impart its bluer-than-blue color to the progeny? Would crossing chicory with the alpine aster (*Aster alpinus*) or *Aster ×frikartii* 'Monch' extend its blooming schedule even further, and would the offspring carry its flower display through the afternoon and into the evening? Would the hybrids exhibit the extraordinary drought tolerance, soil tolerance, and hardiness of chickweed? These are all worthy considerations for the pursuit of new hybrids of chicory and other members of the daisy family.

Coreopsis Tickseed

Coreopsis is yet another genus in this large family containing some of the most useful and popular garden ornamentals. A uniform-from-seed, 18-in (46-cm) tall, double yellow called 'Early Sunrise' (*Coreopsis grandiflora* 'Early Sunrise') received the AAS and Fleuroselect Gold Medal awards. *Coreopsis verticillata* 'Moonbeam', an 18-in (46-cm), pale yellow threadleaf coreopsis, was chosen perennial of the year in 1992 by the Perennial Plant Association. A few years earlier, the stoloniferous, 3-in (7.5-cm) tall, shade-tolerant *C. auriculata* 'Nana' was all the rage; then it was the moisture-tolerant, pink-flowering *C. rosea* that captured center stage. The dwarf (about 5 in (12.5 cm) in bloom) *C. grandiflora* 'Goldfink' has also been popular for many years. Undoubtedly, a large and enthusiastic gardening public eagerly awaits the next new variety of coreopsis.

Unfortunately, *Coreopsis lanceolata* 'Brown Eyes', with its brown-spotted yellow flowers, is at best reluctantly perennial. As yet, no white coreopsis, no dwarf threadleaf coreopsis, and no drought-tolerant pink coreopsis have emerged. Some of these gaps can probably be filled without leaving the genus—cross *C. rosea* with *C. grandiflora* 'Goldfink' to get a dwarf pink coreopsis, for example. If pale-yellow or white miniatures are desired, maybe *Bellium minutum* can be enlisted to help. Crosses of 'Goldfink' with *Rudbeckia* 'Rustic Colors' might yield semidwarf plants with the desired browns but with stronger perennial tendencies than is found in the latter plant. Crossing tickseed plants with painted daisy might add red coloring to the coreopsis but on a neater plant than the painted daisy.

Cosmos   PLATE 20

Cosmos bipinnatus has been one of the most popular of all annuals, valued both for cutting and garden displays. White, pink, red, or bicolored flowers, some with tubular petals, may be as much as 5 in (12.5 cm) across and are borne throughout the summer and into the fall. The taller forms (to 4 ft (1.2 m)) have a disheveled appearance in spite of the finely scissored foliage. However, much more attractive shorter cosmos, like the 2-ft (0.6-m) 'Sonata' cultivar, have been introduced and will probably take the place of the taller kinds.

Could *Cosmos*, in combination with *Coreopsis*, *Aster*, or *Erigeron*, become a perennial plant? Such things have happened: the annual *Gaillardia pulchella* has been crossed with the perennial *Gaillardia aristata* to yield a wide variety of popular zone 3 perennials called *G.* ×*grandiflora*. In the case of *Cosmos* (not knowing of any existing hardy perennial varieties of the plant) an intergeneric cross would be required—but if it works, there are great possibilities.

Cotula New Zealand Brass Buttons

Adaptable, zone 4 hardy, tough enough to withstand some foot traffic, and only 1 in (2.5 cm) tall, *Cotula potentillina* is a little-known plant of enormous potential. The finely cut gray-green leaves have a fernlike delicacy and remain on the plant all winter, although cold weather gives them a bronze tint. *Cotula potentillina* does flower, but the tiny buttonlike blooms have little garden impact. This charming New Zealander has the makings of one of the most useful of all groundcovers.

I see no way to improve *Cotula potentillina* except by selecting still hardier and tougher clones. It might, however, be used to dwarf Compositae such as *Erigeron*, *Chrysanthemum*, and *Santolina*. In particular, a cross of *Cotula potentillina* with *Chrysanthemum haradjanii* might yield a plant taller than the cotula but shorter and tighter than the chrysanthemum, with delicately exquisite leaves in a shade of silver.

Dahlia

In a family not noted for the subtlety of its flowers, the dahlias may be the brashest of them all. Some dahlia plants are 5 ft (1.5 m) tall, with shaggy 10-in (25-cm) blooms so heavy-headed that they need to be tied to the mast to remain upright. Then there are those, such as the 'Figaro' cultivar, that are barely 1 ft (0.3 m) tall, with single or semidouble 1-in (2.5-cm) blossoms. Between these two extremes, dahlias come in all heights, with flowers of all colors (except blue and green) and flower shapes that include anemone, cactus, pompon, formal, and informal.

Dahlia is grown as a perennial in zone 10, but in colder climates the roots are dug up and stored over winter. Perhaps a cross between a *Dahlia* and some other Compositae would be fortuitous. The resulting plant might be hardier than the dahlia, and yet share its variety of flower shapes, colors, and sizes. A cross between *Dahlia* and *Chrysanthemum weyrichii* 'Pink Bomb' or 'White Bomb', for example, might do just that, as might a cross with *Erigeron* or *Aster*.

Erigeron Fleabane
PLATE 18

The fleabanes (*Erigeron*) comprise a varied genus, with some plants barely 1 in (2.5 cm) tall and others reaching a height of nearly 3 ft (0.9 m). Some of the miniatures have silvery, finely cut foliage, and others have narrow spatulate basal leaves of no great distinction. Flowers can be white, yellow, orange, or blue, with several rows of petals and a yellow center. Most erigerons are hardy into zone 4, some even to zone 2, and almost all are drought tolerant and adaptable to most soils.

Among my favorites are *Erigeron chrysopsidis* 'Grand Ridge', *E. aurantiacus*, *E. pinnatisectus*, and *E. melanocephalus*. *Erigeron chrysopsidis* 'Grand Ridge' has yellow 1.5-in (4-cm) daisies on plants barely 1 in (2.5 cm) tall throughout summer. The 2-in (5-cm) orange flowers of *E. aurantiacus* appear in late spring on stems to 1 ft (0.3 cm) tall. *Erigeron pinnatisectus* has startlingly large 1.5-in (4-cm), yellow-centered blue flowers only 1 in (2.5 cm) above finely dissected leaves, and *E. melanocephalus*'s 1-in (2.5-cm) white blossoms sit on 4- to 10-in (10- to 25-cm) stems above compact mounds of foliage. All four of these plants are hardy to at least zone 4. These and many other similar species are likely candidates to breed with the asters, chicory, chrysanthemums, or garden erigerons in the hope of obtaining new long-blooming, cold-hardy, drought-tolerant miniature daisies in a wide variety of colors.

Gaillardia Blanketflower
Another show-stopper of enormous popularity, *Gaillardia* ×*grandiflora* is a hybrid of *G. aristata* and *G. pulchella*. *Gaillardia aristata* is a zone 3 perennial with yellow flowers and a central cone of reddish brown; the latter parent-plant, *G. pulchella*, is a Mexican annual with raging color contrast in mahogany-red and gold. The hybrid is available in sizes ranging from 6 in (15 cm) to 5 ft (1.5 m), and colors range from golden yellow to burgundy—those with burgundy petals tipped with gold are the most garish and the most popular of all. Gaillardias flower throughout the summer.

Unfortunately, the larger blanketflowers are floppy to the point of being sloppy, and the smaller ones, like *Gaillardia* ×*grandiflora* 'Goblin', are usually grown from seed, resulting in plants that are frustratingly variable as to height, form, flower color, floriferousness, and longevity. To my eye, none of the garden forms compare with the natural beauty of the wild brown-eyed Susan (*G. aristata*).

The best wild forms may be the choicest gaillardias to select for in cross breeding. Let us try for some softer colors, in selfs and patterns. Maybe blending *Gaillardia* with *Chrysanthemum weyrichii* 'White Bomb' or *C. weyrichii* 'Pink Bomb', or with the white-flowered *Erigeron melanocephalus* will do the job without loss of hardiness or perennial constitution.

Gazania African Daisy   PLATE 21
Perhaps the most brilliantly colored and strikingly patterned of all the daisies, *Gazania* species and hybrids enliven many an otherwise dun and droughty landscape. Perennial only in zones 9 and above, African daisies are cherished annuals elsewhere. These trailing or mounding plants, to 1 ft (0.3 m) in height, feature stunning blossoms in white, yellow, orange, or red. The blossoms are nearly 4 in (10 cm) wide, some with an inner circle of black and some with longitudinal markings of lighter hues or a contrasting color on the petals.

Can the incomparable color brilliance and markings of *Gazania* be brought down to cooler zones? Genes from *Aster alpinus*, *Erigeron chrysopsidis* 'Grand Ridge', *Coreopsis lanceolata* 'Goldfink', or *Chrysanthemum weyrichii* could provide the vehicle.

Gerbera

A major showoff in a family noted for its lack of modesty in floral displays, *Gerbera jamesonii* is a wildly popular perennial in zones 8 to 10, and a wildly popular annual in colder climates. Although the coarse, lobed, 10-in (25-cm) leaves would disgrace most gardens, *G. jamesonii*'s 4-in (10-cm) flowers—singles, semi-doubles, and doubles in yellow, orange, and deep red, some with contrasting stripes on the petals—are magnificent. Surely, there must be an opportunity to interject hardiness and better plant form into this genus, even if something may be lost in the flower display. Suppose one were to breed *Chrysanthemum weyrichii* or *Aster alpinus* with *Gerbera jamesonii*—that would be a step in the right direction.

Helenium Helen's Flower, Sneezeweed

One of the great standbys in the autumn garden, Helen's flower or sneezeweed (*Helenium autumnale*) is a zone 3 perennial with a profusion of 2-in (5-cm) blossoms in yellow, red, or near brown, with slightly drooping petals surrounding a prominent cone. The flowers are borne on plants 2 to 5 ft (0.6 to 1.5 m) tall and, although the name "pumilum" means dwarf, even the cultivar 'Pumilum Magnificum' can reach the tallest height. These tall plants often need support, at which time they take on a disheveled look that is not likely to enhance the landscape.

A cross between *Helenium* and *Heliopsis* might yield a sturdier plant, maybe in a variety of colors characteristic of *Helenium*, and maybe with a desire to bloom throughout summer and autumn. If we wanted to create something of smaller size, we could try crossing *Helenium* with all sorts of Compositae, from *Arnica* to *Zinnia*.

Melampodium Blackfoot Daisy

The blackfoot daisy (*Melampodium leucanthum*), less than 1 ft (0.3 m) in height and 1.5 ft (0.45 m) in width, is a zone 4 plant found in the dry prairies. Its 1-in (2.5-cm) wide, yellow-centered white flowers have wide petals notched at the tips—lovely and distinctive. Best of all, the plant is in bloom from midspring to midfall.

The blackfoot daisies possess some variation in height, habit, floriferousness, and perennial proclivity—all of which should be exploited by selection. The most exciting use of this splendid little plant might be in hybridizing with other Compositae such as *Aster, Chrysanthemum,* and *Echinacea* in order to reduce plant size and, perhaps most important, to increase flowering time.

Raoulia Scab Plant, Vegetable Sheep

Among the most miniature of all garden plants, *Raoulia* is a genus of exquisite New Zealanders that are grown as ground-covers in the alpine rockery. They are called "scab plants" because they form a hard, thin groundcover. As tiny as the individual plants are, a patch of *Raoulia* can be recognized from ten feet away—they are that distinctive and that beautiful.

My favorite species of scab plants are *Raoulia australis* and *R. glabra*. They are rated as zone 6 hardy, but both species can be found growing as perennials in zone 5 (perhaps 4 would be more realistic) at the Denver Botanic Garden in Denver, Colorado. *Raoulia australis* is a shiny silvery gray; the other is bright green. Both *Raoulia* species need sun and good drainage, and they bring the look of moss to places where a true moss could not survive. *Raoulia australis* is my personal favorite, with its tiny aluminum-colored leaves barely 0.25 in (0.5 cm) off the ground. It has shown considerable dieback after every severe winter in my Colorado garden, and I can never grow enough to satisfy my wants.

The potential of these plants is so great that an effort should be made to find the hardiest and most adaptable varieties. Maybe intergeneric crosses will bring some hybrid vigor, or perhaps polyploidy can solve the problem. Another possible direction is the use of *Raoulia* in hybridizing in order to radically reduce size or enhance leaf color of other Compositae. To this end, *Cotula potentillina* or *Chrysanthemum haradjanii* are possible partners. Hardy, adaptable, silvery mat plants with the texture of lichen or moss—that is the promise.

Rudbeckia Coneflower

Coneflower, particularly the cultivar *Rudbeckia fulgida* 'Goldsturm', is rated as one of the top perennials for summer and fall bloom. The 4-in (10-cm) flowers, bright orange-yellow with a prominent black central cone, are set atop stems that can reach a height of 2.5 ft (0.75 m). The 6-in (15-cm), long-stalked leaves appear late enough in the spring to provide an ideal follow-up to early-flowering bulbs.

Other *Rudbeckia* cultivars are also quite attractive: *R. hirta* 'Green Eyes', with paler yellow flowers and a green cone, and 'Rustic Colors', with copper-colored flowers embellished with proximal washes of brown. Unfortunately, these two cultivars are not reliably perennial, contrary to the claims of some seed advertisements.

Of course, shorter forms of all three of these cultivars of cone-flower would be nice garden newcomers, and perennials with the colors of 'Green Eyes' and 'Rustic Colors' would be very appealing. Polyploidy might give us shorter plants (as it has with daylilies), but how do we impart a perennial constitution? Long-lived dwarf coreopsis like *Coreopsis lanceolata* 'Goldfink', and some not-so-long-lived brown-eyed forms like *C. lanceolata* 'Brown Eyes', might be suitable partners for *Rudbeckia*. *Aster alpinus* or *Chrysanthemum weyrichii* might also be used in this endeavor.

Senecio   PLATES 22, 23

Perhaps the largest genus of all, *Senecio* has an estimated 1500 species distributed worldwide. The genus includes an extraordinary diversity of shrubs, vines, perennials, and annuals, and its members are found growing in an extraordinary diversity of climates, from tropical, moisture-rich lowlands to droughty alpine tundra.

The popular cineraria (*Senecio* ×*hybridus*) is one of the moisture-loving tropical forms. A proper outdoor perennial in zones 9 and 10, elsewhere it is widely grown as an indoor or glasshouse plant. The profuse long-blooming daisylike blossoms, available in a wide variety of colors and patterns clustered atop a mound of unlovely foliage, make this plant easily recognizable. The zone 8 dusty miller (*S. cineraria*) is grown primarily for its finely cut silvery foliage to 2 ft (0.6 m) high—its corymbs of pale yellow flowers are less significant. *Senecio greyi* is a zone 7 evergreen shrub to 5 ft (1.5 m) in height, with silver-edged leaves and a profusion of yellow 1-in (2.5-cm) daisies that last over a long period in summer. Chain-of-beads (*S. rowleyanus*) is a succulent zone 9 plant, often grown indoors in hanging pots so that the perfectly pendant stems can be properly displayed. Hoary senecio (*S. canus*) is a zone 3 Rocky Mountain wildling, an inhabitant of the driest south-facing hillsides. Its large, felted, silvery gray leaves provide an excellent foil for the corymbs of small yellow flowers on 2-ft (0.6-m) stems. From lower altitudes and slightly moister terrain, black-tipped senecio (*S. atratus*) is similar to hoary senecio, but it has silvery green leaves and shows more of a tendency to form colonies.

This tiny sampling of the diversity of *Senecio* only hints at the possibilities of creating new and useful ornamentals without ever leaving the genus. In particular, why not bring some of the super-hardy, extra-drought-tolerant alpine and subalpine *Senecio* off their mountains and cross them with cineraria. Any boost in the hardiness and drought tolerance of cineraria, while retaining the extraordinary flower colors and floriferousness, is bound to be welcomed by many gardeners. Intergeneric hybrids involving *Senecio* are always a possibility, but an enormous number of possibilities already exist within this vast and diverse genus.

Zinnia

It may be a surprise to some to learn that there is a perennial *Zinnia*, *Z. grandiflora*, that is native to zone 4 regions of Colorado. It is a beautiful plant with brilliant yellow, single blossoms more than 1 in (2.5 cm) wide on a 10-in (25-cm) mound of grayish green, finely cut leaves. Extraordinarily floriferous when well sited, this perennial can flower from late spring to early fall. It thrives in full sun and drought—in fact, these conditions are a must for the plant's very survival.

The common garden zinnias are derived from *Zinnia elegans* and are grown as annuals. These widely popular plants come in shades of white, yellow, orange, and a brownish red so deep that one could call it mahogany. There are solid colors and bicolors, singles, semidoubles, and doubles. The flowers range from barely 1 in (2.5 cm) across to more than 4 in (10 cm) across, on stems from 3 in (7.5 cm) high to more than 2.5 ft (0.75 m) high. They need sun and some watering, but garden zinnias are otherwise very adaptable.

Hybridize *Zinnia grandiflora* with the annual zinnias—it is a plan that begs to be carried out—and we could get a clan of zinnias in all the forms of the annuals but perennial, hardy, and tolerant of all soils, from desert-dry to garden-moist. These new zinnias would be guaranteed winners.

CORNACEAE

Dogwood family　　　　　　12 genera, 90 species

GENERA DISCUSSED　　*Aucuba • Cornus*

Only two genera and not many species in the dogwood family are of garden importance. In this small collection, however, are some of our most cherished shrubs and flowering trees—among the finest ornamentals to be found anywhere. With this sparse but choice collection of garden-worthy trees and shrubs there is an obvious need to develop new plants in the family Cornaceae, and there are great opportunities to do so.

Aucuba

The Japanese aucuba (*Aucuba japonica*) is a magnificent evergreen shrub with 8-in (20-cm), lustrous dark green leaves. It can reach a height of 15 ft (4.5 m), but dwarf cultivars grow to only 3 ft (0.9 m) or so. The many forms with leaves speckled with white or yellow give *A. japonica* its nickname "gold dust plant." Other forms have leaves boldly patterned white or gold on the interior and green on the margins. Female plants in the presence of suitors will exhibit showy red berries throughout most of the winter. The plant is a shade lover, indifferent as to soil type and pH, and will even accept some drought once established. The catch? It is hardy only into zone 7.

Some shrubby dogwoods, on the other hand, are hardy in zone 2 and have superb, highly variegated foliage: *Cornus alba* 'Gouchaultii' has leaves variegated in golden yellow and rose; *C. sericea* 'Silver and Gold' has leaves variegated in white and winter stems of gold. Suppose we hybridize these dogwoods with the Japanese aucuba. How will the traits average out in the offspring? Will the progeny be hardy halfway through zone 4? Will they be semievergreen? What about the color patterns? What about the F_2 generation—how will the traits be distributed there? Can the second generation favor us with the best of both parents? Other dogwoods are also available for breeding. Shall we give the gold dust plant flowers to brag about by crossing it with a flowering *Cornus*—or would that be serving the greedy, not the needy?

Cornus Dogwood   PLATES 24–27

When those silly arguments arise as to which flowering trees
are the most magnificent of all, dogwoods are always among the
top contenders. Top among the tops are the eastern flowering dogwood (*Cornus florida*) and the kousa dogwood (*C. kousa*). How can
one argue against them? After all, both are stunning in bloom,
both have an interesting layered structure (more striking in *C.
florida*), and both show superb autumn tints (again, more striking
in *C. florida*). The extraordinary mottled bark of *C. kousa* is reason
enough to grow this dogwood. Although not as well known because of its more finicky requirements, the Pacific dogwood (*C.
nuttallii*), with blossoms (bracts really, like the others) up to 6 in (15
cm) in diameter, is another contender.

Horticulturists have responded to the demand for these
plants, and they have fueled it by finding many new cultivars and
by creating several wonderful hybrids. These can come with pink
blossoms or red blossoms, and with reddish purple leaves or variegated leaves. Dwarf forms and weeping forms have also been
developed. Notable hybrids include *Cornus* 'Eddie's White Wonder' (*C. florida* × *C. nuttallii*) and the superb series of galaxy crosses
(*C. ×rutgersensis* = *C. florida* × *C. kousa*), made by Elwin Orton of
Rutgers University, including 'Aurora', 'Constellation', and 'Stel-
lar Pinks'. These hybrids have traits, including bloom time, that
are intermediate between those of the parents.

Unfortunately, these magnificent trees are not for every garden. They prefer soils on the acidic side, moist but perfectly
drained. Late frosts may not kill the plants, but they will nip the
flower display. Dry winds and baking sun are also not easily tol-
erated by any of the varieties. The Pacific dogwood is barely hardy
in zone 7, and the anthracnose blight poses a significant threat to
the flowering dogwood. All these considerations strongly limit
the range in which these trees can be grown.

Shrubs like the red osier dogwood (*Cornus sericea*) and the
Tatarian dogwood (*C. alba*), among others, thrive under the most
miserable conditions of heat, cold, and soil. They need neither perfect drainage nor acidity and are happy in sun or shade. The
flower display of these shrubs is insignificant, to be polite, when
compared to that of the eastern flowering dogwood, kousa dogwood, or Pacific dogwood, although it does go on for months from
late spring through much of the summer. Nevertheless, the red

osier dogwood and the Tatarian dogwood have attractive foliage, commendable autumn tints, and spectacular winter twig color. Variants of the red osier dogwood range in size from the cultivar 'Kelsey's Dwarf Dogwood', at 3 ft (0.9 m), to a 16-ft (5-m) clone. Selections have been made for stem color (deep red, yellow, and green) and leaf color (variegated in green and silver or in green and gold), but more needs to be done, especially with the yellow-twig varieties of *C. sericea*, to select for resistance to twig blight— and resistant forms do exist.

The opportunity and promise seem obvious: cross the flowering trees with the hardier shrubs. What might you get—some "brown-thumb" concoction with lousy stem color and unnoticeable blossoms? Possibly, but there might also be a chance of creating an unprecedented assortment of flowering dogwoods. These new hybrids could come in a variety of sizes and forms, from small shrubs to trees of moderate size, and trees and shrubs could be made available for almost every climate and growing condition. It is a gamble, but what a prize should the gamble pay off.

And while we are conjuring up these fantastic new beasts, let us entertain the possibility of admitting another player into the game. The bunchberry (*Cornus canadensis*), humble in size (4 to 9 in (10 to 23 cm) tall) but mighty in flower power (bracts to 2 in (5 cm) across), could be the key to producing truly big-flowered shrublets with great cold tolerance. The bunchberry's dissimilarity to other dogwoods has recently caused some taxonomists to reconsider its classification, and they now place this gem in a genus of its own. The late Lincoln Foster, of rock garden fame, suggested crossing this miniature with some of the big dogwoods in order to test their genetic affinity—an excellent idea, but there are so many more reasons to give it a try.

Other worthy dogwoods might also be considered as breeding partners for the flowering dogwoods, such as the cornelian cherry (*Cornus mas*), the pagoda dogwood (*C. alternifolia*), and the giant dogwood (*C. controversa*), and these suggest all sorts of other crosses; but I will place my bets on those mentioned earlier. If such hybrids can be made, and if backcrosses or the F_2 generation can be realized, it is certain that they will be winners.

CRUCIFERAE

Mustard family   390 genera, 3000 species

GENUS DISCUSSED   *Stanleya*

OTHER ORNAMENTAL GENERA   *Aethionema* • *Alyssum* • *Arabis* •
Aubrieta • *Draba* • *Erysimum*

Stanleya Prince's Plume   PLATE 28

Most of the genera in our Wishlist contain well-known garden
plants, but the prince's plume (*Stanleya pinnata*) is an exception.
A plant of the high plains of Colorado, Arizona, Utah, and farther
west, *S. pinnata* is remarkably drought tolerant and would be a
striking addition to any xeriscape, although it is adaptable enough
to grace any sunny zone 4 site with good drainage.

Above a rosette of basal 6-in (15-cm) leaves—some linear,
some pinnate—rises a 3-ft (0.9-m) raceme of 1-in (2.5-cm), brilliant
yellow cruciform blossoms. These open from the bottom of the
spike to the top in a display that lasts for weeks—months in some
strains. Kelly Grummons of Paulino Gardens in Denver, Colorado, knows of a dwarf *Stanleya* that matures at 16 in (41 cm) and
flowers for most of the summer. Unfortunately, prince's plume
sets only a few seeds at a time, and this makes it difficult to gather
enough seeds to supply commercial growers.

There is no doubt that prince's plume would be a top perennial if it were readily available. After all, it is hardy, drought tolerant, long flowering, and distinctively beautiful. What we need to
do is learn how to propagate it more efficiently. We are not asking
that this plant be remade in any way, but if older propagation
techniques such as root cuttings or leaf cuttings will not work,
then maybe tissue culture will succeed.

CUPRESSACEAE

Cedar or Cypress family   17 genera, 113 species

GENERA DISCUSSED   *Chamaecyparis • Cupressus • Juniperus*

OTHER ORNAMENTAL GENERA   *Libocedrus • Platycladus • Thuja*

The Cupressaceae offer a fine selection of coniferous evergreen shrubs for the garden, particularly from *Chamaecyparis* and *Juniperus*. Both of these genera have contributed an enormous variety of cultivars. Couple this with significant variations in hardiness and adaptability, and all sorts of hybridizing opportunities become evident.

Chamaecyparis False Cypress

Included in the genus *Chamaecyparis* are two species of extraordinary genetic variability: the hinoki false cypress (*Chamaecyparis obtusa*) and the sawara false cypress (*C. pisifera*). Both species contain dozens of garden forms, with colors ranging from green and blue to yellow and silver, and sizes ranging from 3 to 70 ft (0.9 to 21 m). These plants also come in an assortment of textures. The hinoki false cypress and sawara false cypress have varieties that form flat mounds and others that form narrow spires. The foliage of some have the velvety softness of moss, whereas in others it can be clumpy and ragged. Many threadleaf varieties are found in these two species, and some of the shrubs hold their foliage in twisted fans layer upon layer. Both false cypress species are zone 4 hardy, but there are provisos. Many of the cultivars are cold hardy to zone 6 only, and few are happy where there is dry heat in summer and drying winds in winter, even within their range of cold tolerance. Considering their unique forms and their great popularity in climates where they are currently grown, the false cypresses could use some hardier, more adaptable look-alikes that would do the gardening public a great service.

Chamaecyparis has been crossed with *Cupressus* to yield ×*Cupressocyparis* and this suggests the possibility of other intergeneric crosses within the family Cupressaceae. A likely candidate for a partner is *Juniperus,* a genus rich in variety that has species widely adapted to heat, wind, and zone 2 cold. The junipers, too, at least intragenerically, have shown a willingness to hybridize.

Cupressus Cypress

The true cypress of the genus *Cupressus* offers little that cannot be had in other genera, but the Monterey cypress (*Cupressus macrocarpa*) is an exception. It is one of the most picturesque of all trees, particularly when its trunk and limbs are flattened and twisted into wind-shaped sculptures. Even sited out of the wind, the Monterey cypress's multitrunked, flat-topped, and wide-spreading form makes this tree a prize. Unfortunately, this fine tree has a very limited natural range, and its horticultural range, too, is limited. Away from the cool moist air of the North American Pacific coast and places with similar climate, the Monterey cypress languishes and usually succumbs to disease.

With a little work, *Juniperus* cultivars such as 'Sea Green' and 'Hetzii' can be trained to resemble *Cupressus macrocarpa*, but such pretenders grow to only 10 ft (3 m) or so, compared to the 50-ft (15-m) height of the Monterey cypress. Maybe a cross between a juniper and this cypress will yield a proper tree with the striking form of the Monterey cypress and some of the hardiness of the juniper. Perhaps such a cross would be more disease resistant and more adaptable to inland sites.

Juniperus Juniper

Perhaps the most popular genus of evergreen shrubs and trees, *Juniperus* is found coast to coast in North America, from upper Canada to the lower United States. Many varieties and several intergeneric hybrids are widely known and grown. Junipers come as mat-forming groundcovers to 2 in (5 cm) high, pyramidal trees to 60 ft (18 m), and shrubs in almost every shape and size in between.

One juniper species, the alligator juniper (*Juniperus deppeana*), is seldom grown despite its magnificent and highly distinctive form. This 60-ft (18-m) tree is native to zones 7 and 8 in the arid regions of the American Southwest. It takes its name from the striking checkered pattern of its bark, like that of an alligator's hide. Mature specimens are thick-boled and gnarly—definitely treelike and decidedly picturesque.

Surely, bringing something like the alligator juniper into more and more climates is a goal worth pursuing. Some sort of hybrid between it and another juniper, say one of the larger *Juniperus* ×*media* cultivars or a stocky *J. virginiana* or *J. scopulorum*, might be the most expedient way to attain this goal.

EQUISETACEAE

Horsetail family   1 genus, 29 species

GENUS DISCUSSED   *Equisetum*

A lone genus in the family Equisetaceae is all that remains of a group of plants that dates back to the Paleozoic era, 345 million years ago. At that time they were the most advanced plants on the planet, some species growing to 30 ft (9 m). Today's horsetails range in size from 8 in (20 cm) to 6 ft (1.8 m), barely a hint of their former stature.

Equisetum Horsetail   PLATE 29

With hollow stems and no woody core, *Equisetum* stems incorporate silica into their tissues to increase their structural strength. The abrasive quality of the silica earns *Equisetum* the name "scouring rushes." Even without a knowledge of the fossil record one would be struck by the primitive look of these plants.

The design of most plants in this genus is that of a narrow upright tube. In some species, the jointed stem is ornamented with whorls of drooping slender stems, reminding one of umbrella frames stacked at intervals one above the other. A few species are evergreen, but most are deciduous. Some of the smaller horsetails form tangled grasslike mounds, but the larger ones form dense colonies of upright parallel stems—superb vertical accents, both elegant and emphatic. All forms like sun and sandy soil and most require abundant moisture at the roots. Most run, some aggressively so, and few plants are as difficult to eradicate once established.

These supremely elegant plants are unappreciated by gardeners except in Japan, where numerous varieties and hybrids are cultivated. Horsetails are often grown in containers that are sunk in the ground up to the rim, curbing the spreading tendency of the trees and allowing them to be given the amount of moisture they need. Otherwise, they require little care. Access to the abundant varieties of *Equisetum* that are so coveted in Japan and success in cloning them is probably enough to fire up a fad among westerners.

ERICACEAE

Heath family   103 genera, 3350 species

GENERA DISCUSSED   *Arbutus* • *Arctostaphylos* • *Enkianthus* • *Kalmia* •
Leucothoe • *Oxydendrum* • *Pieris* • *Rhododendron*

Only the Rosaceae and the Leguminosae rival the Ericaceae in the number of shrubs of garden merit they contain, and no family has received more attention from breeders interested in creating new forms and improving old ones than the heath family. Hybridizers have created numerous interspecific crosses among the rhododendrons, pieris, leucothoes, and others. Many of the forms are distinctive enough and desirable enough to have been patented and distributed worldwide. The effort has not only produced a wondrous variety of new plants but has also succeeded in bringing hardier forms of existing plants into entirely new regions both northward and southward.

Bravo! Keep up the good work. But on the other hand, maybe we have enough for awhile, at least in the directions currently being pursued. Maybe we should turn our attention to other genera of Ericaceae; maybe we should entertain some intergeneric crosses; maybe there are more significant challenges to tackle, challenges that promise a whole new set of rewards.

Arbutus Madrona, Strawberry Tree
The Pacific madrona (*Arbutus menziesii*) and the strawberry tree (*A. unedo*) are singularly beautiful trees, and they are prized wherever they grow, which unfortunately excludes most of the globe. *Arbutus menziesii* is native to California, found near the Pacific coast from zone 7 to zone 9. It can tolerate a variety of soils, droughty to moist and of low or high pH. This shrubby tree can reach 30 ft (9 m) in height. It has evergreen leaves and lovely but not spectacular drooping panicles of flowers. The red and shredding bark is extraordinarily beautiful on stems that twist and turn in a most picturesque way. It is considered a messy tree, dropping this and that here and there, and it is difficult to transplant when it outgrows the sapling stage. Nevertheless, the Pacific madrona's compelling beauty makes it a coveted showpiece wherever it can be grown.

The Pacific madrona's Mediterranean sibling, *Arbutus unedo*, is also an evergreen tree or shrub, with leaves and bark much like those of the madrona. It can reach a height of 10 ft (3 m) or 30 ft (9 m), depending on how it is grown and on the climate, and a 5-ft (1.5-m) bushy dwarf form is available as well. Although hardy only to zone 7, the strawberry tree can survive in many kinds of soils and is quite drought tolerant, yet it is more capable of coping with humidity than the madrona. Moreover, these two *Arbutus* have been hybridized with each other and the hybrid is more adaptable than either parent.

Why not try a cross between an *Arbutus* and a tough and hardy *Arctostaphylos*. Maybe we can develop a range of arbutus-like plants for inland regions—broadleaf evergreens in a range of sizes, with interesting shape and character, and beautiful bark for four-season interest. Any improvement in the adaptability of trees and shrubs like *Arbutus* would be greatly appreciated.

Arctostaphylos Bearberry, Kinnikinick, Manzanita

The humble bearberry (*Arctostaphylos uva-ursi*) is being recognized more and more as a premier groundcover. It is evergreen and tight, and its hardiness ranges from zone 2 to zone 6 (depending on the variety). The bearberry comes in small-leaved forms and relatively large-leaved forms. There are forms that remain green in winter and others that color bronze or red. Some varieties of *A. uva-ursi* are only 1 in (2.5 cm) high, whereas others grow to a full 1 ft (0.3 m). Forms have been selected for flower proclivity and the size of their red berries, and new selections appear every year. The popularity and availability of the bearberry are rapidly increasing, for this plant is not only beautiful and remarkably heat and cold hardy, but it also withstands drought and thrives on a wide range of soil pH. It is the exception: an ericaceous shrub that is both drought tolerant and pH tolerant. In fact, in the foothills of the Rocky Mountains of North America the plant is often found growing in huge patches in soils with pH levels over 8.5. The author has several patches growing in his own garden, some in full sun, others in nearly full shade, all in miserable bentonite clay with pH near 9.

Other *Arctostaphylos* plants are found in the high plains near the Rocky Mountains, such as *Arctostaphylos patula* and *A. nevadensis*. These are open, small- to medium-sized evergreen shrubs rather than groundcovers, and they are modestly attractive in flower and fruit. *Arctostaphylos patula* is hardy to zone 5, and *A. nevadensis* to zone 4, with a bit of help. Both shrubs are remarkably tolerant of drought and high pH. Hybrids between these and other species have been made, and that is encouraging.

The genus also offers some superb plants from the more mild climates of the western coast of the United States, particularly evergreens like the 6-ft (1.8-m) Stanford manzanita (*Arctostaphylos stanfordiana*), with dense panicles of bright pink bell-like flowers, and the similar silver manzanita (*A. canescens*). The stems of these plants are often quite contorted and display a superb patchwork pattern of tans and reddish mahogany. Flowering occurs over a very long period from winter into spring, and blossoms are often produced in spectacular abundance. The Stanford and silver manzanitas call zones 6 to 8 home, although I cannot speak for their pH tolerance.

Why not cross the shrubby manzanitas with the bearberry? Heat- and cold-tolerant broadleaved evergreens, particularly ones that can tolerate a dry atmosphere and alkaline soil, are not common. Anything new in this direction would be welcomed, and a shrubby, free-flowering manzanita would have the field to itself.

Enkianthus, Oxydendrum Sourwood, Sorreltree

For their long season of interest redvein enkianthus (*Enkianthus campanulatus*) and sourwood (*Oxydendrum arboreum*) are two of the most desirable small trees. The redvein enkianthus grows to 8 ft (2.5 m) and the sourwood to 30 ft (9 m), and both are inclined to a multistemmed shrubbiness, which is the way I like to see them grown. The *Enkianthus* flowers in the spring, with blueberrylike clusters of white to pink blossoms; the *Oxydendrum* flowers in early summer and has drooping, pierislike fragrant panicles. Both plants are deciduous and disrobe with a scarlet color-flourish second to none. *Enkianthus* is hardy to zone 5, although I have been growing one in a specially prepared bed in my zone 4 garden for several years—it has not yet reached 3 ft (0.9 m) and does not seem particularly happy. The sourwood is best in zone 6 and higher, although it can take zone 5 conditions if well sited. Both require moist acid soil.

Can we bring either of these small ericaceous trees or a facsimile into colder regions and onto alkaline soils? Probably, if we can cross them with *Arctostaphylos*. Since the redvein enkianthus and the sourwood are deciduous and the *Arctostaphylos* is evergreen, one might expect that, as in crosses within the genus *Berberis* (in the family Berberidaceae), the result will be semievergreen, at least in more rigorous climates. What will this do to the spectacular fall color display of the trees? Be prepared to give a little and take a little.

Kalmia, Leucothoe, Pieris Andromeda   PLATES 30, 31

Kalmia, Leucothoe, and *Pieris,* three cherished genera, all take zone 5 temperatures; indeed, mountain laurel (*Kalmia latifolia*) courts zone 4 without much difficulty, and a miniature alpine gem, the 6-in (15-cm) bog laurel (*K. polifolia*), is at least zone 3 hardy. All three genera are well known and popular, but they require fast-draining, moisture-retentive, acid soil, and none is happy in the desiccating path of a dry wind. Can *Kalmia, Leucothoe,* and *Pieris* be crossed with some *Arctostaphylos,* and if so will the latter contribute increased hardiness and pH tolerance to the other three? Surely it is worth a try.

Rhododendron Rhododendron, Azalea   PLATES 32, 33

Azaleas and rhododendrons may be the most popular shrubs in cultivation, with the possible exception of roses. Included in this vast genus are shrublets barely 6 in (15 cm) high, multi-stemmed trees to 40 ft (12 m), and all sorts in between, in both evergreen and deciduous varieties. *Rhododendron* species are found from near sea level in the deep south to as high as 6500 ft (2000 m) on the Japanese island of Yaku Shima. The leaves of these shrubs are varied and beautiful, and most rhododendrons make a splendid contribution to the garden all year long. But it is the flowers that steal the show: flowers 3 in (7.5 cm) across in packed panicles 14 in (36 cm) in diameter; small flowers in small clusters so profuse as to hide the foliage altogether; single flowers, double flowers, hose-in-hose flowers; flowers in white, pink, red, yellow, orange, green, and near blue—this splendid variety captivates gardeners around the globe.

The rhododendron clan seems to be made up of the most promiscuous plants on the planet. Crosses and backcrosses are made almost at will, and the offspring are usually fertile. The genus has been a hybridizer's dream, and breeders have created plants that thrive in muggy heat and crackling cold. In many places, however, growing rhododendrons requires heroic efforts. As is the case with some of their fellow Ericaceae, rhododendrons can often be difficult to grow because of their intolerance of alkaline soil and dry air. Additional hardiness for this genus would also not be spurned.

The zone 3 roseshell azalea (*Rhododendron prinophyllum*) and the zone 4 royal azalea (*R. schlippenbachii*), both magnificent species, are claimed to have a tolerance for mildly sweet soils. Maybe, then, there is hope for creating cold-hardy, alkaline-tolerant rhododendrons and azaleas. (The royal azalea is reluctant to hybridize and might require some help from biotechnological processes to do so.) Whether this approach works or not, it might be worthwhile to attempt a cross between *Rhododendron* and *Arctostaphylos*. Here again, the proposed cross is between such seemingly disparate parents, and the stakes are so high, that an F_2 generation should probably be pursued, utilizing, if necessary, the new biotechnological methods.

EUPHORBIACEAE

Spurge family   321 genera, 7950 species

GENERA DISCUSSED   *Codiaeum* • *Euphorbia*

Euphorbiaceae is a large family that represents taxonomy at its most tangled and most controversial. If the "splitters" (see Chapter 2) have their way, this family might be divided into several families; if the "lumpers" prevail, Euphorbiaceae might include everything that is green. In either case, the spurge family is a collection containing extraordinary diversity, already with much to offer and hinting at a great deal more.

Codiaeum Croton
    It is with some hesitation that I mention the crotons (*Codiaeum*) since I find them all too garish indoors and I can barely suffer them outdoors even in the tropics. Looking at the extraordinary range of colors and patterns in the leaves, however—designs so beautiful and varied that they could foster an entire art movement—I can easily see why these plants remain so popular for indoor and outdoor decoration.
    Those of us living in zones colder than zone 10 need not worry about giving in to such crass temptations. But once in a while it is fun to succumb to the outrageous, and if I could liven up a dull spot in the garden with the sparkle of a croton (*Codiaeum variegatum*), I probably would do so. How can we introduce this plant to winter? Maybe crossing it with a *Euphorbia* will broker the meeting.

Euphorbia Spurge
    Euphorbia—with 1600 species worldwide—is the largest genus in a large family. Some of the most noxious, persistent, and aggressive weeds belong to this genus, as do some particularly sturdy, useful, and beautiful plants. It is all a question of when spurge goes to scourge.
    Cushion spurge (*Euphorbia polychroma*, syn. *E. epithymoides*) is probably the most popular of the garden euphorbias. It is a neat plant for most of the season, forming 15-in (38-cm) high mounds of glaucous green foliage. Effectively set off against this foliage are greenish yellow bracts that last for up to a month before dis-

cretely fading from view. In the fall the foliage colors nicely in hues of orange and red. This zone 3 hardy plant, unlike most of its brethren, will tolerate a bit of wetness at the roots and a bit of shade, and although almost any soil is acceptable, cushion spurge is well behaved and not at all weedy.

Myrtle euphorbia (*Euphorbia myrsinites*), on the other hand, is a weed—free-seeding, hardy to zone 4, and widely adaptable— but it is a beautiful weed, with lax stems of blue-green oval leaves that bring to mind some of the eucalyptus. The stems can reach a length of 12 in (30 cm) or more, but rising to more than 8 in (20 cm) is a struggle. Heads of greenish yellow bracts crown the branches for a month in spring, but the plants are showy for most of the year because of their structural quality and their glaucous color.

What can we do to improve *Euphorbia myrsinites*? First and foremost, tame it. Myrtle euphorbia has so much going for it that all it needs is a bit of discipline. Exposing the plant to radiation or some chemical mutagen might work to reduce its fertility or render it sterile—after all, it is easy to reproduce by stem cuttings. Maybe crossing *E. myrsinites* with *E. polychroma* would yield a hybrid of reduced fertility but with some of the sculptural form of *E. myrsinites*. This would be a welcome addition to the gardenworthy spurges.

Another delightful and adaptable zone 3 hardy euphorbia is the cypress spurge (*Euphorbia cyparissias*). With upright stems to 1 ft (0.3 m) clad in narrow leaves, cypress spurge looks somewhat like a miniature of its namesake. Come spring, the stems of *E. cyparissias* are topped with full heads of greenish yellow bracts. Beautiful in flower as well as in form, it would make a superb garden plant were it not for its cursed proclivity to seed itself around. Make no mistake, cypress spurge is a weed—a pernicious, tenacious, ineradicable weed. How, then, might we improve the cypress spurge? As with *E. myrsinites*, controlling its fecundity would yield a truly superior plant. What's more, a reduction in fertility might also increase the already lengthy bloom period of the plant.

Euphorbia griffithii, in its various garden forms such as 'Fireglow', is quite a different plant. This spurge has lancelike leaves along 2- to 3-ft (0.6- to 0.9-m) upright stems. In late spring the stems support showy heads of red bracts that subtend insignificant flowers. *Euphorbia griffithii* puts on another show in the fall, when the leaves recall the red color of the earlier display. It is zone 5 (maybe 4) hardy and tolerates both a bit of shade and a bit of moisture—not common traits in this genus. After flowering, however, the stems become too lax to be tidy and too stiff to be gracefully sprawling, at which time the plant's appearance may be described as somewhere between mediocre and downright shabby—that is, until it takes on its autumn coloring. Weediness is not a concern for this species of *Euphorbia*, but it would be nice to have shorter and stiffer plants with increased hardiness. A cross of *Euphorbia griffithii* with *E. polychroma* or *E. cyparissias* might achieve these goals; at the very least it is likely to be different.

Perhaps the most striking of all garden euphorbias is *Euphorbia characias*. It has an immense, spherical, yellow-green inflorescence atop a 4-ft (1.2-m) erect stem furnished with narrow glaucous leaves 5 in (12.5 cm) long. I would sacrifice any of the other species of *Euphorbia* to be able to grow this one, but it is only hardy to zone 8. Again, *E. cyparissias*, *E. myrsinites*, or *E. polychroma* might contribute hardiness to a cross with *E. characias* and give us a smaller, more usable form as well.

What about all the other species in this vast genus? They seem to fall roughly into two categories: noxious but not necessarily unattractive weeds annoyingly common in the temperate regions, even into zone 2, and those sculpturally superb and highly ornamental tropical and subtropical succulents. Why not cross some from the former group with some of the latter? How would hardiness transfer? How would succulence be distributed? Size, color, and all sorts of other features might be allocated in new and interesting ways. Such a breeding program could result in a vast gallery of new garden-worthy plants. Of course, it could also result in trash. Any gamblers out there?

FAGACEAE

Beech family   7 genera, 1050 species

GENERA DISCUSSED   *Carya* • *Castanea* • *Fagus* • *Nothofagus* •
Quercus

Many of the most majestic trees are found in the beech family
(Fagaceae), trees of value for their timber, their bark, and their ornamental qualities. Nature supplies such a grand diversity of species that wanting more from the Fagaceae might seem ungrateful,
but I think that much more is not only very possible but also quite
likely.

Carya Hickory, *Castanea* Chestnut

Even before the American native chestnut (*Castanea dentata*)
was all but eliminated by the chestnut blight, the tree was never
considered to be a serviceable ornamental. It is too coarse and
much too messy. The hickories, however, do have some ornamental value, particularly the shagbark hickory (*Carya ovata*). The
zone 4 shagbark hickory can reach a straight and fairly narrow 80
ft (24 m), imposing enough even in this family of giants. The leaves
turn golden-tan in autumn, and the tree's shaggy bark, shredding
in long, silvery gray strips, is a distinctive feature throughout the
year.

The nuts of *Carya ovata* are perfectly palatable, but to avoid the
litter and the squirrels, sterile clones could be vegetatively propagated, or anther culture could be used to give us haploid or dou-
ble-haploid (two identical copies of a haploid genome) male trees.
The big problem with shagbark hickory is that it is tap-rooted. Although this gives the tree some drought tolerance, it makes it difficult to transplant the tree beyond the seedling stage. Maybe root
pruning two or three times is all that is needed, or maybe a judicious cross with some oak would solve the problem of the tap root,
as well as introduce more variety in leaf shape and fall color. There
does seem to be an opportunity to add something new to the very
short list of drought-tolerant, pH-adaptable, and cold-hardy
shade trees.

Fagus Beech PLATE 34

The two grand beeches for gardens and private estates are the European beech (*Fagus sylvatica*) and the American beech (*F. grandifolia*). Both species are large and massive at maturity—a height of 70 ft (21 m) for the European beech and as much as 100 ft (30 m) for the American. Both have smooth gray bark stretched over a thick fluted trunk. The leaves of the two beech species are similar, turning a pleasant bronzy yellow in the fall. The European beech seems to have the richer gene pool, and selections have been made for leaf color (purples, yellows, and variegated), leaf shape (miniature, fluted, and lancinated), and habit (dwarf, weeping, and others). Beeches are usually grown as isolated specimens, given enough room to display their grandeur to the fullest. But strolling in the heavy shade among the massive trunks of a dense beech forest brings its own pleasures.

As popular as they are over much of Europe, South America, and the coasts of North America, these two grand beech trees are not often seen in the interior of North America. They are cold-hardy enough (zone 3 for the American beech, zone 4 for the European beech), but either the soil or the drying winds or the heat does not suit the trees. In their larger forms, *Fagus sylvatica* and *F. grandifolia* dominate the landscape, leaving little room for anything else, and their hungry, extensive near-surface roots assure their hegemony. Few plants grow happily under a beech, and this too may lessen their usefulness.

On the other hand, with so many varieties of European beech, one can expect some variation in adaptability. Several of the purple-leaved clones of European beech seem to be hardier and more adaptable than the species. Perhaps one of the dwarf or semidwarf clones, from 10 to 20 ft (3 to 6 m) in height, would stand up better under wind and snow, and maybe it would be more appropriate for gardens of less-than-estate size. Maybe popularizing this tree and exploiting its usefulness is mainly a question of the availability of special clones.

Nothofagus Southern Beech

Many other spectacular beeches are available in addition to the European and American beeches—strange and wonderful trees from the southern hemisphere, trees I have seen in Chile and parts of California but nowhere else. These are the southern beeches of the genus *Nothofagus*. So different are they from those of the north that one might guess the southern beeches belong to a different family. Some of these, such as *Nothofagus betuloides* and *N. solanderi* among others, display their tiny leaves in a herringbonelike spray, reminiscent of *Cotoneaster horizontalis* (in the family Rosaceae). Others, such as *N. procera*, have corrugated, 4-in (10-cm) hornbeamlike leaves. In many, fall color is a spectacular mix of orange, red, and yellow; others are evergreen. In general, the southern beeches are smaller and more graceful than their northern relatives, and many tend to a sinuous, multistemmed shrubbiness that can be remarkably picturesque.

Could a fortuitous cross with American beech or European beech extradite some of the traits of the southern beeches to the north? Then again, crossing a beech with an oak (*Quercus*) is an obvious possibility. After all, many different oaks, from imperial trees to modest shrubs, have that legendary oak hardiness to cold, wind, snow, heat, and miserable soil. Why not try it? We might get some wonderful new plant forms, and some interesting leaf colors and patterns as well.

Quercus Oak   PLATE 35

Wherever they grow, the great oaks—including the red oak (*Quercus rubra*), the white oak (*Q. alba*), the English oak (*Q. robur*), the live oak (*Q. virginiana*), and the California live oak (*Q. lobata*)—dominate the landscape with their imposing size and widespreading undulating frame. They live for centuries, becoming more and more imposing with every year.

Depending on the species, oaks are valued for the shape of their leaves, their fall color, their sturdy and impressive form, and their hardiness. Several of the great oaks thrive in zone 4, but others, such as the live oak (*Quercus virginiana*), are hardy only to zone 7. Some oaks are notably drought tolerant, as in the case of the burr oak (*Q. macrocarpa*), and will take some alkalinity in the soil. The pin oak (*Q. palustris*) and others prefer more acidic soil. Northern oaks—the white oak, the red oak, and the burr oak, for example—are strong enough to withstand heavy winds, and many are both heat and drought tolerant.

Like the beech species, oaks will outgrow most of today's suburban lots long before their full landscape potential is realized. Several much smaller oaks, however, are under appreciated and seldom used. Gambel oak (*Quercus gambelii*) is one of the small ones, as fine and useful as any. It is extraordinarily variable, and so it is not so easy to describe. There is a 30-ft (9-m) specimen in a cushy canyon in Mesa Verde National Park, Colorado, but nearby other mature shrubby specimens stand less than 8 ft (2.5 m) tall. The Gambel oak can grow a single straight trunk, or form a clump with many sinuous stems. The leaves, too, are variable, but most are about 4 in (10 cm) long and shaped like those of a white oak. Fall color can be a soft gold or a solid orange-red, and like many oaks, the leaves are held late into fall. *Quercus gambelii* is a tough little tree, hardy at least into zone 4, tolerant of drought, high wind, heavy snow, and alkaline soil (to some degree), and it is essentially pest and disease free.

Other shrubby evergreen dwarfs are also found in this genus. The huckleberry oak (*Quercus vacciniifolia*) keeps its small leaves through the winter, even in zone 5. It is a rather sprawling shrub, about 2 ft (0.6 m) tall, but perhaps in warmer zones it will reach greater heights.

Numerous hybrid oaks are currently bring evaluated at the University of Utah in Salt Lake City, Utah. If Gambel oak or one of the hardier dwarf evergreen species has not yet been crossed with one of the northern giants, we may be missing a great opportunity: the possibility of creating super-hardy, widely adaptable, moderate-sized oaks, maybe even some evergreen types. There aren't many tree-sized broadleaved evergreens to be found far from the coasts.

GENTIANACEAE

Gentian family   74 genera, 1200 species

GENERA DISCUSSED   *Eustoma* • *Gentiana*

Eustoma Prairie Gentian

A member of the genus *Eustoma* (syn. *Lisianthus*), the prairie gentian (*Eustoma grandiflorum*) is enjoying a surge in popularity in the United States and Japan, and it deserves every bit of it. The species has stiff upright stems from 2 to 5 ft (0.6 to 1.5 m) in height and exquisite blossoms that open from roselike buds to flaring trumpets 3 in (7.5 cm) across. The seed-propagated cultivars of prairie gentian range in height from 9 to 24 in (23 to 60 cm), some bearing single blooms, some double. The blossoms come in a very wide range of colors, including white, pink, and blue, as well as various bicolors. The plants have an extraordinarily long flowering season—from July through August—and some optimists consider prairie gentians to be perennial, although most of us grow them as annuals. This matter might be easily solved by crossing the prairie gentians with some of the truly perennial gentians.

Gentiana Gentian   PLATE 36

The taller gentians are sometimes grown in a border, but here I focus on the small alpine gentians, like the 4-in (10-cm) spring-flowering *Gentiana acaulis* and the 8-in (20-cm) summer-flowering *G. septemfida*, those bluer-than-blue flowered gems that are the darlings of the rock garden enthusiasts. Generally, the dwarf gentians have rather finicky requirements, some needing soil that is definitely acid, others needing soil that is definitely alkaline. Some shade is appreciated by most. The two high-country gentians mentioned here are quite adaptable and easy to grow.

Gentians show a great willingness to hybridize among themselves, but what I wish to suggest is crossing one of the alpine gentians with prairie gentians. It would be interesting to take the colorful *Eustoma grandiflorum* and cross it with one of the hardier perennial gentians like *Gentiana acaulis* or *G. septemfida*. The result could be a committed perennial, in a very usable height range intermediate between the alpine gentians and prairie gentian, accommodating as to soil and sun requirements, and having absolutely beautiful blossoms in all shades of white, pink, and blue.

GERANIACEAE

Geranium family   14 genera, 730 species

GENERA DISCUSSED   *Erodium* • *Geranium* • *Pelargonium*

The garden interest in the family Geraniaceae is focused on only three genera. However, within this restricted realm are found several cherished perennials—some cherished for their flowers, some for their foliage, and some for their scent. Not all of these traits are present in every member, however, and each has a contribution to make.

Erodium Hawksbill, Heron's Bill, Storksbill
The hawksbills, such as *Erodium chamaedryoides*, with their pink flowers and scalloped foliage, look like miniature (3 in by 3 in (7.5 by 7.5 cm)) geraniums. Erodiums are considered weeds by some since many forms are known to seed themselves rampantly. I, however, have not been that lucky. In my zone 4 garden, hawksbills often last only one season, and they do not set much seed.

Geranium
Geranium—the flagship genus of the family—includes some of the finest of all garden perennials. The flowers, depending on the species or cultivar, are white, silvery pink, bright red, or blue. Individual blossoms, ranging from 1 to 2 in (2.5 to 5 cm) across, last over a long period from early spring to midsummer on plants 6 in (15 cm) to 2 ft (0.6 m) in height. The leaves, dissected into various snowflake patterns or scalloped, are 1 to 5 in (2.5 to 13 cm) across and are as beautiful as any, whether seen as a groundcover or sited in the perennial border. Clearly there are many reasons to grow geraniums, and since types are available from zone 3 to zone 10, suitable for all sorts of soils and exposures (including shade), many gardeners worldwide grow them.

Perhaps one could use erodiums to miniaturize the geraniums, creating a variety of geraniumlike plants in the 3 to 6 in (7.5 to 15 cm) range, with all the flower colors and leaf patterns of the geraniums in a much smaller package. Too precious? Not with all the current interest in diminutive plants.

Pelargonium

   Among the pelargoniums is the big, blowzy geranium *Pelargonium* ×*hortorum*, sold by the millions for patio pot culture. The genus *Pelargonium* also includes the scented geraniums—lemon scented, apple scented, rose scented, and others—so popular as indoor windowsill plants. It is the bedding geranium that is of interest to us here, however. *Pelargonium* ×*hortorum*, a complex hybrid involving *P. inquinans* and *P. zonale*, is a zone 10 perennial but it is primarily grown as an annual. In accordance with the philosophy that bigger and brasher is better, these plants boast 1.5-in (4-cm) flowers on spherical heads up to 5 in (13 cm) across, in all shades of white, pink, orange, and red. Some, like the 'Martha Washington' pelargoniums (*P.* ×*domesticum*, complex hybrids involving *P. cucullatum*, *P. grandiflorum*, and others) have patterned blossoms in looser sprays—less garish in color and more subtle in effect. The zonal geraniums (*P.* ×*hortorum* cultivars) feature exceptionally beautiful leaves with scalloped margins and concentric bands of color that may include hues of purple, green, cream, and pink.

   Why not cross 'Martha Washington' geraniums or zonal geraniums with the true geraniums? The purpose would be to offer the larger flowers of the 'Martha Washington' geraniums and the color pattern of the zonal varieties to gardeners in colder climates. Maybe the color pattern of the zonals can be superimposed on the snowflake shape of the leaves of the true geraniums. If so, we might get some of the most striking foliage plants to be seen in the garden. And if some find these hybrids too bold, maybe smaller versions could be created with the help of the erodiums.

GRAMINEAE

Grass family 635 genera, 9000 species

GENERA DISCUSSED *Cortaderia* • *Erianthus*

OTHER ORNAMENTAL GENERA *Alopecurus* • *Arrhenatherum* • *Avena* • *Bambusa* and other bamboos • *Briza* • *Calamagrostis* • *Carex* • *Deschampsia* • *Festuca* • *Glyceria* • *Hakonechloa* • *Helictotrichon* • *Imperata* • *Koeleria* • *Miscanthus* • *Panicum* • *Pennisetum* • *Phalaris* • *Stipa*

No family of plants is more important to human civilization than the Gramineae (also known as Poaceae). All our food grains—barley, millet, oats, rice, rye, wheat, and so on—belong to the grass family. Here, too, are the bamboos, which are used for so many different purposes, particularly in Far East Asia. The family also supplies us with our turf grasses, as well as many ornamentals. (See Plate 37.)

For those of us interested in ornamental horticulture, the turf grasses should be our main concern. More than half of the water use in urban and suburban areas in the United States is consumed in the upkeep of bluegrass lawns, and in many climates the maintenance of bluegrass lawns must now be seen as environmentally irresponsible. It is time to find alternatives.

The environmentally-responsible alternative that would also provide the greatest contribution to ornamental horticulture would be the development of hardy, low-maintenance, long-season, and pest- and disease-resistant turf grasses with an additional, singularly important feature—drought resistance. Extensive programs for developing new grasses with these attributes are currently underway, and a Canadian project is making significant progress using prairie grasses. Another approach is to use some other groundcover in place of grass—*Thymus serpyllum* or *Veronica repens*, for example.

As far as the taller ornamental grasses are concerned, so many beautiful, hardy, and adaptable species are available, and so many new varieties are introduced each year, that we can only complain about the limitations of one such species. That single exception, pampas grass, may be the most spectacular grass of all.

Cortaderia Pampas Grass, *Erianthus* Northern Pampas Grass

The pampas grass familiar to most of us is *Cortaderia selloana*. A superb ornamental to 12 ft (3.7 m) tall (with inflorescence it rises to as much as 20 ft (6 m) tall), it is topped with massive white, cream, or pink plumes—a showpiece that is impossible to ignore. Unfortunately, *C. selloana*'s cold-hardiness is suspect below zone 8.

In zones 4 to 9, gardeners can grow the northern pampas grass (*Erianthus ravenae*). Its foliage mass grows to a height of 8 ft (2.5 m) and its inflorescence can tower 7 ft (2 m) above that. Northern pampas grass almost compares with pampas grass in height, but its flower panicles are dingy in color and stingy in size by comparison.

Perhaps some fortuitous union can be struck by crossing the two ornamental grasses. Maybe the progeny will share the drought tolerance common to both, yet be hardier than *Cortaderia* and showier than *Erianthus*. Such a grass would make a choice addition to northern gardens.

1 Vine maple (*Acer circinatum*) sporting its autumn finery

2 Amur maple (*Acer ginnala*) in autumn

3 Flame Amur maple (*Acer ginnala* 'Flame'), selected by the United States Department of Agriculture for its brilliant red fall color, showing its keys in summer

4 Bigtooth maple (*Acer grandidentatum*) in autumn

5 Japanese maples (*Acer palmatum*)

6 *Alocasia micholitziana*

7 *Anthurium andraeanum* naturalized on the island of Dominica in the Caribbean Sea (photo by Seth Malitz)

8 *Arisaema ringens*, with leaves 18 in (46 cm) across, in the Japanese Garden of the United States National Arboretum, Washington, D.C.

9 Gray birch (*Betula populifolia*), more adaptable than the European white birch (*B. pendula*) and nearly as lovely, Gorham Mountain Trail, Acadia National Park, Maine

10 Trumpet vine (*Campsis radicans*) flowering for months during summer

11 *Catalpa speciosa* in bloom during much of June

12 *Catalpa speciosa*

13 Golden elder (*Sambucus canadensis* 'Aurea') in full flower during early summer

14 Cutleaf golden elder (*Sambucus racemosa* 'Plumosa Aurea'), Jasper, Canada

15 Nannyberry viburnum (*Viburnum lentago*) flowering in late spring

16 *Achillea* 'Coronation Gold' flowering throughout most of the summer

17 *Anaphalis margaritacea* flowering in August, Trail Ridge Road, Rocky Mountain National Park, Colorado

18 Pussytoes (*Antennaria pulcherrima*), a superb drought-tolerant, evergreen groundcover, and *Erigeron compositus*, one of several dwarf erigerons common in the mountains of Colorado

19 *Chrysanthemum weyrichii* flowering in September

20 *Cosmos bipinnatus* 'Sonata Mix' flowering from late spring to fall

21 *Gazania* hybrids provide all-summer bloom

22 *Senecio atratus* flowering in August at 10,000 ft (3000 m), Trail
Ridge Road, Rocky Mountain National Park, Colorado

23 Hoary senecio (*Senecio canus*) flowering in summer on scree and
tallis slopes from the subalpine to the alpine region throughout the
Rocky Mountains

24 Bunchberry dogwood (*Cornus canadensis*), summer-flowering, Banff National Park, Canada

25 Eastern flowering dogwood (*Cornus florida*) flowering in midspring

26 Kousa dogwood (*Cornus kousa*)—a tree for all seasons

27 *Cornus kousa* displays bracts that in some forms can span 4 in (10 cm) from tip to opposing tip

28 Prince's plume (*Stanleya pinnata*) in summer, Arches National Monument, Utah

29 Tall scouring rush (*Equisetum hyemale*), an elegant 4-ft (1.2-m) accent, as primitive as it looks, Golden Gate Park, San Francisco, California

30 Bog laurel (*Kalmia polifolia*) flowering in July on the shores of Timber Lake, Rocky Mountain National Park, Colorado

31 *Pieris japonica*, an evergreen shrub of four-season interest, flowering in May

32 Azalea hybrid
(*Rhododendron*) in
May, Brooklyn
Botanic Garden,
New York

33 An unabashedly brilliant grouping of azaleas, Brooklyn Botanic
Garden, New York

34 European beech (*Fagus sylvatica*), with its unmistakable burly bole

35 Gambel oak (*Quercus gambelii*) holds its leaves throughout most of the winter

36 Arctic gentian (*Gentiana algida*), with jadelike 1.5-in (4-cm) blossoms, flowering in August at 12,000 ft (3600 m) on the shores of Chasm Lake, Rocky Mountain National Park, Colorado

37 Various grasses: varieties of silver grass (*Miscanthus*), Japanese blood grass (*Imperata cylindrica* 'Red Baron'), and blue oat grass (*Helictotrichon sempervirens*), Elizabeth Park, Hartford, Connecticut

38 Ohio buckeye
(*Aesculus glabra*),
distinctive color
in October

39 *Aesculus ×plantierensis*, a backcross of *A. ×carnea* × *A. hippocastanum*,
showing its exquisite blossoms in May

40 Cliff jamesia
(*Jamesia americana*) in
October,
Rocky Mountain
National Park,
Colorado

41 Mockorange
(*Philadelphus*
'Galahad')
displaying its
fragrant, single
white flowers in
June

42 *Iris pseudacorus* blooming in May

43 *Iris* 'Paltec', a cross between a crested iris (*Iris tectorum*) and a bearded iris (*Iris pallida*)

44 Roof iris (*Iris tectorum* 'Alba') blooming in May, with an unpretentious natural grace not often found in today's hybrid iris

45 Goldenchain tree (*Laburnum ×watereri*) flowering in May (photo by Susan Malitz)

46 Black locust (*Robinia pseudoacacia*), with highly fragrant flowers from mid-May to June

47 Japanese wisteria (*Wisteria floribunda*) in May, Brooklyn Botanic Garden, New York

48 Fireweed (*Epilobium angustifolium*) blooming in July, along Icefields Parkway, Canada

49 Prickly poppy (*Argemone polyanthemos*) blooming throughout most of the summer

50 *Cedrus atlantica* 'Glauca Pendula'—a suberb specimen in the Gotelli collection of the National Arboretum, Washington, D.C.

51 *Picea pungens* 'Girard's Dwarf Blue', one of many dwarf varieties of the Colorado blue spruce, stands 2.5 ft (0.75 m) tall after fifteen years in the author's garden

52 *Pinus griffithii* 'Zebrina': "as striking and interesting a cultivar as one could hope to see among the pines," according to Michael Dirr (1990). In the Gotelli collection of the National Arboretum, Washington, D.C.

53 Sargent's weeping hemlock (*Tsuga canadensis* 'Sargentii'), an attractive weeping form of the eastern hemlock

54 *Primula japonica* blooming in May, New York Botanical Garden, New York

55 *Clematis occidentalis*, Rocky Mountain National Park, Colorado

56 Subalpine buttercup (*Ranunculus eschscholtzii*), a silky, diminutive beauty, in July at nearly 12,000 ft (3600 m), Poudre Lake Trail, Rocky Mountain National Park, Colorado

57 The crabapple 'Profusion' (*Malus ×moerlandsii* 'Profusion') living up to its name during three weeks of May

58 Shrubby cinquefoil (*Potentilla fruticosa*), near Mills Lake, Rocky
Mountain National Park, Colorado

59 Flowering cherry, exquisite in April, Golden Gate Park, San
Francisco, California

60 Japanese flowering cherry (*Prunus serrulata* 'Kwanzan') in May,
Cape Cod, Massachusetts

61 Wild rose (*Rosa woodsii*) with July bloom, Tonahutu Trail, Rocky Mountain National Park, Colorado

62 European mountain ash (*Sorbus aucuparia*) showing its long-lasting fruit in October

63 Plains cottonwood (*Populus sargentii*) putting on its autumn show, Boulder, Colorado

64 Quaking aspen (*Populus tremuloides*), Rocky Mountain National Park, Colorado

65 Yellowhorn (*Xanthoceras sorbifolium*) blooming in May, Arnold
Arboretum, Boston, Massachusetts

66 Flowering pitcher plants (*Sarracenia* spp.) in the outdoor bog garden of the US Botanic Garden, Washington, D.C.

67 Indian paintbrush (*Castilleja miniata*) in flower throughout July, subalpine regions, Rocky Mountain National Park, Colorado

68 Little elephant head (*Pedicularis groenlandica*), near Poudre Lake, Rocky Mountain National Park, Colorado

69 *Sequoia sempervirens*, Redwood National Forest, California

70 *Stewartia sinensis*, a shrub or small tree, with magnificent purple-red-orange fall color, exquisite white flowers in late summer, and a bark pattern that is second to none, Arnold Arboretum, Boston, Massachusetts

GROSSULARIACEAE

Currant or Gooseberry family   23 genera, 340 species

GENERA DISCUSSED   *Escallonia* • *Ribes*

Escallonia
   The genus *Escallonia* has several shrubs, a few shrubby trees, and some hybrids. Of limited adaptability to low temperatures, they are, nevertheless, fairly tolerant of wind, shade, salt, and pH. Although some have drooping branchlets, most *Escallonia* plants have an upright habit. Shiny, elliptic leaves and abundant small cymes of flowers in white, pink, or red (depending on the species), borne over a very long season (continually in favored climates), add to the value of these plants and contribute to their popularity, particularly in England and parts of California. With cold tolerance only to zone 7, however, this plant's popularity is obviously restricted.

Ribes Currant, Gooseberry
   Delectable fruit is the principal virtue of some of the ribes, but others are notable for their ornamental qualities. Alpine currant (*Ribes alpinum*) is a neat, twiggy shrub to 3 ft (0.9 m), with 1-in (2.5-cm), scalloped leaves lasting long into fall and showing early in spring. Drought tolerance and zone 2 hardiness also contribute to its popularity. *Ribes alpinum* prunes well to make a hedge, and it is also quite acceptable as a small specimen or in a shrub border. The small, nondescript yellow-green inflorescence is of no consequence.
   In contrast, the flowering or winter currant (*Ribes sanguineum*) bears drooping 3-in (7.5-cm) panicles of blossoms in white, pink, or red—a standout in the early-spring garden but not a knockout. Although it is hardy to zone 5, *R. sanguineum* flowers early enough to be nipped in the bud in those regions with late frosts. Out of flower, it is a rather ungainly upright shrub to 10 ft (3 m), with no great distinction except for its 3-in (7.5-cm), maple-shaped leaves. Several cultivars of *R. sanguineum*, like the red-flowered 'King Edward VII', are shorter, to about 6 ft (1.8 m), and more compact.
   The principal garden interest of clove currant (*Ribes odoratum*) is the scent of its blossoms—a penetrating, spicy, clovelike fra-

grance that is always an attention getter in the late-spring garden. The small, bright yellow flowers borne in short racemes are quite showy, however, and gardeners may purchase the clove currant for this feature alone. The 3-in (7.5-cm) leaves remind one of a ragged-edged maple leaf, and the clove currant's fall color—scarlet, as bright as any, even when grown in partial shade—is not dimmed by comparison. Otherwise, the shrub is rather ordinary: 6 ft (1.8 m) tall, fairly upright, and less than neat. As with the alpine currant and flowering currant species of *Ribes*, clove currant has considerable shade tolerance and is hardy to zone 4, at least.

Where might we go from here? Judging from the popularity of the flowering currant in those places where it can be grown, a hybrid between the flowering currant and the alpine currant—if it honors the flowering proclivity of the first and the hardiness of the second—might be well received. Maybe the form will also be improved and the stature reduced. Maybe clove currant should be added to the mix for scent and fall color or to give an even wider range of flower color.

An *Escallonia* × *Ribes* hybrid might yield evergreen or semievergreen shrubs of great distinction, hardy enough to survive in those regions that are most in need of such plants. Of course, one can also entertain the possibility of increasing the showiness of the *Escallonia* blossoms by such crosses.

HIPPOCASTANACEAE

Horse Chestnut family   2 genera, 15 species

GENUS DISCUSSED   *Aesculus*

Aesculus Buckeye, Horse Chestnut   PLATES 38, 39
     After most of the cherries and crabapples have blossomed, the buckeyes of the genus *Aesculus* take the stage and put on a floral display of tropical flamboyance. Panicles to 16 in (41 cm) in length hold blossoms extending to 1 in (2.5 cm) across. Varieties come in white, red, and salmon, and some even show blends of white, rose, and yellow all on the same flower. The huge (to 12 in (30 cm)) compound palmate leaves are distinctive and boldly attractive.
     Many people see these trees as being irredeemably coarse and much too large for the small garden. Some criticize the lack of fall color, and some condemn the larger species as messy and disease-prone. Smaller species are available, however. The zone 4 red-flowered red buckeye (*Aesculus pavia*) grows to 35 ft (11 m); the superb bottlebrush buckeye (*A. parviflora*) is a suckering shrub to 12 ft (3.7 m) that blooms in early summer, more than a month after the others have finished; and the Ohio buckeye (*A. glabra*) is a tree to 40 ft (12 m), but usually much shorter, with flowers less remarkable than the others and with smaller leaves that color orange in the fall.
     The opportunities are obvious: hybridize the larger buckeyes to the smaller ones in the hopes of achieving a class of trees and shrubs of moderate size with an assortment of flower colors and an extended period of bloom. The Ohio buckeye can contribute its fall color and smaller leaves. Another union to consider is between the bottlebrush buckeye and the red buckeye. This, too, should yield dwarf trees and large shrubs with the superbly shaped distinctive foliage typical of the family. In addition, we might see the extraordinary length of the panicles of the bottlebrush buckeye in combination with the vivid coloring of the red buckeye.
     It should be mentioned that the bottlebrush buckeye (*Aesculus parviflora*), widely praised as one of the most ornamental large shrubs, is not easy to find on the market. Forestfarm Nurseries, in Williams, Oregon, has listed the plant on occasion, but the nursery

admits that it is very difficult to obtain viable seed in quantity. On the other hand, the shrub does sucker, and this might provide a reliable and economical means of propagation. If not, then *in vitro* culture methods might be used to bring this choice plant to more people.

No intergeneric crosses within the family Hippocastanaceae hold much promise, but there are reasons to entertain crosses between buckeyes and members of the soapberry family (Sapindaceae). The two families are thought to be very closely related; the palmate leaves and larger seed of the Hippocastanaceae primarily account for the distinction. The Sapindaceae contain two superb garden plants: the popular golden rain tree (*Koelreuteria paniculata*) and the little-known yellowhorn (*Xanthoceras sorbifolium*; Plate 65). The golden rain tree is common enough to mention without description, but the *Xanthoceras* is far less common. Given its own way, the yellowhorn is more of a shrub than a tree, reaching only 20 ft (6 m) in height. It is hardy at least into zone 4, and in midspring the plant bears exquisite trumpet-shaped, yellow-throated white blossoms that are 1-in (2.5-cm) across and held in loose racemes. The 9-in (23-cm) pinnate leaves are reminiscent of a refined sumac.

A buckeye crossed with a yellowhorn might yield small trees or large shrubs with superb blossoms and foliage that is not coarse like that of the buckeye trees. Buckeye crossed with the golden rain tree might do the same, with the promise of introducing a good yellow flower color into the mix. All are worthwhile goals.

HYDRANGEACEAE

Hydrangea family   17 genera, 170 species

GENERA DISCUSSED   *Fendlera* • *Hydrangea* • *Jamesia* • *Philadelphus*

Some of the garden's most extravagant flowering shrubs belong to the hydrangea family, and some of the most fragrant shrubs belong here as well. Several lesser-known plants in the family have more modest attractions, but they nevertheless hold considerable promise.

Fendlera Fendlerbush

The 5-ft (1.5-m) tall cliff fendlerbush (*Fendlera rupicola*) and the 2-ft (0.6-m) tall Utah fendlerbush (*F. utahensis*) are little-known natives of the United States that are beginning to attract the attention of xeriscape designers. Both plants are fine-textured and a bit ungainly, but the white, 1-in (2.5-cm) wide, four-petaled spring blossoms that follow the pink buds are delightful, and even the seed pods are ornamental. The cliff fendlerbush is hardy in Zone 4 and *F. utahensis* is hardy in zone 6 at least. Both survive prolonged drought and gravelly soil. There is considerable variability in the field, and selections should be made for form, height, and flower quality. Of course, crossing fendlerbushes with other members of the Hydrangeaceae might bring some worthwhile rewards— maybe something like a drought-tolerant hydrangea.

Hydrangea

The hydrangeas are loved by some, despised by others—their beauty is certainly in the eye of the beholder. Some praise these plants for their enormous inflorescences, for their long season of bloom, and for their ease of cultivation. Others damn them as being blowzy and ostentatious in flower and ungainly in habit.

It is true that some of the most popular hydrangeas lack any hint of grace. 'Pee-gee' hydrangea (*Hydrangea grandiflora* 'Pee Gee') is just such an example. Grown as a tree to as much as 30 ft (9 m), it is irredeemably coarse, in bloom or out, in almost every garden setting. I grow *H. paniculata* 'Tardiva', a late-flowering cultivar, as a shrub and almost as a perennial, cutting it to the ground every few years. In one season it grows to 5 ft (1.5 m) and bears prodigious quantities of 10-in (25-cm) panicles with more fertile flowers than the species, making the bloom of the cultivar airier and far more graceful; and the display goes on and on, from midsummer to midfall.

'Annabelle', a cultivar of *Hydrangea arborescens*, is a shrub to about 5 ft (1.5 m) that dies back to ground level in zone 4. In both the species and the cultivar, the shrub smothers itself in enormous 1-ft (0.3-m) pillows of white, mostly sterile florets for most of the summer. It is an odd-looking shrub, but I do love to see it in bloom—preferably in someone else's yard.

The oakleaf hydrangea (*Hydrangea quercifolia*) is my favorite. A suckering 6-ft (1.8-m) shrub with bold 8-in (20-cm) leaves shaped like those of a white oak (*Quercus alba*, in the family Fagaceae) and with superb purple-red fall color, it is worth growing for the foliage alone, although the long-lasting, sterile, 1.5-in (4-cm) flowers set on 1-ft (0.3-m) long panicles are also spectacular. If this superb plant survives at all in zone 4, it behaves like a perennial, dying to the ground each year, and it does not flower. Even in most parts of zone 5 the oakleaf hydrangea's performance is only so-so.

In zone 6 through zone 9, the most popular hydrangeas are the cultivars of the bigleaf hydrangea (*Hydrangea macrophylla*), with their huge (up to 1 ft (0.3 m)) hemispherical heads of flowers in blue, pink, or white—the color is somewhat dependent on the pH of the soil, with pink reflecting the higher end. Coarse and inelegant when out of flower, *H. macrophylla* becomes insufferably crass in flower.

The climbing hydrangea (*Hydrangea anomala* subsp. *petiolaris*, formerly *H. petiolaris*) is a vine that can reach 80 ft (24 m), but if pruned and given some support, it can be grown as a shrub. The flowers are born in platelike corymbs to 10 in (25 cm) across and are arranged in the lacecap pattern. Small beadlike fertile blossoms are ringed by 1.5-in (4-cm) sterile blossoms. The plant blooms in early summer and the blossoms are fragrant. This is one of the tougher sorts, hardy to zone 4.

Breeding goals for the hydrangeas suggest themselves. Hybridize the oakleaf hydrangea with 'Pee-gee' or other cultivars of *Hydrangea paniculata* primarily to increase hardiness, and maybe a reduction in leaf size for *H. quercifolia* would also be appreciated. Cross the oakleaf or climbing hydrangea with 'Annabelle' or some other form of *H. arborescens*, again to increase hardiness but also to give us lacecap inflorescences and oaklike foliage in a smaller package.

In some classification systems, the hydrangeas are classified as Saxifragaceae, a vast family of plants embracing *Astilbe*, *Bergenia*, *Heuchera*, *Saxifraga*, and other genera. To the extent that it is a valid perspective, this alternative classification suggests all sorts of strange possibilities for the exchange of genetic material. But let us keep the lacecap flower pattern of the hydrangeas.

Jamesia PLATE 40

The cliff jamesia (*Jamesia americana*) is a superb wildling, with a wide distribution in the Rocky Mountain range from zone 3 in Montana to zone 7 in New Mexico, usually on rocky cliff sides. It is a shrub to 4 ft (1.2 m) in height, densely foliaged with deeply veined and felted 2-in (5-cm) leaves. In the spring, pale pink buds open to fill 2-in (5-cm) cymes of white flowers. In the fall, the shrub turns a deep pink hue, making spectacular splashes of color in the mountains. This plant does grow well at more modest elevations and is quite tolerant of sun and shade, of heavy soil and light soil, and of both heat and cold. In the garden, *J. americana* gives three full seasons of pleasure with its modest but satisfying spring flowers, lovely summer foliage, and spectacular autumn display. The only thing it lacks is recognition.

Besides selecting and breeding jamesias for shape and floriferousness, how else might these shrubs be used? Could they impart a neater habit and some fall color to the mockoranges (*Philadelphus*) in return for more flower power and a scent worth remembering? Could it do the same for the hydrangeas: tidy them up a bit, give them some fall color, maybe impart more hardiness to the *Hydrangea macrophylla* hybrids? It seems worth the try.

Philadelphus Mockorange PLATE 41

To my nose, there is no finer scent-shrub than the mockorange (*Philadelphus*) and its time of bloom (late spring to early summer) provides a wonderful follow-up to the viburnums and daphnes. It is true that some of the larger mockoranges become leggy and disheveled to the point where they may be considered closer to "unkempt" than simply "casual"; but to level this accusation against the entire clan is pure slander. The white flowers of many mockoranges are extraordinarily beautiful. Indeed, many of the singles, like *P. ×lemoinei* 'Belle Etoile' with its 2.5-in (6-cm) blossoms, and many doubles, like *P. ×lemoinei* 'Innocence' with 2-in (5-cm) blossoms, would be considered superb even without their scent. The form of these plants is also often more than merely fair. The 4-ft (1.2-m) tall *P. ×lemoinei* 'Avalanche' forms cascading mounds of pleasing foliage, and dwarfs like the 3-ft (0.9-m) 'Miniature Snowflake' are perkily upright, with neat, bright green foliage. Some of the older and larger ones, however, such as *P. ×virginalis* 'Virginal', are at best mediocre for eleven months of the year.

Given today's smaller plots, one would think that few gardeners would want to allot room to a large shrub that is a shabby mess for eleven months out of the year, no matter how delightful it is in flower. Nevertheless, the mockoranges remain among our most popular shrubs—they are that irresistible in flower. The need and the desire for developing new varieties is there—more hardy dwarfs in a variety of shapes and flower forms—and the means are there also, since the mockoranges cross willingly and the gene pool is fairly rich. But if one wanted to add flower color or fall color (at the risk of decreasing scent), the hydrangeas and cliff jamesia might be considered as breeding partners. If one wanted to increase drought tolerance, then fendlerbush should be considered as well.

IRIDACEAE

Iris family   92 genera, 1800 species

GENERA DISCUSSED   *Acidanthera • Belamcanda • Crocosmia • Dietes •*
Iris • Moraea • Sisyrinchium • Tigridia

OTHER ORNAMENTAL GENERA   *Crocus • Curtonus • Ixia •*
Pardanthopsis • Schizostylis • Sparaxis

Gathered together in the family Iridaceae is a grand assortment of bulbs, corms, and tubers drawn from around the world. Only the lily family (Liliaceae) rivals this one in garden popularity, and the two families are close enough to be in the same order and to have some of their members classified under one and then reclassified under the other.

Iris   PLATES 42–44

The many sorts of unnatural-looking plants that are currently established in my otherwise naturalistic garden is testament to my own iris addiction. The genus *Iris* contains over 200 species, and hybridizers have created more than 10,000 cultivars and hybrids. The modern German bearded iris itself is a mix of six or more species. Flowers come in all colors except green and red, although a hint of even these colors can be found in some versions of the hybrids. There are selfs and bicolors, picotees and anemones, and crazy-quilt patterns that are too difficult to describe and too erratic to be defined. The flowers can be flared or relaxed, neat or pinked, ruffled, fluted, or laced. If you can imagine some combination of color or shape involving these traits, then it probably is already available in a German bearded iris. One can even have a plant with petals of one color and beards of a contrasting color. One of the most exciting trends is the development of reblooming and everblooming beardeds, and even the fanciest and most modern German bearded iris can take zone 3 cold. They are well adapted to dry soil, and pH is generally not a factor.

Of course, not all the interest in iris is confined to the German bearded cultivars. In fact, many gardeners think that these are the most overbred, the most crass, and the least graceful of the entire genus, and turn their attention to other iris.

The Japanese iris derive from *Iris ensata*. This iris has cultivars with three petals, others with six petals, and even some with nine. The flowers can reach 10 in (25 cm) in diameter, and they come in all shades of blue, pink, and white. Some are fantastically patterned with speckles and splashes and rays and rims. The fluted petals often give the flower the appearance of a rumpled kimono of the finest silk or, in the case of the singles, a silken umbrella. *Iris ensata* has been hybridized with *I. laevigata* and with *I. pseudacorus*, the latter contributing yellow blossoms.

A bit more formal, more elegant, and less ostentatious are the Siberian iris (Series *Sibiricae*). Like the German beardeds, modern cultivars of Siberian iris are complex plants involving several species, although the gene pool here seems to be a little stingier. Nevertheless, progress toward diverse colors and shapes has been commendable, and there are whites, lilac-pinks, pale yellows, and a full palette of wonderful blues. Cultivars are available as 10-in (25-cm) dwarfs and 4-ft (1.2-m) giants, all hardy to zone 3 at least. I would grow the Siberians for their foliage alone, but I do love their refined blossoms as well.

Hybrids involving beardless species from the southeastern United States gave rise to the Louisiana iris (Series *Hexagonae*), a remarkably diverse group with particularly graceful flowers coming in many shapes and in all the colors found in iris, including red. In spite of the considerable progress that has been made with the Louisiana iris, these have not yet become as popular as the three groups already mentioned. Maybe that is because their foliage lacks the refinement of the Siberian or Japanese iris, though the Louisiana iris's foliage is certainly not bad compared to that of the German bearded iris. Hardiness cannot be the problem, since some of these southerners are hardy well into Canada.

The greatest range of colors, patterns, and flower shapes among the iris are offered by the Pacific Coast or California iris (Series *Californicae*), another clan of complicated hybrids, and they are also among the most floriferous of all. Unfortunately, these iris are more limited in their adaptability; otherwise they would no doubt be in every garden. Perhaps too little attention was given to the problem of hardiness and adaptability during their development.

The breeding of plants is something of a sport, and, where there are rules, you have to play by them in order to have your prowess in the game recognized and rewarded. For example, yellow has only recently found expression in the Siberian iris, thanks to the patient work of Dr. Currier McEwen. This accomplishment has been duly recognized and rewarded, having been realized within the framework of Siberian iris breeding. Hybrids between Siberian and Pacific Coast iris yield, among other delights, some clear yellows of superb form, and unlike the Pacific Coast iris, the hybrids are hardy almost everywhere. Unfortunately, these Cal-Sibe hybrids are sterile, at least in the conventional sense, and so the game ends there and the pursuit of such unconventional crosses goes largely unnoticed. Because such worthwhile crosses are not easily accomplished in the usual way, perhaps some of the new techniques described in Chapter 4 are exactly what is needed to bring them about more readily. Tissue culture may then provide a vehicle to propagate Cal-Sibes in sufficient numbers.

While I love all the forms of iris mentioned above, my particular passion is for the crested iris. This group includes such gems as *Iris cristata*, *I. tectorum*, *I. tenuis*, *I. gracilipes*, and *I. japonica*. The first three species, *I. cristata*, *I. tectorum*, and *I. tenuis*, are hardy to zone 3, *I. gracilipes* is barely hardy in zone 5, and *I. japonica* is a bit risky even in zone 6. These are exquisite flowers—much more delicate and graceful than any of the German beardeds, Japanese, Siberians, Louisianans, or Californians—and they are as well suited for the natural garden as they are for the vase (although the small size and short stems of the first four crested iris species argue against decapitation). The colors found in the varieties of crested iris include white, mauve, blue, violet, and purple, and some are beautifully patterned. If I had to choose favorites among them it would be *I. gracilipes* and *I. japonica*, unfortunately the least hardy of the bunch. How wonderful it would be if we could toughen them up by involving *I. cristata*, *I. tectorum*, or *I. tenuis* in a cross—it is thought that *I. tenuis* is particularly close to *I. gracilipes*.

In addition to these many rhizomatous iris, the bulbous iris also hold considerable promise, particularly the Dutch iris (*Iris* ×*hollandica*, a *I. xiphium* × *I. tingitana* hybrid) and the English iris (*I. latifolia*). The Dutch iris comes in a wide range of blues, yellows, whites, and browns, both in solids and bicolors; the English iris features white and an extraordinary range of blues. The Dutch iris is not dependable in zone 4, and although the English iris can be zone 4 hardy, it is not so in the presence of heat and drought. Other bulbous iris, such as *I. danfordiae* and *I. reticulata*, are superb in their own right, and are hardy in zone 4. *Iris danfordiae* has flowers of brilliant yellow, and *I. reticulata* offers white, purple, and a large range of blues. Both do well almost anywhere, at least where there is a winter. The opportunities for cross breeding are clear and promising.

So far all the speculation about the family Iridaceae has been about the genus *Iris*. But the family embraces many other genera that are rich with garden favorites and have great potential for producing new plants with even more usefulness. Let us consider a few of the other possibilities.

Acidanthera Abyssinian Gladiolus

Abyssinian gladiolus (*Acidanthera bicolor*, syn. *Gladiolus callianthus*) is a summer-blooming plant, growing from a corm, with 2-in (5-cm) nodding blossoms shaped like those of a daylily. The flowers are white with distinct purple blotches at the base of the petals. Abyssinian gladiolus is a spectacular yet graceful plant, but it is only hardy to zone 8. A little boost in hardiness from intergeneric crosses with other related Iridiceae might widen the appeal of *Acidanthera*.

Belamcanda Blackberry Lily

The blackberry or leopard lily (*Belamcanda chinensis*) is popular enough to be sold in several forms, varying in height between 2 and 4 ft (0.6 and 1.2 m). The 2-in (5-cm) flowers are borne on branched stems, and when a flower is spent, the petals curl and twist into tight corkscrews that remain an attraction for several days before falling. They come in yellow, orange, and near red, many with the spotting that earned the plant the name leopard lily. *Belamcanda* has been crossed with *Pardanthopsis* to give ×*Pardancanda*, and the hybrid shows a greater range of colors than the blackberry lily and a longer flowering period. Given that the species and the hybrid bloom throughout August and into September, one has to wonder if *Belamcanda* could be crossed with any one of the many species of *Iris*. Such a hybrid could be an improvement for both genera, with flowers larger and showier and in a greater range of colors than those of the blackberry lily, and with a longer season of bloom and less of a need for dead-heading than *Iris*.

Crocosmia

Crocosmias (*Crocosmia aurea*, *C. masoniorum*, *C. pottsii*, and various hybrids and cultivars) are highly prized landscape plants wherever they can be grown, valued for their graceful daylilylike foliage and the arching racemes of summer flowers in brilliant shades of yellow, orange, and near red. Some claim that crocosmias are hardy in zone 4, but most gardeners will agree that the plants are a bit touchy even in zone 5. *Crocosmia* has been hybridized with the related genus *Curtonus* by Alan Bloom to produce a series of beautiful cultivars with intensely colorful blossoms. What is needed now is to increase the hardiness of crocosmias a zone or two, for there is no reliable plant like it for northern gardens. Judicious selection or a cross with blackberry lily or some iris might do.

Dietes Fortnight Lily, *Moraea* Peacock Lily

Unfortunately for those of us living in the colder regions of the globe, the closely related *Dietes* and *Moraea* are hardy only in zone 9 and warmer regions. These are superb plants, 3 to 6 ft (0.9 to 1.8 m) tall, with excellent foliage and exquisite blossoms that are shaped like those of a Siberian iris, in white and various shades of blue. Moraeas have a peacock plume's eyespot at the base of each petal, earning the plant its vernacular name, the peacock lily. The flower stems of these two lily genera continue to lengthen, producing flowers over a period of months or even years. What can be done to encourage these plants to bestow some of their blessings on us northern folk? Can they be bred to the Siberians or maybe the crested iris? How about crossing them with *Sisyrinchium*? Would that extend the plant's flowering time as well as its hardiness? Any advance northward would garner millions of new fans.

Sisyrinchium Blue-eyed Grass

Sisyrinchium is a genus of plants that give pleasure way out of proportion to their size. Blue-eyed grass (*Sisyrinchium montanum*) is zone 3 hardy (at least) and bears brilliant blue, 0.5-in (1.5-cm) solitary flowers on 5-in (13-cm) stems. The 18-in (46-cm), zone 7 hardy *S. striatum* has 1- to 2-ft (0.3 to 0.6 m) racemes of 0.5-in (1.5-cm) cream-colored blossoms, and several other superb species have yellow flowers and violet flowers. If these plants have a fault, it is that they seed themselves about too freely. I wonder if these exquisite plants could be bred to some of the iris, say a Siberian iris, or a Pacific Coast iris, or some crested iris. Would that herald an entirely new race of perky gems that are at home in the border or in the rockery? One would think that such miniatures would be able to compete with the dwarf bearded iris in class and style but have the advantage of much better foliage and flowers borne over a much longer season.

Tigridia Mexican Shell Flower, Tiger Flower
       Even more exciting (or, perhaps, more preposterous) than bringing the fortnight and peacock lilies (*Dietes* and *Moraea*) below zone 9 is the prospect of bringing something like the Mexican shell flower (*Tigridia*) into northern gardens. This summer-flowering bulb may be the most flamboyant of all the Iridaceae: flowers to 6 in (15 cm) in whites, yellows, reds, and browns, both solids and bi-colors, with or without stippling. The plant grows to 2 ft (0.6 m) and is hardy only to zone 8. It is tempting to try to cross it with one of the hardy bulbous iris, or even one without bulbs. Try a cross, let's say, between the Mexican shell flower and a Siberian iris, or a peacock iris, or any old iris, or *Sisyrinchium*, or whatever else would work to bring the Mexican shell flower northward. A *Tigridia*-like flower on a hardy perennial plant—now that would be quite a prize.
       A similar plan might be tried for *Ixia*, *Schizostylis*, or *Sparaxis*, each a genera of superb, summer-flowering, non-hardy plants. What can we make of them? Probably nothing by the old techniques, but what about the new methods?

LABIATAE

Mint family   221 genera, 5600 species

GENUS DISCUSSED   *Salvia*

OTHER ORNAMENTAL GENERA   *Ajuga* • *Lamium* • *Mentha* •
Monarda • *Perovskia* • *Phlomis* • *Physostegia* • *Stachys* • *Thymus*

The family Labiatae (also known as Lamiaceae) contains several important genera of garden ornamentals, some grown primarily for their extraordinary foliage, some for their showy bloom. Others in the family, less striking in appearance, are nevertheless popular groundcovers. The mints (*Mentha*) contain useful groundcovers, as well as a number of important culinary herbs. The popularity of *Monarda* and *Salvia* has been encouraged by the work of breeders who have increased the color and size ranges of plants in each of the two genera. Breeders have also obtained mildew-resistent monardas, and these are likely to quickly replace older varieties in popularity. Here, however, the discussion will focus on the salvias.

Salvia

The genus *Salvia* contains both perennial and annual members. *Salvia* ×*superba* (a hybrid involving *S. nemorosa*, *S. pratensis*, and *S. villicaulis*) and the cultivars 'Mainacht' and 'Ostfriesland' are among the very best garden perennials from zone 4 to zone 10. These plants have a basal cluster of attractive 3-in (7.5-cm) leaves and panicles, to 26 in (66 cm), of blue or purple blossoms—superb, as its name implies.

On the other hand, mealy-cup sages (*Salvia farinacea*) are perennial only in zones 7 and above; elsewhere they are grown as annuals. With varieties from 1 to 3 ft (0.3 to 0.9 m) in height, and flowers in every hue but green, they are among the most popular of all bedding plants, flowering for a very long time from summer into autumn. Since neither red nor white cultivars of *S.* ×*superba* have made an appearance, why not cross *S.* ×*superba* (or one of its ancestors) with a cultivar of *S. farinacea*? After all, the salvias have already shown a willingness to hybridize.

One might also consider a cross between *Salvia* ×*superba* and a salvia like silver sage (*S. argentea*). Silver sage is grown for its huge (to 6 in (15 cm) long), heavily haired and felted leaves of silvery grey. Its flowers are boring at best and ideally should be removed from the plant. The plant itself is short-lived, behaving more like an annual or biennial than a perennial. But just imagine the deep purple panicles of *S. ×superba* set against the silvery grey leaves of *S. argentea*. Not that setting the scarlet blossoms of some *S. farinacea* against the leaves of *S. argentea* would be a bad idea, but this would not advance the quest for greater hardiness and longevity for silver sage.

LEGUMINOSAE

Legume family   657 genera, 16,400 species

GENERA DISCUSSED   *Acacia* • *Amorpha* • *Bauhinia* • *Caragana* •
Cassia • *Cladrastis* • *Delonix* • *Erythrina* • *Gleditsia* • *Laburnum* •
Robinia • *Wisteria*

OTHER ORNAMENTAL GENERA   *Albizia* • *Baptisia* • *Caesalpinia* •
Calliandra • *Cercis* • *Cytisus* • *Genista* • *Gymnocladus* •
Indigofera • *Lespedeza* • *Lupinus* • *Maackia* • *Sophora* •
Thermopsis

The vast legume family, with members throughout the tropical and temperate regions, holds many of our most desirable, useful, and exotic ornamentals. The family Leguminosae (or Faba-
ceae) also includes some of our shabbiest plants—those that are
grown where nothing else will grow, garden plants of last resort.
There is a great deal of potential for creating new plants in this
family, but I will consider here only a few of the possibilities.

Acacia Mimosa, *Caragana* Pea Shrub, *Cassia* Senna
   Acacia and *Cassia* contribute dozens of trees and shrubs to the
gardens of the southwestern United States and similar hot and
dry climates. The shrubs range in size from 4 to 12 ft (1.2 to 3.7 m)
and the trees from 12 to 50 ft (3.7 to 15 m). The best among them
flower prodigiously, covering themselves in fragrant blossoms
ranging in color from creamy yellow to near orange. Some bloom
in late winter, others in spring, and still others during summer.
For many, the flowering season spans months. Unfortunately,
these exceedingly showy and drought-tolerant shrubs are at home
only in zones 9 and 10.
   On the other hand, the pea shrubs (*Caragana arborescens, C. frutex*, and others) are hardy in zone 2. *Caragana arborescens* grows to
20 ft (6 m) and can be trained into a small tree, and *C. frutex* grows
to be a 9-ft (2.7-m) shrub. Both bear 1-in (2.5-cm) yellow blossoms
in short pendulous racemes in the spring—a pleasant display but
not comparable to mimosa or senna. Soil tolerant and drought tolerant to the extreme, these shrubs are as tough as they get.
   Surely, there are opportunities here for some improvements
through hybridizing. Cross *Acacia* or *Cassia* with a *Caragana*, and

keep the drought, soil, and heat tolerance of the parents, but aim for hybrids closer to the pea shrub in cold tolerance and closer to senna or mimosa in flower production and length of flowering time.

Amorpha Leadplant, *Bauhinia* Orchid Tree, *Delonix* Poinciana, *Erythrina* Coral Tree

The genera *Bauhinia*, *Delonix*, and *Erythrina* are to be seen only in zones 9 and 10, where they convey the outrageous flamboyance of the tropics—no tree is more spectacular in bloom than these. The Chinese orchid tree (*Bauhinia* ×*blakeana*) grows to 25 ft (7.5 m) and its 5-in (13-cm) blossoms in shades of pink or purple do remind one of *Laelia* orchids, hence the tree's common name. The royal poinciana (*Delonix regia*) grows to 50 ft (15 m) and flowers in the summer. Its 4-in (10-cm) scarlet blossoms also resemble those of orchids—*Oncidium* orchids. The coral tree (*Erythrina caffra*) grows to 60 ft (18 m) and has 2-in (5-cm) scarlet flowers borne in late winter in panicles to 8 in (20 cm) long.

Can any of these marvels be approximated farther north? Again, the pea shrubs (*Caragana*) might hold the key. Otherwise, we might risk sullying the reds with the orange-centered blue blooms of some leadplant, such as *Amorpha fruticosa* or *A. canescens*. *Amorpha fruticosa* is a zone 4 shrub to 20 ft (6 m) in height, and *A. canescens* is a zone 2 shrub to 4 ft (1.2 m). Admittedly, it does not seem a likely prospect, but the promise is surely worth the gamble.

Cladrastis Yellow-wood, *Gleditsia* Honeylocust, *Robinia* Locust   PLATE 46

Both the honeylocust (*Gleditsia triacanthos*) and the black locust (*Robinia pseudoacacia*) are common trees—the *Gleditsia* planted as an ornamental shade tree, the *Robinia* for soil conservation and sometimes for ornament. They both have the ferny pinnate or bipinnate foliage so common in the legume family, and they cast light shade. The honeylocust and the black locust are large trees (to 100 ft (30 m) and 70 ft (21 m) respectively) and they boast excellent and reliable golden-yellow autumn color in any climate with a proper autumn. Both are highly soil and wind tolerant and are cold tolerant to zone 3. The flowers of *G. triacanthos* are insignificant except for their pervasive scent, which I love. The black locust, too, has fragrant flowers, but these are white, displayed on hanging panicles to 8 in (20 cm) long, and quite showy. These trees do have their problems, however. Even the thornless, podless varieties of honeylocust are not always neat. They will drop twigs and leaves in a heavy wind or rain, and flower parts are shed in midspring. Where present in sizable numbers, the locust pod midge causes the leaflets of the honeylocust to roll up, giving the tree a sickly, shabby, emaciated look. The black locust is brittle, suckers aggressively, and has a rampant root system, and it is prone to borers.

Why not wed these two trees? With such a mixture of good points and bad points it might take more than one generation to sort things out favorably, but given the current popularity of each of these genera of locust trees it might be worth the wait. The pod midge and locust borer seem so specific in choosing their hosts that a hybrid might confuse them both. Furthermore, there is the possibility that the hybrid will have the attractive and fragrant flowers of *Robinia pseudoacacia* and the structural integrity of *Gleditsia triacanthos*.

Other locusts, such as *Robinia fertilis* and rose acacia (*R. hispida*), are worth considering as garden ornamentals, particularly in hot, dry, windy sites with alkaline soils. These two in particular are especially attractive in flower, with rosy panicles to 4 in (10 cm). Unfortunately, they have many of the same faults as the black locust. Maybe a cross with *Cladrastis* will rescue the better features of the locusts while avoiding their worst features.

American yellow-wood (*Cladrastis lutea*) is a superb tree to 50 ft (15 m), with a muscular trunk covered in smooth gray bark like that of the European beech (*Fagus sylvatica*, in the family Fagaceae). The foliage is pinnate, but the 4-in (10-cm) leaflets present a more substantial picture than in *Robinia* and *Gleditsia*. In addition, the yellow-wood cannot match the intensity of the golden-yellow fall color of the locusts or the honeylocust. On the other hand, the yellow-wood's pendant 14-in (36-cm) panicles of white flowers are as showy as the best of the locusts. The tree is hardy to zone 4, but it is not altogether happy in droughty climates with severe temperature fluctuations, and even when growing well yellow-wood may take twenty years to flower.

What about a *Robinia* × *Cladrastis* hybrid, say between the black locust (*Robinia pseudoacacia*) or the rose acacia (*R. hispida*) and the yellow-wood? We could get the best of both worlds: a tree of moderate size that is adaptable, hardy, and early flowering, maybe with pale rose or creamy white blossoms, and the superb bark of yellow-wood for winter interest.

Laburnum Goldenchain Tree   PLATE 45

The goldenchain tree (*Laburnum* ×*watereri*, a hybrid of *L. alpinum* and *L. anagyroides*) is a lovely small tree (to 15 ft (4.5 m) in height) that is prized for its late-May showing of bright yellow 0.75-in (2-cm) flowers in pendulous 15-in (38-cm) racemes. Although the tree is considered to be zone 5 hardy, over much of that region *L.* ×*watereri* needs some protection, particularly where there are drying winds and high temperature fluctuations, and even then it is often not reliable, cracking easily and flowering poorly.

The flowers of the goldenchain tree resemble those of Japanese wisteria (*Wisteria floribunda*) closely enough in size and shape to suggest crossing the two plants. Maybe a bit of hybrid vigor will bring out the hardiness purported to be inherent in each of the parents. At least we might hope for a treelike vine or a sinuous tree with startling long racemes of creamy white, or pink, or purplish hue—that alone would be a prize. A cross between *Laburnum* ×*watereri* and the zone 3 yellow-wood (*Cladrastis lutea*) or black locust (*Robinia pseudoacacia*) is more likely to yield a tree, perhaps intermediate between yellow and white in flower color and intermediate in cold tolerance. If greater cold tolerance and general adaptability are the most important goals, then the zone 2 pea shrubs (*Caragana*) might once again be the logical choice as breeding partners. Since there are several intrageneric *Laburnum* hybrids and a chimera involving *Laburnum* and *Cytisus* (+*Laburnocytisus*), success with some of these crosses proposed might not be unreasonable even by "old-fashioned" methods.

Wisteria   PLATE 47

Big, bold, and supremely beautiful in flower, the Japanese wisteria (*Wisteria floribunda*) may be the most cherished vine in the garden. Everyone is familiar with the long pendant racemes (to 4 ft (1.2 m) in some cultivars, although 1.5 ft (0.45 m) is more common) of fragrant flowers in white, rose, or violet. Everyone is also familiar with the huge (to 15 in (38 cm)) pinnate leaves that give the vine its lush, almost tropical look, and with the gnarled and braided trunks that make the vine so impressive during winter. Not everyone can grow these vines well, however, not even in zones 4 through 9 where Japanese wisteria is supposed to be hardy.

Where it does grow well, wisteria grows at a weed's pace. It is rambunctious and powerful enough to threaten structures and requires massive pruning several times a year to limit its hegemony. Over much of the western and midwestern regions of North America, *Wisteria floribunda* will grow but it will flower sparsely, sporadically, or even not at all. Maybe it is bad soil (although these vines are supposed to be quite soil tolerant), maybe it is the droughty summers and freeze-drying winds of winter, or maybe it is the wrenching temperature changes or the frosts in early fall and late spring that prevent these glorious vines from displaying their true worth. Maybe that is the reason why most of the heavy population centers of wisterias (not to mention people) are near the coasts.

Perhaps we can bestow the blessings of Japanese wisteria on more places by breeding it with other Leguminosae. Perhaps we can retain a large measure of the vine's flowering proclivity, reduce its aggressive growth, and increase its adaptability all at the same time. The black locust (*Robinia pseudoacacia*) may be a likely candidate to broker these benefits. After all, black locust is hardy (zone 3), adaptable, and has showy racemes of flowers with the fragrance and colors of Japanese wisteria. What's more, the black locust can be had in cultivars ranging from 20 ft (6 m) to 80 ft (24 m) tall. There is even the possibility of introducing yellow foliage color in a wisterialike plant.

Another possible partner for breeding with Japanese wisteria is the American yellow-wood (*Cladrastis lutea*). It, too, has racemes like wisteria, but the flowers of the yellow-wood are more modest in size and come only in white. The tree's 50-ft (15-m) height, supported by a massive bole clothed in smooth gray bark, might add to the interest of such a cross. In either case, it would be interesting to see how the treelike tendencies of black locust or yellow-wood play against the vining tendency of wisterias.

LILIACEAE

Lily family   294 genera, 4500 species

GENERA DISCUSSED   *Agapanthus • Alstroemeria • Anthericum • Calochortus • Camassia • Clivia • Hemerocallis • Hippeastrum • Liriope • Lycoris • Nerine • Ophiopogon • Pancratium • Sprekelia*

OTHER ORNAMENTAL GENERA   *Allium • Amaryllis • Chionodoxa • Convallaria • Eremurus • Erythronium • Fritillaria • Galtonia • Hyacinthus • Hymenocallis • Kniphofia • Lilium • Narcissus • Polygonatum • Puschkinia • Scilla • Tricyrtis • Trillium • Tulipa*

The Liliaceae are a vast family containing many of our most cherished garden plants. Would winter ever end without daffodils, hyacinths, snowdrops, and tulips? Would spring be spring without the scent of lily-of-the-valley? Would we survive the heat of summer without daylilies and hostas, and could we adjust to the closing of the season without the late-blooming lilies? Probably, but what a blessing it is not to have to do without these pleasures.

The wondrous richness of the Liliaceae gene pool has been greatly augmented by plant breeders. Many of the garden forms of daylilies, hostas, lilies, and tulips are complex hybrids involving many species. Some crosses between lily species that had been unsuccessful were subsequently achieved using embryo rescue techniques and embryo culture. All this points to the possibility of even wider crosses, hybrids that would bring us even more pleasure from this wonderful family.

Agapanthus Lily-of-the-Nile
    In zones 8 through 10, lily-of-the-Nile (*Agapanthus africanus, A. campanulatus, A. praecox*, and other species, hybrids, and cultivars) is one of the most popular and useful perennials. The flowers are borne in an umbel atop stems 1.5 to 4 ft (0.45 to 1.2 m) tall, depending on the variety. Some *Agapanthus* plants have white flowers, but blue is what the flowers of lily-of-the-Nile are noted for, from the lightest shades to the darkest, and these plants send up stalk after blooming stalk throughout the summer. The strap-like leaves grow like those of a hyacinth.
    Unfortunately, in colder regions there is nothing like the lily-of-the-Nile, at least not in the summer. It may be a real reach, but

could we insert the hardiness of *Chionodoxa, Puschkinia, Scilla,* or *Hyacinthus,* genera hardy to zone 4 and some to zone 2, into the *Agapanthus* genome and bring a little lily-of-the-Nile up north?

Alstroemeria　Peruvian Lily

The Peruvian lilies (such as *Alstroemeria aurantiaca, A. psittacina,* and many hybrids and cultivars) are among the showiest of the Liliaceae, another family not noted for floral modesty. Atop 3-ft (0.9-m) tall leafy stems emerge loose clusters of blossoms, each blossom as much as 2 in (5 cm) across. Three prominent petals and conspicuous stamens give the blossoms a distinctive appearance. A broad range of colors—white, yellow, orange, pink, red, and lilac—is available, as well as finely striped, dotted, and picotee patterns. Peruvian lilies are vigorous growers under a wide variety of conditions from zone 8 (maybe 7) to zone 10, unfortunately well out of the reach of a vast number of gardeners.

Subjecting cell cultures to cold might provide an efficient way to select hardier strains, but it is unlikely to move Peruvian lilies all the way into zone 4. Maybe crossing some Peruvian lily with a hardy lily, like the zone 2 *Lilium bulbiferum,* will yield progeny that are significantly hardier than *Alstroemeria.* One has to wonder if such a hybrid is survivable, however, since the lilies grow from bulbs and alstroemerias are fibrous-rooted.

Anthericum

The zone 3 St. Bernard's lily (*Anthericum liliago*) looks like a giant white-flowered Siberian squill (*Scilla siberica*) when it sends up its 3-ft (9-m) flower spike, but this plant blooms in early summer. White is its only color, so plant breeding schemes suggest themselves; crosses between *Anthericum* and *Agapanthus, Camassia,* or *Hyacinthus* are among those that might broaden the palette.

Calochortus　Mariposa Lily

Even among the Liliaceae, the mariposa lilies are outstanding for the beauty of their flowers. These flowers look more like tulips than lilies, the petals of most forming flaring goblets in various shades of white, yellow, orange, pink, rose or red, a palette of purples, and even browns, depending on the species. Many have a near-black eyespot in the center of the flower, and others have golden or brown eyespots, often reticulated with darker mesh.

One species of mariposa lily, *Calochortus coeruleus*, has pale blue flowers so profusely covered by hair that its shape is obscured. The dark-eyed sego lily (*C. nuttallii*) has forms that come in white, yellow, orange, and brilliant pink. Some mariposa lilies flower in the spring and some flower in the summer. The plants range in size from 2 to 18 in (5 to 46 cm). This genus contains approximately sixty species, most of which are native to the west and midwest of North America.

With all their beauty and diversity, how is it that these lilies are largely unknown to gardeners? Several things work against them. In many cases, the bulb does not split or yield bulblets, and the plants remain as single plants. There are exceptions, however, as in the case of *Calochortus venustus* and *C. luteus*, whose bulbs split readily to yield clusters of plants. Many mariposa lilies require up to seven years to reach flowering size from seed, but some may bloom after only three years. Many are sensitive to summer watering, although this is less true for those growing in the Rocky Mountains, such as the Gunnison mariposa (*C. gunnisonii*), a beautiful and enormously varied species with flowers in white, pink, or lavender, many with prominent markings at the base of the petals. Most members of the genus *Calochortus* are only hardy to zone 6, but again, *C. gunnisonii* and several other Rocky Mountain species are exceptions that are hardy in zone 4 at least.

One method that might bring these superb plants into more of our gardens is the use of various chemicals known to promote the formation of bulblets. If these chemicals could be used to propagate plants *in vitro*, this could greatly curtail the time required for flowering. Tissue culture techniques have shortened the maturation time for many orchid genera from seven years to three years, so perhaps this will work similarly for mariposa lilies. What about interspecific crosses, such as with *Calochortus venustus*, to increase the tendency of the plants to form colonies, and crosses with those of the northern Rockies to increase hardiness? Maybe crossing some mariposa lilies with tulips will give us something that is easier to cultivate.

Camassia Camass, Quamash

Imagine a gigantic spidery-flowered hyacinth and you have some idea of what quamash or camass (*Camassia*) look like. Several easy-to-grow species are hardy to zone 3 but need abundant moisture, at least during the period of active growth. They flower in late spring or early summer, and flowers come in white and a wide range of blues. Included among the species of camass are *Camassia cusickii*, which grows to 3 ft (0.9 m), *C. leichtlinii*, to 4 ft (1.2 m), and *C. quamash*, to 2 ft (0.6 m). Several selections have been made for color, but none of the camass is commonly available. That is my main complaint and motivates my wish for this genus: make camass more available.

Merely making them more available may not exploit the full potential of camass, however. Perhaps they can be hybridized with some hyacinth to stretch the flowering time and expand the color range. On the other hand, many of the Liliaceae are not hardy beyond zone 7 and an infusion of camass genes might do a great deal to address that problem.

Hemerocallis Daylily

Most modern daylilies are the result of crosses involving several species, including *Hemerocallis dumortieri, H. middendorffii, H. fulva, H. nana*, and others. More than 1000 new cultivars are registered each year and to date more than 30,000 are already on the books. Daylilies have received the benefit of colchicine-induced polyploidy, tissue culture, and endless hybridization. There are daylilies to satisfy every taste, from the most subtle and sophisticated to the most crass and flamboyant. But these plants still suffer from a major fault that no one seems interested in addressing: daylilies have to be dead-headed every day in order to be at all presentable. If not, the wilted blossoms hang like rotting bananas on the inflorescence for a day or two—a terrible eyesore. An isolated plant can be easily managed but a collection presents a chore. Can we breed strains that are self-cleaning? Can we use genetic engineering to cause spent flowers to drop cleanly overnight? Botanists are close to isolating genes in certain plants that govern the aging of flowers, so maybe something can be done for daylilies to accelerate the aging process.

Liriope, Ophiopogon Turf Lilies

The turf lilies, *Liriope* and *Ophiopogon*, are evergreen grasslike plants with cultivars between 4 and 18 in (10 and 46 cm) tall. Although grown mostly for their foliage, turf lilies do bear racemes of white or pale purple flowers that have modest appeal in late summer. These are tough plants, tolerating shade or a bit of sun, a variety of soils, considerable heat, and a bit of drought. *Liriope* is hardy in zone 4; *Ophiopogon* only into zone 6. Turf lilies are not the showiest of plants, but they do have a subtle and sophisticated beauty that makes them desirable in the border, as small specimens along streams and ponds, and as groundcovers. The green-and-white striped turf lilies are quite popular, such as several cultivars of *O. jaburan*, and a cultivar with black leaves, *O. planiscapus* 'Nigrescens', is a show stopper. The liriopes are a bit larger than the ophiopogons, a bit coarser, and more aggressively stoloniferous (the ophiopogons tend to form neat clumps). Some striped liriopes are available, but there are no black-leaved ones.

Why not cross the black-leaved ophiopogon with the hardiest of the liriopes, or even with one of the hardier (zone 3) daylilies? That might net a prize: a dwarf, black-leaved, evergreen plant with daylilylike flowers, perhaps in off-white, yellow, or orange.

Clivia, Hippeastrum Amaryllis, *Lycoris* Spider Lily, *Nerine, Pancratium* Sea Daffodil, *Sprekelia* Aztec Lily

Some taxonomists place the genera *Clivia, Hippeastrum, Lycoris, Nerine, Pancratium,* and *Sprekelia* into a family of their own, Amaryllidaceae, but most consider them to be members of the Liliaceae. Which classification is correct? Why not put the question to the genetic test and try to cross these tender (generally zone 8 and above for all of them) bulbs with some of the zone 2 and zone 3 members of the family Liliaceae?

Just imagine the elegant new shapes that the spider lily (*Lycoris*) and the sea daffodil (*Pancratium*) might bring to more northern gardens. Anything resembling the Aztec lily (*Sprekelia*), with its scarlet orchidlike blossoms, would be a prize indeed anywhere colder than zone 9. Can we realize these hopes by some judicious cross? Maybe we can hybridize these plants with something very hardy and with graceful blossoms but something that is not over-bred—tulip species such as *Tulipa dasystemon* or *T. clusiana* perhaps, or a daylily, or some true lily. Perhaps all this is pushing visionary to imaginary, but then again, who can say?

LYTHRACEAE

Loosestrife family   26 genera, 280 species

GENERA DISCUSSED   *Lagerstroemia* • *Lythrum*

It may surprise some to learn that crape myrtle and purple loosestrife are both members of the family Lythraceae. Crape myrtle (*Lagerstroemia indica*) is a woody plant, the darling of the South; purple loosestrife (*Lythrum salicaria*) is one of the most useful and popular perennials for northern gardens as well as southern gardens. (However, because of its extremely invasive and weedy nature, purple loosestrife is now prohibited in many areas of the United States.) Yet both plants are members of the loosestrife family, and so there may be promising prospects for creating a radically new plant from a cross between the two.

Lagerstroemia Crape Myrtle

Crape myrtle (*Lagerstroemia indica*), deciduous and many-branched and able to grow as a waist-high shrub or a 30-ft (9-m) tree depending on the cultivar, is one of the most spectacular of all woody plants. On the trunk and thicker stems of the crape myrtle, the bark flakes off to create a jigsaw-puzzle design in brown, red, cream, and gray—a garden highlight throughout the winter. The 6- to 8-in (15- to 20-cm) panicles of 1.5-in (4-cm) crinkled flowers in white, pink, or purple put on a show from midsummer into fall that is the envy of all gardeners and plant lovers of the northern United States.

Lythrum Loosestrife

In contrast to crape myrtle, loosestrifes (*Lythrum alatum, L. salicaria,* and *L. virgatum*) are bushy perennials, with cultivars ranging in height from the 15-in (38-cm) *L. salicaria* 'Happy' to the 5-ft (1.5-m) *L. salicaria* 'Purple Spires'. They flower in midsummer for three weeks or more, with pink, rose, or purple panicles up to 1 ft (0.3 m) in length, depending on the cultivar. These tough plants are hardy from zone 3 to zone 10, but loosestrife, particularly purple loosestrife (*L. salicaria* and certain cultivars), can be a very destructive weed and is a serious environmental threat to wetland areas. *Lythrum salicaria* is currently outlawed in several states.

Could it be possible to cross these two genera of the family Lythraceae, and at the same time tame the noxious nature of loosestrife? As asked earlier, how will a cross between a herbaceous plant and a woody plant determine woodiness in the offspring? Is it conceivable that such a cross can be fertile? What then of the F_2 generation? Hardy but manageable crape-myrtlelike shrubs for us northern folk! That could be a dream come true.

MALVACEAE

Mallow family   116 genera, 1550 species

GENERA DISCUSSED   *Callirhoe* • *Hibiscus* • *Lavatera* • *Malva* •
Sidalcea • *Sphaeralcea*

OTHER ORNAMENTAL GENERA   *Abutilon* • *Alcea*

The mallow family (Malvaceae) has a number of popular plants with unabashedly showy flowers and hopelessly coarse foliage or habit; hollyhock (*Alcea rosea*) is a prime example. There are some less-familiar members, however, that are small in stature, elegant in leaf, more modest in flower, and both durable and hardy. Here is where the greatest prospects lie for this family of plants.

Callirhoe   Poppy Mallow, Wine Cups

Currently finding favor as a xeriscape plant, wine cups (*Callirhoe involucrata*) is a straggly drylander 6 in (15 cm) high, wandering without rooting to 3 ft (0.9 m). It bears a profusion of 2-in (5-cm), wine-colored and cup-shaped blossoms throughout summer and into fall, and has the finely cut palmate leaves of a Japanese maple (*Acer palmatum*, in the family Aceraceae). The leaves and stems of *Callirhoe* create an interesting tracery wandering over rocks. It is zone 4 hardy and enjoys sun, heat, and drought, but it will suffer some shade and a bit of moisture.

A cross between wine cups and its fellow Malvaceae *Malva neglecta* might yield pastel colors and a much tighter plant than wine cups. Since both parents are tap-rooted and unwilling to root from stems, tissue culture might be the only feasible means of propagating hybrids or special clones.

Hibiscus

In the genus *Hibiscus* one finds perennials like *H. moscheutos*, which grows to 8 ft (2.5 m) in height and bears flowers up to 12 in (30 cm) across. The hibiscus of the tropics (*H. rosa-sinensis*), a popular indoor plant even in non-tropical locales, and *H. syriacus*, a garden shrub barely hardy into zone 4, with flowers similar to the tropical species but more modest in size (to 3 in (7.5 cm) across), are other popular (and large) members of this genus. *Hibiscus syriacus* flowers during high summer and puts on quite a show. I even enjoy the 3-in (7.5-cm) maplelike leaves.

It would be nice to have smaller versions of these hibiscus, smaller in both plant and flower size. To this end we might look to *Malva neglecta* or some *Sphaeralcea* species for help—neither should compromise the leaf shape or flower form of hibiscus.

Lavatera, Malva Mallow, *Sidalcea*

In leaf and flower shape, the three genera *Lavatera, Malva,* and *Sidalcea* resemble refined hollyhocks. *Malva alcea* 'Fastigiata', one of my favorites, is bushier than hollyhock, grows to a height of 3 ft (0.9 m), and is very drought tolerant. It is usually in bloom from early summer to midfall. *Lavatera cachemiriana* is only weakly perennial, but it is more upright, to 8 ft (2.5 m), and has larger flowers, to 4 in (10 cm). *Sidalcea malviflora* may be the most graceful of these three, although its 4-ft (1.2-m) stems often need support and it requires more water than the other two and prefers some shade. The *Malva* cultivar and *Lavatera cachemiriana* are hardy to zone 4, and *Sidalcea malviflora* to zone 5.

Malva neglecta, on the other hand, is known as a weed wherever it grows, and it grows wherever it wants. It is an ineradicable, pernicious pest, but it does have some attractive features. The leaves are similar to those of *Alchemilla vulgaris* (in the family Rosaceae) but smaller (to 3 in (7.5 cm)), and the pale violet 1-in (2.5-cm) flowers are quite attractive. The plant forms a neat mound to 8 in (20 cm), and were it not for its insufferably weedy ways, *M. neglecta* would be considered a prize ornamental.

The most important thing to do, therefore, is to tame this weedy mallow, strip it of its hyper-fertility. Maybe some induced polyploidy will do the job. Or maybe a cross of *Malva neglecta* with *Lavatera, Sidalcea,* or other *Malva* species will work to reduce the size of the latter plants and toughen them up. It could result in a very usable clan of hybrids with excellent foliage and plant habit, as well as superb blossoms.

Sphaeralcea

Sphaeralcea is commonly found growing wild in zones 4 to 7. Copper or prairie mallow (*Sphaeralcea coccinea*) and cowboy's dream (*S. munroana*) look like diminutive malva, with silvery gray, lobed leaves on 18-in (46-cm) plants. Several red or clear orange blossoms, to 0.75 in (2 cm) across, emerge atop the stems, and they tend to rebloom from late spring through summer.

As pleasing as these plants are in a xeriscape garden, *Sphaeralcea*'s main contribution to horticulture may come in reducing the size and increasing the color range and flowering period of *Lavatera*, *Malva*, or *Sidalcea*. Crosses of *Sphaeralcea* with various hibiscus species could yield subshrubs with neat habit and leaves, and hibiscuslike flowers—a whole new set of Malvaceae, perhaps with more garden appeal than their ancestors.

NYSSACEAE

Tupelo family   3 genera, 8 species

GENERA DISCUSSED   *Davidia* • *Nyssa*

The family Nyssaceae has only two trees of established garden merit—but what superb trees they are.

Davidia Dove Tree, Handkerchief Tree
The dove tree (*Davidia involucrata*) grows to 20 ft (6 m) in the garden, neat at all times of the year and uniquely fascinating in flower. The flower clusters are small and insignificant, but the inflorescence is subtended by two white bracts, a 4 in by 2 in (10 cm by 5 cm) upper bract and a 7 in by 4 in (18 cm by 10 cm) lower bract, lax enough to flutter in the slightest breeze. To some the bracts suggest handkerchiefs; to others the bracts are reminiscent of doves on the wing. No other tree has such a display.

Nyssa Tupelo
Tupelo or black gum (*Nyssa sylvatica*) grows to 50 ft (15 m), and even 100 ft (30 m) in favored locations. It is a stately tree, with a rounded habit and glossy leaves that turn a fiery red in autumn—a color display as spectacular as any.
Tupelo is hardy in zone 3, but the dove tree is only marginally hardy in zone 6 (although there is a fine specimen growing in zone 5 at the Arnold Arboretum in Cambridge, Massachusetts), just out of reach for a great number of gardens. Both *Davidia* and *Nyssa* prefer moist, acid soil, although some alkalinity seems tolerable.
How fortuitous would a cross between these two members of Nyssaceae be? We might get something intermediate in size, maybe closer to tupelo in hardiness, maybe with some fall color, and maybe, just maybe, a flower bract like that of the dove tree. Not a bad gift for northern gardens.

ONAGRACEAE

Evening Primrose family   24 genera, 650 species

GENERA DISCUSSED   *Epilobium* • *Fuchsia* • *Gaura* • *Oenothera*

The evening primrose family contains only a few plants of established garden merit. However, a glorious wildling is included here—*Epilobium angustifolium*, libelously called fireweed—that would be welcomed in every garden if it could be tamed and made available. The enduringly popular *Fuchsia* also belongs to the Onagraceae. Add evening primrose (*Oenothera*) and the distinctive *Gaura*, and there is more than enough to stir the imagination.

Epilobium   PLATE 48
Fireweed (*Epilobium angustifolium*) is a superb native plant, widespread throughout the Rocky Mountain region, from zone 3 in Canada to zone 9 in the southwestern United States. It is frequently found along roadsides and in areas cleared by fire—hence its common name. Fireweed grows to a stately 5 ft (1.5 m) tall, with terminal racemes of pink 1-in (2.5-cm) flowers. This long-blooming plant puts on a show throughout summer and into fall, at which time the leaves turn a striking red color. *Epilobium angustifolium* prefers moist soil but is otherwise very adaptable. Only its proclivity to seed itself about limits the plant's popularity. Other epilobiums are available in differing heights, habits, and requirements, although none are as showy as fireweed.

Since this plant shows some variation in the field, it might be possible to select for height, floriferousness, and flower color. Maybe hybridizing fireweed with another *Epilobium* will reduce its fecundity, such as breeding it with *Epilobium dodonaei* or *E. fleischeri*, both as hardy but less showy than fireweed; but of course, it could go the other way, and the hybrid might demonstrate the same weedy tendencies as fireweed.

Fuchsia
Almost all the fuchsias seen in gardens today are hybrids, and no one misidentifies a *Fuchsia* in bloom—they are that distinctive. The pendant flowers on these multistemmed shrubs have a corolla of petals emerging from a cuff of reflexed sepals. Blooms vary in

size from 1 in (2.5 cm) long and quite narrow to something closer to the size of a fist. Flower color can delight the eye or it can assault it: solids in red or yellow, bicolors with red sepals and purple corolla or white sepals with red corolla, and many other combinations are possible in *Fuchsia* blossoms. Fuchsias flower continuously for months, from summer until the first frost. Some grow to 10 ft (3 m), but others have stems lax enough to be grown cascading from a hanging basket. They are outdoor hardy in zones 7 to 10, and demand partial shade, cool summers, and atmospheric humidity. In climates lacking these requirements, fuchsias are grown as annuals or as pot plants.

If we crossed *Fuchsia* with fireweed or some *Gaura* species, it seems that no flower color would be unobtainable. The difference in flower shape is so vast between these plants that intermediate forms are hard to imagine. Plant form, too, is hard to predict— after all, we would be crossing a shrub with a herbaceous perennial. The big gain for fuchsias, however, should come in hardiness and adaptability.

Gaura

Gaura lindheimeri is sometimes called whirling butterflies, and the 1-in (2.5-cm) white flowers on 4-ft (1.2-m) panicles do call up some comparisons with the butterfly. This plant is hardy from zone 5 to zone 10 and, being tap-rooted, is very drought tolerant and has become quite popular as a xeriscape plant. *Gaura coccinea* shows pink flowers that fade red, but it has more herbage than flower and so is not as showy as whirling butterflies. Nevertheless, *G. coccinea* might be a source of pink or even red for its fellow gaura.

What if we crossed fireweed (*Epilobium angustifolium*) with *Gaura lindheimeri*? Both are sun lovers, but one prefers moist soils and the other is happy in dry soils. One can spread aggressively, the other usually stays put. One has flowers in screaming pink, the other in demure white, although both flower for a very long time. Fireweed is more stately, whirling butterflies is more elegant. Would a cross yield soft pinks, intermediate plant forms, manageable but dependable spread, and extended adaptability? If so, we could have a real treat for the most difficult sites.

Oenothera Evening Primrose
   Is there a gardener who doesn't grow or at least know evening primrose? The immense 4-in (10-cm) yellow blooms of the straggly, 1-ft (0.3-m) tall Missouri primrose (*Oenothera missouriensis*) are seen in gardens from zone 7 to zone 10, in heavy or light soil, under moist conditions or dry. *Oenothera berlandieri* has smaller flowers, to 2 in (5 cm) in a lovely shade of pink, on 10-in (25-cm) plants. It is a true drought lover, happy in the leanest soils. Both primrose species bloom for a very long time during summer, and both have blossoms that remain open during the day.

   The *Oenothera* that I love most and hate most is *O. caespitosa*, a 4-in (10-cm) tall plant with poppylike, silky white 3-in (7.5-cm) flowers that are nearly stemless. It is amusing to see these huge, solitary blossoms regally perched atop such a small plant. Even more than *O. berlandieri*, *O. caespitosa* loves drought and poor soil. What is its problem? It seeds itself about, thoroughly and recklessly, warranting nuisance status.

   Tame this plant so that it stays put, and it will be a winner. Combining *Oenothera caespitosa* in some way with one of the other two oenotheras mentioned might do the job and introduce a bit of pink or yellow. Hybridizing it with fireweed or gaura might yield something like a refined *Hibiscus* (in the family Malvaceae). And what is the prospect of crossing it with a *Fuchsia*?

ORCHIDACEAE

Orchid family   796 genera, 17,500 species

GENERA DISCUSSED   Bletilla • Calypso • Cypripedium • Epipactis •
Habenaria • Orchis • Paphiopedilum • Phragmipedilum • Pleione •
Spiranthes

OTHER ORNAMENTAL GENERA   Cymbidium • Epidendrum • Laelia

In the orchid family one finds many of the most exquisite, most extravagant, most elegant, most delicate, and most bizarre blossoms in the entire plant kingdom. In addition to the 17,500 species distributed worldwide (most occurring in tropical forests), over 35,000 hybrids have been contrived by people. There are epiphytes (growing on another plant) and terrestrials (growing on land), and even a few saprophytes (living on dead or decaying matter) that spend their lives entirely underground. Some have flowers the size of a pinhead, and others have flowers with petals that grow to 2 ft (0.6 m) in length, finally reaching the ground to provide a ramp for the ants that pollinate them. Some orchid blossoms mimic the flies that pollinate them. Others mimic butterflies, egrets in flight, and all sorts of other creatures, just for fun. Certain members of the genus *Masdevallia* brandish flowers so grotesque that to some they recall Count Dracula himself. (Certain plants classified as *Masdevallia* are sometimes grouped in a separate genus called *Dracula*.) Most orchids, however, are merely supremely beautiful. All this variety makes orchids the most renowned, the most coveted, and the most cherished of all plants.

A more promiscuous lot of plants is hard to imagine. Intrageneric and intergeneric crosses are common. ×*Potinara*, for example, is the name given to a fertile cross involving four genera: *Brassia, Cattleya, Laelia,* and *Sophronitis*. Human-made crosses now outnumber the naturally occurring species, and the rate at which new wonders are being created shows no sign of declining. Meanwhile, tissue culture and other new cultivation techniques have made the latest and best creations more available and affordable.

Almost all of this activity has been in the service of the greenhouse hobby and the cut-flower trade, although many of the exotic kinds can be grown out of doors in certain areas of the United States, such as southern California, Florida, and Hawaii. In northern gardens, however, orchids are seldom seen. Yet dozens of magnificent species native to the United States and Europe are hardy in zone 4, and some even to zone 2. Unlike the tropicals, many of these cold-hardy orchids grow on boggy soils. However, most are difficult to grow even in their native regions. What a blessing it would be to have a wider variety of orchids for temperate gardens, reasonably priced and readily grown. Surely, hardy and easily grown orchids would give iris and daylilies a challenge in the popularity polls.

Bletilla, Calypso Calypso Orchid, *Epipactis, Orchis, Pleione, Spiranthes* Lady's Tresses

The following six orchid genera have members that are hardy enough and adaptable enough to occasionally be represented in temperate zone gardens.

The calypso orchid (*Calypso bulbosa*) is a zone 3 mountain dweller. It is superb as is, looking like a 4-in (10-cm) tall *Cattleya*, complete with pseudobulbs and lilac blossoms, but with a more pouchlike lip. Not much could be done to improve this plant's beauty, although maybe some magic might be worked to bring it into easier cultivation in the garden.

The 10-in (25-cm) hyacinth bletilla (*Bletilla striata*) looks like a windblown version of the calypso orchid. It is successfully grown in the ground in zone 6, and something like it would be much appreciated farther north. The white-flowered form is also truly exquisite.

The pleione orchids (*Pleione*) from China are becoming popular garden plants in zone 7 and above. They have flowers like those of a *Laelia* orchid, in various shades of rose, purple, and white, above narrow leaves to 8 in (20 cm). Let us toughen up these plants, too, and move them northward.

The stream orchid (*Epipactis gigantea*) is a zone 4 waterside dweller from the west coast of North America. It grows from 1 to 3 ft (0.3 to 0.9 m) tall and bears racemes of bronze-colored flowers to 1.5 in (4 cm) that look like starlings with outstretched wings. This one is among the easiest to grow in the garden, at least near water, and might provide an interesting line of breeding.

The lady's tresses orchids (*Spiranthes*) and the genus *Orchis* have several species that make good garden plants. The inflorescence has a different pattern than that of the other orchids mentioned, as it resembles more that of the squill (*Scilla*, in the family Liliaceae).

Cypripedium, Paphiopedilum, Phragmipedium Slipper Orchids

The slipper orchids—those renowned beauties of the genera *Cypripedium, Paphiopedilum,* and *Phragmipedium*—are among the finest of all orchids. *Cypripedium* has members that are hardy in zone 2, but the other two genera are tropical; all are terrestrial. At one time, some taxonomists lumped the three genera together under the genus *Cypripedium,* but now they are thought to be separate. Hybrids abound within the tropical genera, and several intergeneric hybrids exist as well. I know of no crosses between a tropical species and a temperate *Cypripedium,* yet the possibilities and the promise seem limitless. Maybe such crosses will not only be cold hardy but will have enough hybrid vigor to make them easy to cultivate.

Habenaria Fringe Orchid

The *Habenaria* species are the fringe orchids, the orchids with racemes of flowers that look like an egret in flight. Some are white, some yellow, and some purple. They are at home in zones 3 and 4, so cold hardiness is not a problem. Some say that the fringe orchids are difficult to grow, but others claim that that is not so. What are the tropical affiliations of these plants? Do they have some exotic cousins that will combine with them to make even more gorgeous blossoms, or more easily grown plants?

Many orchids from genera other than those discussed here are native in subtropical regions and might contribute to a breeding program. Orchids from such genera as *Odontoglossum, Cymbidium,* and *Laelia* can be grown outdoors in the San Francisco Bay Area of California. Maybe some of these can be hybridized to the truly hardy genera of Orchidaceae. Of course, it is all a romantic mind game—orchids with a tropical flamboyance growing in temperate gardens—but the magnitude of the prize does make one wonder.

PAPAVERACEAE

Poppy family   23 genera, 210 species

GENERA DISCUSSED   *Argemone* • *Macleaya* • *Meconopsis* • *Papaver* •
Romneya

OTHER ORNAMENTAL GENERA   *Eschscholzia* • *Sanguinaria*

Considering their many faults, members of the poppy family (Papaveraceae) must have some extraordinary positive traits to warrant their worldwide popularity. They certainly do, and the debits and credits make this family an ideal venue for the games of the plant breeder.

Argemone Prickly Poppy   PLATE 49
On the matter of adaptability to heat, cold, drought, and miserable soil, the prickly poppy (*Argemone polyanthemos*), native to the western United States, may have a lot to offer besides prickles. I have never seen this plant for sale—too weedy, perhaps—yet its pure white, yellow-centered flowers can be fully 4 in (10 cm) across, crinkled, and well displayed on rigid 2- to 3-ft (0.6- to 0.9-m) stems. What would we get if we crossed the prickly poppy with other members of the poppy family, such as blue poppy (*Meconopsis*), California poppy (*Eschscholzia*), or some species of *Papaver*? Could we see a series of hardy, drought-resistant poppies, sporting all the colors of the spectrum including blue and green? The hardy, adaptable genus *Argemone* has a lot to offer its fellow poppies.

Macleaya Plume Poppy
The plume poppies (*Macleaya cordata* and *M. microcarpa*) are giant perennials with unbranched stems to 8 ft (2.5 m), furnished with huge, deeply lobed, circular leaves and topped by 12-in (30 cm) panicles of small, tan, apetalous flowers. These striking plants are tough and zone 4 hardy. Now, if any of the other poppies will breed with the plume poppy, could we not get a hardy perennial that looks a bit like hollyhock (*Alcea*, in the family Malvaceae) but with better foliage? But that may be pushing it a bit.

Meconopsis Asiatic Poppy, Blue Poppy
    Meconopsis betonicifolia, the legendary Himalayan blue poppy, is among the most beautiful and most frustrating of all plants. Indigenous to regions with acid bogs and cool moist air, *M. betonicifolia* is rarely seen in the United States, and then only in those few places that approximate the plant's native habitat. Is this poppy compatible with the likes of the oriental poppy (*Papaver orientale*), for example? And if so, what can we expect in color, habit, and most important, in adaptability? Perhaps bringing in the prickly poppy could help on this last account.

Papaver Poppy
    When we think of garden poppies, we usually have in mind the varieties of *Papaver orientale*, the oriental poppy. These plants can reach 4 ft (1.2 m) high in flower, and they have blossoms 6 in (15 cm) across with petals like crumpled silk in shades of white, pink, peach, and red, set off by black blotches at their base and a boss of yellow stamens. Unfortunately, bloom time for the oriental poppy lasts only a few weeks. The mound of fuzzy, fernlike leaves is attractive until early summer, and then it is best to cut the leaves back before it becomes a shabby mess. The taller cultivars often need staking, and the size of the plants makes them difficult to accommodate in a garden of modest size. Can we add to the gifts that nature and plant breeders have bestowed upon this already striking poppy? As discussed in Chapter 5, there is some evidence that infertility extends flowering time considerably—this is particularly true in poppies—and that suggests developing male strains by anther culture as a means of improving these plants even more.
    To counter objections to the size and the resulting sloppiness of oriental poppies, developing truly dwarf poppies of the oriental type would be a good plan of attack as well. Creating something considerably smaller than *Papaver orientale* 'Allegro'—a cultivar that is highly variable from seed and can get to be more than 2 ft (0.6 m) tall—would be nice. What would a mix between the dwarf Japanese poppy (*P. miyabeanum*), with its pale greenish white flowers, and a white oriental poppy yield? Could we get a small poppy of the *P. orientale* type with green blossoms? Maybe the alpine poppy (*P. alpinum*) or the Iceland poppy (*P. nudicaule*) will cross with the oriental poppy, giving plants of far smaller size

than the oriental poppy and far greater longevity than the alpine or Iceland species, in a range of color limited only at the blue end of the spectrum. But if the family Papaveraceae will admit some intergeneric hanky-panky, then even more exciting prospects become evident, and even blue color is not out of the picture once we employ *Meconopsis*.

Romneya Matilija Poppy

And let us not overlook *Romneya coulteri*, the famed matilija poppy. This plant is a native to the drylands of southern California, so it is heat and drought tolerant but hardy only into zone 6. It is a superb plant of informal habit, 3 to 8 ft (0.9 to 2.5 m) tall, with creped white flowers to 6 in (15 cm) in diameter that last through most of the summer. In spite of its aggressive roving tendencies, matilija poppy is a garden staple in climates warm enough to grow it. We would love to see it brought down to size and toughened up enough to survive a real winter. What are the plant's genetic affiliations? Can it be crossed with the prickly poppy or the oriental poppy? If so, it might yield all sorts of surprises, including some extraordinary prospects for harsh climates.

PINACEAE

Pine family   9 genera, 194 species

GENERA DISCUSSED   *Cedrus* • *Picea* • *Pinus* • *Pseudotsuga* • *Tsuga*

OTHER ORNAMENTAL GENERA   *Abies* • *Larix* • *Pseudolarix*

The pine family is a small one, but it has a wide distribution in the northern hemisphere, with strong representation in the colder regions. Indeed, as one travels farther north, the trees of this family, particularly pine, spruce, and fir, become the dominant woody plants in the landscape. Given their beauty and hardiness, many of these plants have become garden favorites, and their propensity to mutation has made them the darlings of collectors. Although there are hundreds of varieties of pine, spruce, fir, and cedar, in sizes from 1 to 100 ft (0.3 to 30 m), in foliage colors from silvery blue to yellow and black-green, there are still worthwhile goals to pursue in expanding or improving upon this family.

Cedrus Cedar   PLATE 50
To my eye, the cedars are the most majestic members of this grand family. Many of the other genera in the family Pinaceae are cone-shaped in youth, and then all too often they grow old ungracefully. But the cedars seem to gain more and more character each year. Sometimes multitrunked, often with massive branches springing from the base of the trunk, cedars such as the cedar of Lebanon (*Cedrus libani*), the deodar cedar (*C. deodara*), and the Atlas cedar (*C. atlantica*) can reach a height of 120 ft (37 m) and a spread of 100 ft (30 m)—too large for most private gardens.

Many cultivars of these three cedar species have also been selected, including some chosen for their silvery blue or golden foliage. Some cultivars were chosen for their narrow, spreading, or semipendulous habit, and others for their dwarf stature.

So magnificent are these cedars—so distinctive and so beautiful—that any restriction on hardiness has to be viewed as an affront to gardening and one that must be addressed as soon as possible. Some cedar of Lebanon are hardy in zone 5, the Atlas cedar is hardy in zone 6, and the deodar cedar only to zone 7. A zone 3 fir, such as *Abies balsamea* and *A. concolor*, or a zone 2 spruce, such as *Picea abies* and *P. pungens*, might cross with the cedars to give trees of greater hardiness. Moreover, dwarf forms of fir and spruce could be employed to moderate size, and there is no shortage of clones of fir and spruce with silver or golden foliage color. Of course, the cedars would be expected to contribute a portion of their uniquely individual habit to the mix. A hybrid might bring an entirely new coniferous tree form to vast regions where the only large conifers, other than the pines, are unrelentingly cone-shaped.

Picea Spruce

PLATE 51

The spruces are among the most popular of all evergreen trees, valued for the emphatically upright conical form of the species, the numerous color variants, and the vast assortment of dwarf and miniature forms. Adding to the widespread utility of Norway spruce (*Picea abies*), white spruce (*P. glauca*), and the Colorado blue spruce (*P. pungens*) is a hardiness range from zone 2 to about zone 7.

Some spruces are popular beyond their range of adaptability. The dwarf, densely foliaged cultivars of *Picea glauca*, such as *P. glauca* 'Conica', are hardy enough, but they object to the dry heat, dry winds, and dry winters that are features of the North American midwest. A cross with the drought-tolerant Black Hills spruce (*P. glauca* var. *densata*) might bring the appeal of the white spruce to dryer regions. Since the Black Hills spruce is slow-growing to 40 ft (12 m), its genes could influence the size of the white spruce as well as that of the cedars.

The same considerations regarding the cultivars of the white spruce also hold for the Serbian spruce (*Picea omorika*), a superb stilettolike tree that grows into a narrow spire of 100 ft (30 m) and is hardy from zone 4 to zone 7. It, too, dislikes atmospheric and soil dryness, and a cross with the Black Hills spruce might be useful.

For me, the most exciting prospect for a new spruce is something like Brewer's spruce (*Picea breweriana*), but hardy and adaptable. This rare tree of singular beauty is found in the wild in only a small region of the Siskiyou Mountains in California, and its horticultural range extends only to similar climates with cool, moist summers and moisture-laden winters, to zone 7. The tree languishes on the east coast of the United States and is rare to nonexistent in other places.

What makes this tree so desirable is its unique appearance.

Picea breweriana grows straight-trunked to a height of 80 ft (24 m), and although its branches, which bend downward and then upward in a graceful arc, are not unlike those of many other spruces, the branchlets coming off of these branches are long and steeply pendulous so that each branch, festooned in plush green, takes on the appearance of a gigantic ceremonial banner. This glorious tree makes other pendulous spruces, such as *P. abies* 'Pendula', seem ungainly in habit and unkempt in texture. Nevertheless, it is the pendulous form of the more common spruces that holds the promise for a new hybrid addition to the genus, one with the adaptability of Norway spruce or the blue spruce but with the incomparably noble overall form and graceful habit of Brewer's spruce.

Pinus Pine   PLATE 52

The pines have great worldwide popularity, a reflection of their beauty and wide adaptability. The mugo pine (*Pinus mugo*), the Austrian black pine (*P. nigra*), and the Scots pine (*P. sylvestris*), among other pine species, are exceptionally hardy—the mugo and Austrian black pines are hardy in zone 2, and the Scots pine in zone 4. The many selections of each of these species offer a choice of height, needle color, and habit.

Nevertheless, there are two particularly distinctive pines that most of us have little opportunity to enjoy. Where it grows well, which includes zones 9 and 10 along the Pacific coast of North America, the Monterey pine (*Pinus radiata*) is a superb tree, growing to 100 ft (30 m), with densely packed, bright green 6-in (15-cm) needles. The tree grows quickly for a pine (as much as 6 ft (1.8 m) per year), setting candles, or flushes of new growth, twice a year, which in part accounts for its extremely lush and fresh appearance in all seasons. The tree is easily uprooted by wind, however, and away from its native haunts, the Monterey pine usually succumbs to pests and disease.

The other pine that I wish I could see more of is the Montezuma pine (*Pinus montezumae*). This native of Mexico is not hardy below zone 7. It is a magnificent, wide-spreading pine, growing eventually to 70 ft (21 m) in height. It has the longest needles of any pine—up to 1 ft (0.3 m) in length—arched and gracefully drooping, and that is the tree's most distinctive characteristic.

The Austrian black pine (*Pinus nigra*) has fairly long needles (to 6 in (15 cm) long) of a deep green color. Some of the ponderosa pines (*P. ponderosa*) have even longer needles (to 10 in (25 cm)), but the color is more of a yellow-green. Both trees are hardy to zone 3 and they adapt to a wide range of soils.

Why not try hybridizing the Monterey or Montezuma pine with the Austrian black pine or ponderosa pine in an effort to get the lush growth and superb color of the Monterey pine or the long pendulous needles of the Montezuma pine on a much hardier and more adaptable tree. An extensive breeding program by the United States Forestry Service has succeeded in creating over ninety new hybrid pines, but the work has been directed at improving forest trees; that does, however, lend some plausibility to the crosses proposed here for more ornamental pursuits.

Pseudotsuga Douglas Fir, *Tsuga* Hemlock PLATE 53

Hemlocks are as rare in the North American midwest as they are common on the east and west coasts. The problem is not that of cold tolerance, since the two most popular species of *Tsuga* are quite hardy—the eastern hemlock (*Tsuga canadensis*) from zone 3 to zone 7, and the Carolina hemlock (*T. caroliniana*) from zone 4 to zone 7. The type of soil or the desiccating winters may be what limits the hemlock's wider use. Where they can be grown, hemlocks are highly regarded as the most graceful of all conifers, with an arching leader and relaxed hands of soft, dark foliage. There are other hemlocks of extraordinary beauty, like the western hemlock (*T. heterophylla*), and my favorite, the mountain hemlock (*T. mertensiana*), but these two are even less hardy and adaptable than the other two species mentioned, *T. canadensis* and *T. caroliniana*.

The Douglas fir (*Pseudotsuga menziesii*) is valued primarily as a timber tree. Although it is quite ornamental, the Douglas fir is not as graceful as the true hemlocks, and when full grown it can attain a height of 200 ft (60 m) (usually much less in cultivation). It is hardy in zone 4 and tolerant of a wide variety of soils.

If the Douglas fir can be crossed with a small clone of either the eastern hemlock or the Carolina hemlock, a happy compromise might be struck: a tree with the hardiness and adaptability of the Douglas fir and with the grace of a hemlock but in a more manageable size much closer to that of the latter than the former. There are many places where such a tree would be valued.

POLYPODIACEAE

Polypody Fern family   52 genera, 550 species

GENERA DISCUSSED   *Aglaomorpha* • *Drynaria* • *Platycerium* • *Polypodium*

The family Polypodiaceae has a wide distribution, with members that thrive in zone 2 and others that require zone 9 conditions. Although all have a primitive beauty that recalls their ancient lineage, the most spectacular members of the family are restricted to the tropics. Hybridizing ferns was something of a hobby during the last century, and a purposeful return to that endeavor might yield some extraordinary rewards.

Aglaomorpha, Drynaria
The tree-dwelling ferns of the genera *Aglaomorpha* and *Drynaria* are bold and distinctive to the point of being coarse and bizarre. The bear's paw fern (*Aglaomorpha meyeniana*) can reach a height of 2.5 ft (0.75 m). Its coarsely pinnate fronds are erect, and the pinnae of the upper third of the fertile fronds are narrowed to cordlike dimensions and appear to be strung with beads. All of this is supported by thick rhizomatous roots, furry enough to warrant this fern's common name. The oakleaf fern (*Drynaria quercifolia*) grows to 4 ft (1.2 m) and it, too, has a thick furry rhizome. It gets its common name from the shape of the smaller sterile basal fronds; the fertile fronds of the oakleaf fern are more or less erect.

Both the bear's paw fern and the oakleaf fern are zone 9 dwellers, and both will tolerate a bit of dryness. They are not uncommon in the gardens of Florida and southern California, although nothing like them can be found outside of such hothouse climates. It seems quite possible, however, that this unfortunate situation could be rectified through some intergeneric hybridizing within the family.

Platycerium Staghorn Fern
Arguably, the most singularly spectacular ferns are found in the genus *Platycerium*. There are only seventeen species in this genus, all of them epiphytic, and all are tropical, although *P. bifurcatum* will flirt with zone 8. Most platyceriums have fertile

fronds that do indeed resemble stag horns or moose horns—upright and narrow but flaring toward the fingered ends. The sterile fronds are irregularly circular and overlapping, forming a half-chalice that covers the roots and catches forest debris to provide nourishment for the plant.

Platycerium bifurcatum and its cultivars have exactly this pattern, and they are the most commonly available of the staghorns. When grown as a colony, with dozens of 3-ft (0.9-m) fronds, *P. bifurcatum* is magnificent. But even this fern is upstaged by the regal staghorn fern (*P. superbum*), one of the giants of the genus, with its fanlike sterile fronds to 3 ft (0.9 m) across and fertile fronds to 5 ft (1.5 m) long. Few plants are so distinctive and impressive. Those gardeners living in zones 9 and 10 can grow both of these ferns outdoors. Those of us in colder climates are not so lucky—we grow them indoors and as greenhouse plants.

Polypodium Polypody Fern

The genus *Polypodium* contains seventy-five species, and none is more typical or beautiful than the common polypody (*Polypodium vulgare*). This evergreen fern is found in Africa, Europe, China, Japan, and North America, in zones 3 through 5. It prefers to grow in rock crevices and on decaying wood, but occasionally common polypody grows epiphytically. This plant is a valued addition to many shade gardens, where its dark green, simply pinnate fronds to 16 in (40 cm) make a pleasant contribution throughout the year.

Yet, for spectacular display, no *Polypodium* is a match for its tropical relatives in the genera *Aglaomorpha*, *Drynaria*, and *Platycerium*. But what if we could cross a *Polypodium* with one of the others? Might we not get some bold new ferns of herculean proportions and striking new forms for gardens far removed from the hothouse climates? Maybe some hybrids would come endowed with the enormous furry rhizomes of the bear's paw fern (*Aglaomorpha meyeniana*) or oakleaf fern (*Drynaria quercifolia*), or sport the magnificent shield fronds of the staghorn ferns (*Platycerium*). Maybe they could grow epiphytically on some old apple tree or on a wall. Now that would capture one's attention.

PRIMULACEAE

Primrose family   22 genera, 800 species

GENERA DISCUSSED   *Androsace* • *Cyclamen* • *Dodecatheon* •
Lysimachia • *Primula* • *Soldanella*

The Primulaceae are a treasure-trove of superb woodlanders
and streamside plants. In this family we find the primulas,
preened and pampered by rabid devotees the world over. The demure shooting stars and cyclamens are members, but so are the
bold and rampant loosestrifes, the showy upright ones and the
creepers. So the family contains members that need and deserve
care in cultivation, and others that will bully their way about
almost any site. What more do we need?

Androsace
The androsaces are mat-forming plants, forming rosettes of
leaves 1 to 2 in (2.5 to 5 cm) across, colored gray, green, or rose. The
0.25-in (0.5-cm) flowers come in white or pink, and they are arranged in spherical clusters on stems from 2 to 4 in (5 to 10 cm)
high, depending on the species. It takes little effort to accommodate these highlanders—several are hardy to zone 3, and sun and
fast-draining soil are appreciated.

These are unassuming little plants, attractive and readily
grown just as they come from nature. I don't see how to improve
on *Androsace* in any significant way, but it might have potential as
a breeding partner with other more finicky Primulaceae.

Cyclamen, Dodecatheon Shooting Star, *Soldanella*
Most everyone knows the florist's cyclamen (*Cyclamen per-*
sicum) as an indoor pot plant, with the rosettes of heart-shaped
leaves, often strikingly marbled in white, and the distinctive blossoms with strongly reflexed petals. The garden species of cyclamen, like *C. hederifolium* and *C. coum*, are more modest in size (to
5 in (12.5 cm) in flower), but they also offer remarkably beautiful
foliage and blossoms of the same windswept design as the pot-
plant species. Both of these garden cyclamens are dormant for a
good part of the year, *C. hederifolium* flowering in autumn and *C.*
coum in early spring. The former is hardy to zone 4, the latter to

zone 5. Both require rich, moist soil, and they are seldom grown to perfection away from the coasts. *Cyclamen* is the only tuberous-rooted genus in the family; all the others are fibrous rooted. The shooting stars, such as *Dodecatheon meadia* and *D. pulchellum*, have flowers that resemble small, narrow cyclamen blossoms in white, pink, red, or violet. These two species of *Dodecatheon* are hardy into zone 2, but they lose their leaves by midsummer. Many soldanellas, on the other hand, are zone 4 evergreens, with round leaves and nodding, cup-shaped, fringed purple flowers. *Soldanella* needs a woodsy soil with perfect drainage.

A cross between *Cyclamen* and *Soldanella*, or between *Dodecatheon* and *Soldanella*, could yield exquisite blossoms on plants that tend to hold their foliage over a long season. *Cyclamen* crossed with *Dodecatheon* should leave no doubts about the hardiness of the progeny. To truly toughen up these three genera, to give them a far wider range of soil and light tolerance, a cross with *Androsace* should be considered. But what sorts of blossoms would they beget?

Lysimachia Loosestrife

Lysimachia is a genus of brasher beauties, usually more in need of curbing than pampering. My favorite is the gooseneck loosestrife (*Lysimachia clethroides*), a long-flowering upright plant, with stems to 3 ft (7.5 cm) topped with gooseneck-shaped racemes to 18 in (41 cm). The racemes are studded with 0.5-in (1.6-cm) white blossoms. The yellow loosestrife or circle flower (*L. punctata*) is shorter (to 2 ft (0.6 m) tall), and its 2-in (5-cm) brown-eyed yellow blossoms are borne in the leaf axils along the upper half of the stem. Circle flower blooms for most of the summer. Creeping Jenny (*L. nummularia*) is 5 in (13 cm) tall, with 1-in (2.5-cm) yellow flowers borne singly. It is a creeper—an inexorable, ineradicable creeper—so use with care.

All three of these *Lysimachia* species prefer moist sites and more sun than the others in the family, but they are quite adaptable as to soil, moisture, and sun, and all are zone 3 hardy.

Primula Primrose   PLATE 54

Primula is the flagship genus of the family—400 species and an ever-increasing list of hybrids that fire the passion of hobbyists around the world. Primroses are grown under glass, on the window sill, and in the garden. Some are mountain dwellers that survive with only moderate water, but most are moisture lovers and prefer organically rich soil, atmospheric humidity, and partial shade. These restrictions keep all but the most plebeian of primroses from many gardens where they would be greatly appreciated if only they could survive. My personal favorites are the candelabra sorts, like *Primula japonica*. Although I have lost enough of them over the years to require a second mortgage, I do love the pagodalike structure of their inflorescence.

Suppose we could cross some of the choice primroses with androsaces—crossing moisture- and shade-loving plants with sunloving dryland plants. Might we not get all sorts of new creations that preserve some of the flower forms and colors of primroses, but that have far wider adaptability to normal garden conditions?

The taller loosestrifes, such as *Lysimachia clethroides*, might also be interesting breeding partners for *Primula*, imparting much greater adaptability and a more imposing stature to the primroses. Imagine a waist-high colony of plants with candelabra inflorescences. In return, maybe some of the *Primula* color palette could be transferred to *Lysimachia*.

RANUNCULACEAE

Ranunculus or Buttercup family 58 genera, 1750 species

GENERA DISCUSSED *Anemone* • *Anemonella* • *Clematis* • *Hepatica* • *Ranunculus*

OTHER ORNAMENTAL GENERA *Aconitum* • *Aquilegia* • *Helleborus* • *Pulsatilla* • *Thalictrum* • *Trollius*

We find some of our most popular garden perennials in the buttercup family, including the plant that many consider to be "the queen of all the vines," *Clematis*. Though not large, this family is extremely diverse, and thus the Ranunculaceae have all the promise of new creations that such diversity encourages.

Anemone

Among the most prized flowers in the fall garden is the Japanese anemone (*Anemone* ×*hybrida*, a cross between *A. hupehensis* var. *japonica* and *A. vitifolia*), a graceful plant with maplelike leaves and airy panicles to 5 ft (1.5 m), bearing blossoms to 3 in (7.5 cm) across, single or double, in white, pink, or near red. The Japanese anemone is zone 5 hardy and likes rich, moist, organic soils.

The grape-leaf anemone (*Anemone vitifolia*) has the size and appearance of a single pink Japanese anemone, but it is hardier (zone 4), more tolerant of dry lean soils, and vigorous to the point of weediness. Grape-leaf anemone, too, flowers in the fall.

Quite different is the pasque flower (*Anemone pulsatilla*, syn. *Pulsatilla vulgaris*), a spring-flowering zone 4 mountain dweller that thrives on drought and gravelly soil. Its 2.5-in (6.5-cm), tulip-shaped blossoms in white, wine red, or purple rise to as much as 1 ft (0.3 m) above finely dissected foliage. Even the spherical, feathery seed heads are decorative. But take care, or *A. pulsatilla* will seed itself about the garden.

My favorite is the snowdrop anemone (*Anemone sylvestris*), a zone 4 plant with 2-in (5-cm), yellow-centered white blossoms borne singly on 18-in (46-cm) stems above a loose 10-in (25-cm) mound of deeply cut palmate leaves. Its long flowering display lasts from midspring to early summer. It runs a bit, although I would never consider snowdrop anemone a weed.

Anemone multifida is a much smaller plant, with pink flowers 1 in (2.5 cm) across on stems to 10 in (25 cm) tall. The foliage is very finely cut and forms a mound 4 in (10 cm) high. This gem flowers in midsummer.

In addition to the fibrous-rooted anemones, there are several tuberous-rooted species as well. Two that I admire most are the Grecian windflower (*Anemone blanda*) and the poppy-flowered anemone (*A. coronaria*). The Grecian windflower forms 6-in (15-cm) mounds of 2.5-in (6.5-cm) palmate leaves, above which are displayed semidouble blossoms to 2 in (5 cm), in white, pink, or blue, on 10-in (25-cm) stems. *Anemone coronaria* is a highly variable species, with spectacular blossoms to 2.5 in (6.5 cm) borne on 15-in (38-cm) stems above 12-in (30-cm) mounds of palmate foliage. The flowers of the poppy-flowered anemone can be flat singles or cupped, poppy-shaped singles, as well as semidoubles and doubles, depending on the cultivar, in colors that include red, white, blue, and some bicolors, all set off by prominent black stamens. The blossoms are beautiful and long-lasting in the garden as well as in a vase.

Just crossing the few anemones mentioned here holds the promise of creating something excitingly different. The pasque flower can add purple hues, increase hardiness, and decrease height in crosses with some of the other anemones. A more radical reduction in size might be obtained by using *Anemone multifida*. The poppy-flowered anemone crossed with the snowdrop anemone or the grape-leaf anemone could yield an entirely new race of plants, hardier and more adaptable than *A. coronaria* but more colorful than either *A. sylvestris* or *A. vitifolia*. What will happen to flowering time when those anemones that flower in the spring are crossed with those that bloom in the fall? Will the new plants choose spring or fall, or will flowering time be extended between these seasons? A summer of anemones—it is a pleasant prospect.

Anemonella, Hepatica

In the genera *Anemonella* and *Hepatica* we find the gems of the family Ranunculaceae: truly exquisite miniatures not more than 6 in (15 cm) tall. They flower in spring bearing white, pink, or blue blossoms. Flower form can be single, double, or like a Japanese-style oriental peony with a central boss of small petals surrounded by a collar of larger ones. The beauty and variety of these plants is extraordinary and has gained them an avid following in Japan, where hobbyists have taken a money-is-no-object approach to the acquisition of *Anemonella* and *Hepatica* (cf. the *Bulletin of the American Rock Garden Society*, Vol. 49, No. 1, for a beautifully illustrated article).

Now cross these plants with the Japanese anemone (*Anemone* ×*hybrida*), or the grape-leaf anemone (*A. vitifolia*), or the pasque flower (*A. pulsatilla*). Size, adaptability, hardiness, and flowering time will sort themselves out, yielding plants of suitable constitution for the average garden. If flower shape shows the influence of anemonellas, or leaf shape shows the influence of the fancy-leaved hepaticas, the hybrids would be the dandies of gardens the world over.

Clematis PLATE 55

Often called "queen of the vines," clematis reigns supreme, challenged only by *Bougainvillea* in warmer climes, Japanese wisteria, and the climbing roses. The larger-flowered hybrid clematis are hardy in zone 3, and they are not particular as to soil. Some species flower in the spring, others in the fall. Many of the large-flowered *Clematis* hybrids, however, continue to bloom from late spring to early fall—an incomparable display of exquisite flowers in white, blue, red, and violet in a variety of tints, tones, and patterns, growing to 8 in (20 cm) across.

Depending on the garden, however, vines can be the easiest plants to place or they can be the most difficult. Would it not be a blessing to have clematislike blossoms on a plant form other than a vine? Imagine shrubs, subshrubs, or perennials of manageable size with flowers approaching those of clematis in size, color, and form. Maybe a judicious cross could bring this about, say between *Clematis* and *Ranunculus*, or between *Clematis* and *Anemone* or *Anemonella*, the latter combination suggesting the possibility of low-growing plants with excellent foliage and large flowers of unsurpassable form and color.

There is also a more-or-less self-supporting clematis, *Clematis integrifolia*. It is a herbaceous perennial to about 5 ft (1.5 m) tall, with 1-in (2.5-cm), nodding blue flowers in summer. It is hardy to zone 3 and quite adaptable. This, too, might bring the vining clematis back down to earth, or it might be used in crosses with other Ranunculaceae for some of the same reasons already described.

Ranunculus   PLATE 56
   The namesake genus of the family Ranunculaceae, *Ranunculus*, is familiar to most, if not all gardeners. In zones 7 through 10, the tuberous-rooted Persian ranunculus (*Ranunculus asiaticus*) can be left in the ground all year. In other climates, it is dug up and stored or treated as an annual. These 2- to 3-ft (0.6- to 0.9-m) tall plants sport heavily ruffled double flowers, reaching 5 in (13 cm) across, that come in all shades, except blue and green. Borne in great profusion over a very long season, Persian ranunculus is a sun-lover and requires perfect drainage.

   The zone 2 creeping buttercup (*Ranunculus repens* 'Flore Pleno') is vigorous enough to warrant weed status when in the wrong place. Where it is wanted, however, creeping buttercup is a charmer, with deeply cut leaves and heavily doubled blossoms that form brilliant yellow spheres 1 in (2.5 cm) across on stems 1 ft (0.3 m) high. It thrives in moist soil and prefers shade or semishade.

   How different these two species of *Ranunculus* are. One is tuberous-rooted and the other is fibrous rooted; one prefers moist soil and the other needs perfect drainage; one likes sun, the other shade; one is fairly tall, the other fairly short; one is available in all sorts of warm shades, the other only in yellow. They were clearly meant for each other, and their union might provide plants of extremely wide adaptability in an extremely wide range of colors and heights. Given the popularity of the Persian ranunculus as a cut flower and garden annual, the promise of such a hybrid is enormous.

RHAMNACEAE

Buckthorn family   53 genera, 875 species

GENERA DISCUSSED   *Ceanothus* • *Rhamnus*

The family Rhamnaceae has only two genera of garden merit. One, *Rhamnus*, is of only moderate interest, but *Ceanothus* is very popular and offers unlimited potential for the creation of new plants.

Ceanothus California Lilac, Wild Lilac
    The wild lilacs (*Ceanothus*), unlike their buckthorn relations (*Rhamnus*), are plants to get excited about. In size, these shrubs vary from a creeping 2 ft (0.6 m) high to an upright 12 ft (3.7 m). Wild lilacs can be evergreen or they can be deciduous. Some species and hybrids of *Ceanothus* bloom in the spring, some in the fall, and some bloom over several months from summer into fall. When in bloom, the wild lilacs cover themselves with small lilac-like panicles that lack the scent and size of the common lilac (*Syringa vulgaris* and its cultivars), but they are showy nevertheless. The flowers come in pink, white, burgundy, and a marvelous range of blues. Moreover, *Ceanothus* is drought tolerant and not particular as to soil. Most of the garden ceanothus are hybrids or cultivars of *Ceanothus cyaneus* and *C. griseus*, natives of California, and they do not fare well inland or even in humid coastal climates. They are also hardy only to zone 8.
    Other species of *Ceanothus*, however, such as New Jersey tea (*Ceanothus americanus*), inland ceanothus (*C. ovatus*), and snowbrush (*C. velutinus*), are much hardier. These species all have small heads of small white flowers, and all are about 3 ft (0.9 m) tall. New Jersey tea and inland ceanothus are hardy in zone 4. Snowbrush is found over a large region of the Rocky Mountains, from New Mexico to well into Canada, and it is at least zone 3 hardy. *Ceanothus velutinus* has shiny, leathery, 4-in (10-cm) leaves that are distinctively different from those of its brethren, and they are evergreen.
    With all these feral ceanothus to work with, why not breed for garden-worthy hybrids of greater adaptability and much greater hardiness? Perhaps even wider crosses are possible, say between wild lilac and a *Rhamnus* species. Maybe this would lead to tough

large shrubs and small trees with the ornamental features of the cultivated *Ceanothus*. Anything that works to bring the amenities of the wild lilacs inland from their coastal retreat would be a blessing.

Rhamnus Buckthorn

It is hard to get excited over the buckthorns, but they are serviceable shrubs for cold winters (zone 2) and poor soil. The common buckthorn (*Rhamnus catharticus*) has a 20-ft (6-m) frame, well clothed in attractive glossy green leaves, and fall color is a pleasant pale yellow. The alder buckthorn (*R. frangula*) is shorter, growing to 12 ft (3.7 m), but it has similar foliage. Tall hedge (*R. frangula* 'Columnaris') is the alder buckthorn's most popular cultivar. It grows in a narrow spire, 4 ft (1.2 m) wide and up to 15 ft (4.5 m) tall, and it has its use as sentries or in narrow hedges. Planted in groups, the tall hedges look a bit like dwarf Lombardy poplars (*Populus nigra* 'Italica', in the family Salicaceae), but they are healthier, neater, and much longer lived.

ROSACEAE

Rose family   107 genera, 3100 species

GENERA DISCUSSED   *Crataegus* • *Malus* • *Potentilla* • *Prunus* • *Pyrus* •
Rosa • *Rubus* • *Sorbus* • *Spiraea*

OTHER ORNAMENTAL GENERA   *Alchemilla* • *Amelanchier* •
Chaenomeles • *Cotoneaster* • *Cydonia* • *Kerria* • *Photinia* •
Pyracantha • *Sorbaria*

The Rosaceae are the premier family of flowering trees and
shrubs—only the Ericaceae can be considered a contender. Cherished for the abundance and beauty of their flowers, many
Rosaceae have far more to offer than just a one-season display,
spectacular though that display may be. It is a vast and varied
family, and plant breeders have had great success in exploiting
that diversity. But it is only the beginning.

Crataegus Hawthorn
The best of the hawthorns have it all: stunning cymes of white,
pink, or red flowers, interesting shape, stunning fall foliage color,
and spectacular fruit that can last until winter. Some *Crataegus*
plants are beset by the scourges that are common plagues for so
many of the Rosaceae—rust, fire blight, and scab. Others, however, are less bothered. It is a genus of great promise, particularly
for the central region of North America, where many species are
found that are tolerant of bitter cold, raking winds, dry heat, and
miserable alkaline and dry rocky soil. Thorns are a problem, but
the cockspur thorn (*Crataegus crus-galli*) has a cultivar, 'Inermis',
that has been declawed. The fall color of the cockspur thorn is perfectly incandescent, and in the variety 'Splendens' (*C. crus-galli* ×
C. macrantha) it is even more so—if that is possible.
The Washington thorn (*Crataegus phaenopyrum*) is the most frequently recommended member of this genus. It has all the good
features of a hawthorn, plus maplelike leaves and good diseas
resistance. *Crataegus viridis* 'Winter King' is one of the most nc
table of the hawthorns, glorious in fruit, flower, and sometime
autumn color. Our pinks and reds come from the English tho:
(*C. laevigata*), and this is the most widely planted of all. Unfort
nately, its fruit display is mediocre, its fall color nondescript if r

downright ugly, and its susceptibility to disease is exceptionally high.

There are several opportunities here, and I would add the Russian thorn (*Crataegus ambigua*) to the list of likely breeding partners. This is more of a shrub than a tree, growing to only 15 ft (4.5 m), with multiple stems contorted in a most interesting way. It is floriferous, bears attractive fruit, shows fair fall color, is hardy to zone 4, and has good disease resistance. Perhaps the Russian thorn or the cockspur thorn can add their mettle to the Washington thorn and English thorn, while the latter two add superb leaf shape and flower color to the mix—it would be an interesting experiment. Of course, if the hawthorns can be bred to other members of their family—say crabapples, cherries, potentillas, or even roses—there is no limit to the variety that could be achieved.

Malus Apple, Crabapple   PLATE 57

Crabapples (*Malus*) are the most popular flowering trees in the temperate zone, and for good reason. The best in the genus are four-season performers with superb spring flowers, healthy summer foliage, autumn leaf color, and a striking display of bright fruit from late summer into winter. Included in the hundreds of varieties of crabapples to choose from are cultivars that are treelike or shrubby, cultivars that are spreading, upright, fastigiate, or weeping, and ones that are blessedly resistant to fire blight, scab, and rust, plagues that so bedevil the rose family. Bravo! All I can wish for is more. Might we create more hybrids that choose to grow as multistemmed trees, more that choose to grow as shrubs, more dwarfs, and more with disease resistance? By all means, let us have more crabapples!

Potentilla Cinquefoil   PLATE 58

The cinquefoils have so much to offer that their hybridization and selection has been proceeding apace. A genus of shrubs, subshrubs, and herbaceous perennials, *Potentilla* offers flowers in white, pink, near red, orange, and a full spectrum of yellows, as well as several bicolors. There are singles and doubles, with some blossoms approaching 2 in (5 cm) in diameter. Even in a family where floriferousness is the rule, the cinquefoils are a standout, and some bloom continuously from spring into fall. The leaves are more or less palmate, they can be tomentose or glabrous, silvery or green, and some color a vibrant claret red in autumn. Potentillas are rugged, and the cultivars of *Potentilla fruticosa* are standard recommendations throughout western North America and the droughty Great Plains.

So what more do we need other than simply more? How about a hardy, drought-tolerant, yellow-flowering tree that blooms for most of the growing season? After all, yellow is the strong suit of the *Potentilla* and, for all we know, might be transferrable to the crabapples, cherries, or hawthorns.

Prunus Apricot, Cherry, Peach, Plum   PLATES 59, 60

The Japanese flowering cherry (*Prunus serrulata*), the Higan cherry (*P. subhirtella*), and the Sargent cherry (*P. sargentii*), and their many hybrids and cultivars, would be as popular as the crabapples were it not for a few shortcomings. Only the Sargent cherry is hardy in zone 4, but there it seldom bears a good crop of flowers. The others are likely to have their buds zapped by late freezes in zone 5. Few forms of these species show fall color, and their fruit is nonexistent or inconsequential. Many are troubled by insects and disease, and most are much more finicky in their soil preferences than the crabapples.

In flower, however, the cherries are unbeatable. Consider, for example, *Prunus serrulata* 'Kwanzan', with its 2.5-in (6.5-cm), pink, 30-petaled blossoms; *P. serrulata* 'Shirotae', a semidouble white with 2-in (5-cm) blossoms; or my favorite, *P. serrulata* 'Ukon', with its pendulous 1.75-in (4.5-cm) blooms of pale lime-green set against bronze-colored newly emerging leaves. The weeping Higan cherry (*P. subhirtella* 'Pendula') has single pink blossoms only 0.5 in (1.3 cm) across, yet the profusion of bloom and the weeping habit make it one of the most popular of the group. Among the species, none is finer than the Sargent cherry. This superb tree grows to 50 ft (15 m), bears 1.5-in (4-cm) single pink blossoms in early spring, sports a polished red-brown bark, and is one of the few cherries to feature red foliage in the fall.

For those of us condemned to live outside of the realm of these splendid flowering cherries, fortunately there is hope. After all, many cherries are much hardier, much more disease resistant, and less finicky about soil conditions than the Japanese flowering cherries. Sour cherries, like *Prunus cerasus* 'Montmorency', are hardy in zone 3 and thrive on soils that a proper flowering cherry would turn up its roots at. The double-flowered mazzard cherry (*P. avium*) is hardy to zone 3 and also quite soil tolerant. Both of these trees can be planted as ornamentals without embarrassment, although the fruit of the sour cherry might be a nuisance, unless you find it as tasty as I do.

Even hardier (zone 2) and more soil tolerant are the bush cherries, such as *Prunus besseyi*, *P.* ×*cistena* (*P. cerasifera* 'Atropurpurea' × *P. pumila*), and *P. tomentosa*. All are quite floriferous and bear fruit that is more than just palatable. Other lesser-known tree cherries and bush cherries are truly tough: *Prunus americana*, *P. fruticosa*, *P. japonica*, *P. tenella*, and *P. virginiana*, to name a few.

Moreover, the cherries are not above a bit of promiscuity. Sweet and sour cherries have been hybridized with each other, and cherries have been crossed with plums. Does this mean that the flowering cherries will cross with the shrub cherries, including the super-tolerant, zone 4, purple-leaved plums, like the cultivars of *Prunus cerasifera*? Or better still, can the cherries hybridize with the zone 2 hardy Canada plum (*P. nigra*), a tree to 30 ft (9 m), which has superb 1.25-in (3-cm) double white flowers in the cultivar 'Princess Kay'? There is a wealth of possibilities, not only to increase hardiness but also to create a much greater diversity of forms. We can imagine flowering cherries as dwarf, standard, and tall shrubs, as multistemmed and single-stemmed trees, with single flowers or double flowers in a full range of whites, pinks, and even pale yellows and greens, with superb bark and even a flush of fall color—all hardy to at least zone 4, and all tolerant of poor soils. What pleasure they would bring!

The larger cherries are not the only show stoppers in the genus *Prunus*, however. Few shrubs can out-flower the dwarf flowering almond (*Prunus glandulosa*) or the double-flowering plum (*P. triloba*). The first grows to 4.5 ft (1.4 m) and *P. triloba* to 15 ft (4.5 m), and both cover themselves with double pink blossoms of exquisite beauty in early spring. Even though both shrub cherries are hardy in zone 4, a late frost commonly destroys the buds when in zone 5 and colder regions.

So spectacular are these shrubs in bloom that their popularity may have exceeded their usefulness. It is now fashionable to say that these shrubs are out of fashion, that they are one-season shrubs, and that even their beauty in that one season is too unreliable, too dependant on the weather to be considered first rate. But I find them spectacular when in bloom, and they are at the very least respectable in their off seasons. The double-flowering plum often takes on a soft rose hue in autumn that is quite pleasant.

Rather than arguing whether these shrubs should be admired for their good points or disdained for their bad ones, perhaps breeders should turn their attention to creating new useful and interesting hybrids to improve the situation. Why not cross the flowering almond or double-flowering plum with one of the hardier bush cherries mentioned previously? Would the progeny have double flowers? Would they inherit the toughness of the bush cherries?

Then again, why restrict the crosses to shrubs? How will the propensity to shrubbiness hold up if the flowering almond or double-flowering plum is crossed with the sour cherry tree or the *Prunus nigra* 'Princess Kay' plum tree? Maybe we would get some truly spectacular large shrubs or multistemmed small trees for the effort.

Taking another direction, let us consider what the cherry laurel (*Prunus laurocerasus*) has to offer: moderately showy panicles of flowers like those of the pin cherries (*P. pensylvanica*), and shiny evergreen lanceolate leaves on a conical 18-ft (5.5-m) tree. The species is hardy to zone 6, but the cultivars 'Otto Luyken' and 'Schipkaensis' are supposedly hardy to zone 5—they survive, but they come out of winter in shabby condition. These free-flowering plants are spreading shrubs to about 4 ft (1.2 m), and they have good shade tolerance. Will they breed with zone 2 cherries and give us something hardy in zone 4? Broadleaved evergreens with notable flowers are not that common in zone 5, and new ones would be greatly appreciated. Even a free-flowering semievergreen would be welcome.

Others in the genus *Prunus* can also be thrown into the arena. The Japanese or flowering apricot (*Prunus mume*) is cherished in East Asia for its late-winter blooms, fragrant and very double, in shades of pink and white, to 1.25 in (3 cm). It is hardy to an optimistic zone 6, but the Manchurian apricot (*P. mandshurica*) is hardy into zone 3. *Prunus mandshurica* flowers in the spring, with 1.25-in (3-cm) single pink blossoms, and this small tree, to 20 ft (6 m) in height, has golden fall color. Why not mix the two apricots? We should also note that apricots have been bred with plums to create a new fruit, the pluot—delicious, in spite of its name. Surely, there are all sorts of other possibilities.

Pyrus Pear

Why grow an ornamental pear when there are so many crab-apples and flowering cherries? After all, flower color in *Pyrus* is limited to white, there are no doubles, habit is less varied and less picturesque than that of the crabs, and the bark is less attractive than that of the cherries. Moreover, pear trees suffer many of the same diseases as the crabapples—fire blight, in particular, can be a fast killer.

The most renowned ornamental tree in the genus is the Callery pear (*Pyrus calleryana*) and its cultivars 'Bradford', 'Aristocrat', 'White House', and others. All are stiff and formal in habit and they are somewhat touchy in zone 4. The Ussurian pear (*P. ussuriensis*), my personal favorite, has the same lovely white flowers as the calleries but is much more casual in habit and is thoroughly hardy in zone 2. Why grow pears rather than cherries or crabapples? Because the pears offer a fall foliage display unmatched by the others: a blazing coppery red for the Ussurian pear and a deep burgundy color for the Callery pear.

I do not see that staying within the genus holds much promise for significant new developments among pears. Of course, if the ornamental pears can be crossed with the flowering cherries or crabapples, then it is a whole new ball game, one in which the winners might sport the finest of flowers and have spectacular fall color as well. Furthermore, pears are fairly cold hardy and they are tolerant of heavy clay soil—other desirable traits that might be passed on to their progeny.

Rosa Rose   PLATE 61

The rose is the archetype of the Rosaceae. The modern garden roses constitute a vast and complicated collection of interspecific hybrids. Cultivated since 600 B.C., roses are cherished for the beauty and scent of their blossoms—few would be grown for their foliage and habit alone. As a group, the hybrid roses require a regular regimen of spraying, fertilizing, and pruning in order to look their best. Most of the fancy hybrid teas, grandifloras, and to a lesser extent, floribundas are somewhat touchy even in zone 5.

On the other hand, some of the species and modern hybrid

shrub roses are quite tough, and some show good fall color as well as attractive fruit. Several of these roses bear single flowers of simple elegance, their unpretentious sophistication making them much better candidates for the informal garden than their fifty-petalled, overbred brethren. *Rosa rugosa*, with red, white, or pink flowers, and *R. virginiana*, with pink flowers, are among several worthwhile species. Notable hybrids include 'Nearly Wild', 'Carefree Beauty', and the Meidiland series, with flowers in white, pink, and scarlet, some single and some double, and in a variety of heights from a mounding 2 ft (0.6 m) to an upright 5 ft (1.5 m). All of these hybrids are hardy in zone 4 and they are relatively carefree. The Meidiland shrub roses are a fairly recent innovation with an exceptionally long flowering season. Let us hope that this breeding trend continues; we certainly could use more easy-care, long-flowering, single whites, yellows, reds, and near blues that can fit neatly into the landscape.

Suppose that roses can be bred to crabapples (*Malus*), cherries (*Prunus*), hawthorns (*Crataegus*), or mountain ashes (*Sorbus*). Maybe some tree forms would result, forms with flowers in various shades of yellow and mauve, as well as white, pink, and red. Maybe tall shrubs would result that are less lethally endowed with spines. Maybe the crosses would have the tendency to flower repeatedly or even perpetually. Perhaps crossing a rose with *Potentilla* will yield hardy, highly adaptable, thornless shrubs, with better habit than that of the rose and with colorful, scented flowers showier than those of the *Potentilla*. Maybe such a hybrid would inherit the popularity of both parents.

Rubus Raspberry

For noshing, there is nothing like a raspberry; but as garden ornamentals, most raspberries are second rate. At least two species of *Rubus*, however, deserve more consideration for their ornamental offerings: the Boulder raspberry (*Rubus deliciosus*) and *R. calycinoides*.

Rubus deliciosus grows to 10 ft (3 m), is drought tolerant, hardy to zone 4 at least, and is showy in bloom, with large, yellow-centered white blossoms. The shrub shows a great deal of variability, and plants can be found on Green Mountain, to the west of Boulder, Colorado, that are less than 2.5 ft (0.75 m) high but sport flowers nearly 2.5 in (6.5 cm) across. The shrub is rather unkempt in growth, but given its xeriscape potential and variability, clones of unusual merit should be located and propagated.

Rubus calycinoides is a delightful evergreen groundcover, a rambling bramble with lobed, kidney-shaped leaves of bright green that turn a bit bronzy in cold weather; the flowers of *R. caly-cinoides* are insignificant. Contrary to most sources that list it as zone 6, the plant is perfectly hardy in zone 4. Broadleaved ever-greens of such hardiness are far from common, so any addition to the list would be most welcome. Crossing *R. calycinoides* with some other *Rubus*, say the Boulder raspberry, might yield a slow-growing semievergreen or evergreen shrub with superb foliage and good-sized blossoms. If not, pursuing these goals into the F_2 generation might garner the rewards.

Sorbus Mountain Ash   PLATE 62

What more can one ask for in a tree or shrub than what one gets with mountain ash? *Sorbus* is a genus of plants renowned for its four-season beauty: abundant spring cymes of (rather smelly) white flowers; elegant, almost ferny foliage (with a few excep-tions); blazing fall color (again with a few exceptions); clusters of brilliant red, orange, yellow, or white fruit; cherrylike bark; and excellent habit. Unfortunately, most *Sorbus* plants are beset by the usual maladies that plague the rose family: apple scab, rust, and fire blight. Fire blight can often be the tree's final affliction, and if not, it can cause such unsightliness that the gardener will most likely finish what the bacteria started.

The Korean mountain ash (*Sorbus alnifolia*) is a fairly disease-resistant species and it is a worthy ornamental. It bears superb flowers and fruit and has a pleasing golden fall color. The leaves are simple, more like the leaves of an elm than the pinnate leaves of most other *Sorbus* plants. A cross between the Korean moun-tain ash and the European mountain ash (*S. aucuparia*) might re-sult in hybrids of greater disease resistance. Of course, it may be possible to find disease-resistant clones, and such precious plants should be propagated.

The genus has a dwarf member, *Sorbus reducta*, that is a stolo-niferous, zone 4, thicket-forming, 2-ft (0.6-m) tall shrublet. It of-fers all the favors expected from the genus: delicate white blos-soms in the spring, ferny foliage coloring nicely in the fall, and a show of red berries from fall into winter. As of yet, this promising plant is not well known, but as a partner in crosses with other *Sorbus*, it might yield delicate dwarf shrubs of considerable beauty and with a long season of interest.

Spiraea

Among the spiraeas we find shrubs in sizes from 1 to 8 ft (0.3 to 2.5 m). There are spring-flowering shrubs whose branches are densely sheathed in white flowers along their entire length, such as bridalwreath spiraea (*Spiraea prunifolia*) and the Vanhoutte spiraea (*S.* ×*vanhouttei* = *S. trilobata* × *S. cantoniensis*). Some spiraea shrubs have summer cymes of white, pink, or red blossoms, such as 'Anthony Waterer' and other *S.* ×*bumalda* cultivars and 'Little Princess' and other *S. japonica* cultivars, and some have panicles of rose-red flowers, such as *S.* ×*billardii* (*S. douglasii* × *S. salicifolia*). The genus is largely unremarkable in habit and leaf shape, but cultivars like *S. japonica* 'Goldmound' and *S.* ×*bumalda* 'Limemound' are descriptively named for their foliage color (both have pink flowers).

Besides crossing them with other Rosaceae that need to have flowering time extended or hardiness and soil tolerance improved, what is *Spiraea*'s potential? Still more is to be explored.

RUBIACEAE

Madder family   630 genera, 10,400 species

GENERA DISCUSSED   *Galium* • *Gardenia*

The Rubiaceae are a large family, but they contain relatively few genera of garden interest. Here we consider only two members, so different in appearance that most gardeners are surprised to find that they are in the same family.

Galium Bedstraw, Woodruff
    Bedstraw (*Galium odoratum*) is a deciduous, herbaceous, 5-in (13-cm) groundcover, and it is quite beautiful in foliage, with upright stems holding whorls of dark green leaves. Tiny white flowers liberally sprinkle the plant in early spring and give off a very pleasant fragrance. This zone 4 plant will take sun or shade, moisture and some drought, heavy or light soils, and is accommodating to a wide range of pH. Where not wanted, bedstraw's vigor and adaptability will put it on the weed list; otherwise, it is a reliable and attractive groundcover.

Gardenia
    Gardenias are shrubs, 3 ft (0.9 m) to over 10 ft (3 m) tall, that are richly clothed in dark green shiny leaves and have fragrant, waxy white blossoms to 5 in (13 cm) across. No shrub is more renowned for its scent than the gardenia (particularly *Gardenia jasminoides* and its cultivars).
    Its midwinter to midspring bloom, its lack of bud-hardiness below freezing, its need for fast-draining acid soil, and its reliance on abundant moisture at the roots as well as in the air, however, make *Gardenia* a shrub of very limited usefulness—highly desirable, but out of reach to the great majority of gardeners.

So here we have two members of the Rubiaceae: one hardy, adaptable, and vigorous to the point of weediness; the other finicky, tender, and quite restricted in its growing range. What about some alliance between the two? Can we significantly boost the hardiness of gardenias while retaining the superb blossoms and their heady scent? Will the herbaceous stems of bedstraw yield to woodiness? Will the deciduous nature of *Galium* yield to the evergreen disposition of *Gardenia*? Any hybrid between the two is sure to yield surprises, and there certainly seems to be room for some very pleasant ones.

RUTACEAE

Rue family   161 genera, 1700 species

GENERA DISCUSSED   *Citrus* • *Dictamnus* • *Phellodendron* • *Ptelea* •
Skimmia

OTHER ORNAMENTAL GENERA   *Choisya* • *Poncirus* • *Ruta*

The most important members of the family Rutaceae are the
citrus—orange, lemon, lime, grapefruit, tangerine, mandarin, and
others. They are grown primarily for their fruit, but they offer
many desirable ornamental features as well. Although *Citrus* can
be grown only in warmer climates, other members of the family
are widely adaptable.

Citrus
Evergreen foliage, attractive habit in a variety of sizes (from 5-
ft (1.5-m) shrubs to 30-ft (9-m) trees), handsome fruit, and an
abundance of waxy white blossoms with legendary fragrance over
a long period all contribute to the value of citrus as landscape ornamentals. Unfortunately, the pleasures of growing citrus out of
doors is not to be enjoyed by those of us who live outside of zones
9 and 10. Even in those favored climates, adequate moisture and
perfect drainage are essential. There are, however, other members
of the rue family that might remedy these shortcomings.

Dictamnus Gas Plant
The gas plant is a long-lived, zone 3 perennial, sturdy enough
when well grown to give the impression of a shrub. The plant in
flower reaches a height of 3 ft (0.9 m), and the blossoms—purplish,
pink, or white, 2 in (5 cm) across on sturdy panicles—remind
me of *Laelia* orchids. *Dictamnus* is a superb, tap-rooted, drought-
tolerant plant, and I do not see how to improve it.
On the other hand, what if it can be bred to one of the other
trees or shrubs in the rue family. The prospects are as exciting as
the plants are different. Again, the question arises as to how the
propensity toward woodiness would be sorted out in a cross between the gas plant and the woodier Rutaceae. Might we hope for
shrubs with stiff upright stems bearing dictamnuslike racemes?

Phellodendron Cork Tree

The Amur cork tree (*Phellodendron amurense*) grows to 45 ft (14 m) in height and spread. Its sinuous branches originate close to the ground, making mature specimens difficult to accommodate in small landscapes. That is too bad, because this is a sturdy tree, hardy to zone 3 and very soil tolerant, with strikingly corky bark and a picturesque shape.

Crossing the Amur cork tree with the 20-ft (6-m) hop tree (*Ptelea trifoliata*) might yield something of intermediate size and with a form better suited to the garden than that of either parent. Crossing the cork tree with a citrus might do the same, and also give us a chance at the fragrance of the citrus's lovely bloom on a hardy semievergreen tree.

Ptelea Wafer-ash, Hop Tree

The hop tree or wafer-ash (*Ptelea trifoliata*) is a member of the rue family—a drought-tolerant, shade-tolerant, wind-tolerant, heat-tolerant, and pH-tolerant, zone 3 hardy relative of the orange! If the taxonomists are correct, maybe the hop tree can be wed to a citrus to improve the citrus's hardiness—not that the hop tree is unworthy in its own right. This 20-ft (6-m) tall, adaptable shrubby tree, with interesting trifoliate leaves and heavily fragrant (too heavy to some), nondescript blossoms, is little known and seldom grown. Maybe the hardiness of the hop tree can be combined with the citrus's proclivity to flower month after month. Maybe the flowers of the mix will have the legendary scent of orange blossoms and their waxy substance. Maybe the progeny will have glossy leaves and a tendency to keep them evergreen, as in the citrus, but in colder climates. Even a semievergreen or deciduous tree with the floral scent and beauty of those offered by orange, lemon, or lime would be a prize to millions of gardeners in climates more harsh than zone 9.

Skimmia

Skimmia japonica is a choice shrub, at least for those who can make their choice in zone 7 or higher. The plant has several desirable attributes: a well-branched, dome-shaped habit to about 4 ft (1.2 m); neat evergreen leaves; 3-in (7.5-cm) panicles of small white flowers borne in early spring; and red berries in fall lasting to midwinter. Its yearlong interest cannot be improved upon, although it would certainly be nice to grant those living in climates colder than zone 7 the pleasure of its company.

Again, a cross of *Skimmia* with the hop tree might yield a hardy, semievergreen shrub with ornamental foliage, habit, fruit, and flowers. Maybe large shrubs with the same traits can be obtained by crossing it with the Amur cork tree (*Phellodendron amurense*). *Dictamnus* is another candidate that might cross with *Skimmia* to increase its hardiness.

SALICACEAE

Willow family   2 genera, 435 species

GENERA DISCUSSED   *Populus • Salix*

The trees of the family Salicaceae are among the weediest to ever curse a garden and among the most elegant to ever grace it. In this family we find some of the most bug-ridden, disease-prone, and short-lived trees, as well as some of the most useful, popular, and tolerant trees. There are only two genera, each with enormous potential.

Populus Aspen, Cottonwood, Poplar   PLATES 63, 64
Because its long, thin pedicels allow the leaves to play in the slightest breeze, *Populus tremuloides* is given the name quaking aspen. In summer, the dark green top surface of the leaves and the silvery undersides flicker alternately into view, imparting to each tree a sparkle that can animate entire groves. Autumn, however, is their season of splendor, when, Midas-touched, the quaking aspens spread a shimmering mantle of gold across the landscape. And the trunk—graceful, smooth-skinned, and a pale silvery green—compares favorably to that of the finest birch all year long.

I love these trees and have more than a dozen of them in my garden, even though I should know better. Leaf miners love them as much as I do; gall insects disfigure the branches of *Populus tremuloides* into chains of grotesque lumps; blackspot fungus robs them of their fall color; and scale peppers their bark with ugliness. What's more, the trees are not structurally stable under a heavy snow. Still I love them, and where summer heat, lack of humidity, and alternate freezing and thawing in winter discourage using birch (*Betula*, in the family Betulaceae), aspen is a logical choice. The Japanese birch (*Betula platyphylla* var. *japonica*) has also been suggested as a substitute, but it lacks the casual grace, the animated leaves, and the autumn brilliance of the aspen.

Quaking aspen is a highly variable tree. Some are narrow, and some are wide-spreading; some have golden fall color, others tend toward orange, copper, or even red; some are straight-boled, and others crooked. If this tree varies similarly in disease resistance, structural integrity, and insect resistance, then desirable strains should be sought out, clonally propagated, and offered to a waiting public.

I have a fondness for other "junk" trees as well. The Lombardy poplar (*Populus nigra* 'Italica') forms a stately narrow spire, growing to 80 ft (24 m) in 20 years, and then it is usually taken by cytospora canker. The white poplar (*P. alba*) also has a fastigiate cultivar, 'Pyramidalis', the Bolleana Poplar, that is not as narrow but is tidier and longer lived than the Lombardy poplar. The cultivar and the species have maple-shaped leaves that are silvery gray underneath, and they show excellent fall color. The trunk is superb; white in youth, it becomes black at the base with age, creating a striking contrast that is particularly effective in winter. This beautiful tree has an unmatched propensity to sucker, although one has to admit that the groves it forms are lovely.

Judging by the popularity of the Lombardy and white poplars, there seems an obvious need to find or develop other fastigiate strains that are more disease resistant, longer lived, and less prone to sucker than typical *Populus* trees. Given these poplars' willingness to hybridize, and given the ease with which they can be propagated asexually (including by anther and ovule culture), the creation of such trees is a distinct possibility.

The cottonwoods suffer from many of the same problems as these poplars. Structural weakness and early senescence are particularly damning in trees that reach the herculean proportions that some of these do. The eastern cottonwood (*Populus deltoides*), for example, can reach a height of over 115 ft (35 m) with a 7-ft (2-m) diameter bole. Female trees present another nuisance factor: enormous quantities of seeds that are airborne on cottony appendages. In regions like the Great Plains of the United States and Canada, however, where quick shade is a near necessity, where soils are usually shallow and alkaline, and where gales rake the land and temperatures fall below −20°F (−28°C), not much else will serve as well as the cottonwoods. Furthermore, these trees are supremely majestic, as imposing as white oak (*Quercus alba*, in the family Fagaceae), and the fall color is a brilliant yellow, more reliable than that of quaking aspen (*P. tremuloides*).

Varieties of the plains cottonwood (*Populus sargentii*) have been selected that are cottonless and structurally sound. Others have been selected for altitude hardiness. In China, poplars have been selected for fast, sturdy, straight growth, and then propa-

gated by anther culture, yielding a completely homozygous cottonless clone. Much more work needs to be done with these trees,
however—their potential usefulness for others in the genus war-
rants it.

Salix Willow

Salix is a large genus, with some 400 members widely distributed in temperate regions. Included are grand trees to nearly 100
ft (30 m) and contorted alpine shrubs barely 2 ft (0.6 m) tall. Some,
such as the pussy willow (*Salix caprea*) and *S. discolor*, are grown
for their beautiful, long-lasting catkins, whereas others, like the
white willow (*S. alba*), are grown for the extraordinary red or gold
coloring of their stems. The corkscrew or dragon's-claw willow
(*S. matsudana* 'Tortuosa') and the globe willow (*S. matsudana* 'Um-
braculifera'), among others, are grown for their highly distinctive
habit. Of course, the weeping willows—*S. babylonica*, *S.* ×*blanda* (a
S. babylonica × *S. fragilis* hybrid), and their various hybrids and cultivars—are famed for their grace and have been treasured as
waterside features for thousands of years. There is still more to
recommend this vast genus of trees. Willows are fast-growing—
about as fast-growing as any hardy tree—and most are tolerant
of a variety of soil conditions, acid or sweet. Moisture is appreciated, but many willows are fairly drought tolerant.

Willows do have problems, however, and the big trees among
them have big problems. They pay for their rapid growth by being
weak-wooded, structurally unsound, and short-lived, and they
suffer many of the same plagues (pests, disease) as the others in
the family.

As with the poplars, there does not seem to be a quick and easy
solution for the many problems that afflict willows. Crosses, even
wide ones, that would serve to eliminate the flaws are not imme-
diately apparent, but maybe the development of sturdier, disease-
resistant strains can be hastened by *in vitro* selection and anther or
ovule culture. The poplars and willows are a highly adaptable and
varied lot, and there is no doubt that they will continue to be
among our most useful and popular trees and shrubs, especially if
improvements can be made.

SAPINDACEAE

Soapberry family   144 genera, 1325 species

GENERA DISCUSSED   *Koelreuteria* • *Xanthoceras*

The Sapindaceae are thought to be very closely related to the buckeye family (Hippocastanaceae), and the two trees of particular merit in the Sapindaceae family—the golden rain tree (*Koelreuteria paniculata*) and the yellowhorn (*Xanthoceras sorbifolium*) (Plate 65)—are mentioned in the discussion of the Hippocastanaceae.

SARRACENIACEAE

Pitcher Plant family 3 genera, 15 species

GENERA DISCUSSED *Darlingtonia* • *Sarracenia*

Wondrously adapted and uniquely shaped, pitcher plants are both fascinating and beautiful. The Sarraceniaceae are carnivorous plants that derive their nourishment by dining on insects—and their form follows their function. Their leaves are rolled lengthwise into pitcherlike structures, and in these vessels the plants prepare a brew of water and digestive juices. The lip of the pitcher exudes stuff that attracts insects, and the slippery inside surface of the leaf and the downward pointing hairs unseat the hapless prey, causing it to fall into the liquid and preventing it from climbing out.

Darlingtonia Cobra Lily
Rearing itself up to a height of 2 ft (0.6 m), the cobra lily (*Darlingtonia californica*) has a forked appendage that looks like a snake's tongue. The hood of this plant cobra is tesselated with translucent spots. The purplish red blossoms nod on shepherd's-crook stems up to 4 ft (1.2 m) in height. It is a kind of "beauty-and-the-beast" design, although with much more beauty in it than beast. The plant is found in northern California and Oregon and is hardy to at least zone 7.

Sarracenia Pitcher Plant PLATE 66
The pitcher plants of the genus *Sarracenia* are found along much of the eastern coast of the United States. There are eight species, many of which hybridize freely, and two of the most common are also two of the most beautiful.
The yellow huntsman's horn (*Sarracenia flava*) is the tallest of the genus, reaching a stately 2 ft (0.6 m), with a gently tapering form that justifies its common name; it is also commonly known as yellow trumpet. The yellow blossoms can span 5 in (13 cm). The plant is native along the southeastern coast of the United States from Florida to Virginia, sometimes in vast numbers.
Sarracenia purpurea, the purple pitcher plant (try saying that ten times quickly), is found along the Atlantic coast from New Jer-

sey to Newfoundland and is hardy to zone 4 at least. *Sarracenia purpurea*, also known as the common pitcher plant or huntsman's cap, is less stately than the others in the genus, but its appearance is more robust and sculptural, forming rosettes of stout pitchers to 10 in (25 cm) tall. Often, depending on the variety and the location, they are suffused with a deep reddish purple. The 2-in (5-cm) flowers, too, are suffused with this color, and they tilt downward at the top of 10-in (25-cm) stems. The popularity of purple pitcher plants as terrarium plants testifies to their requirements: they need acid soil, considerable moisture, salt-free water, and some humidity, conditions often met along a pond or stream.

Even in gardens with water features, however, one seldom sees a display of pitcher plants. Why? Given the extraordinary appearance of *Sarracenia* and the current interest in native plants, this lack of favor is inexplicable. Maybe these plants are more difficult to grow than one might expect knowing their wide range and their good performance in terraria. On the other hand, perhaps all that these plants need to increase their popularity is a good publicist.

Given the genus's proclivity to hybridize, there might be a chance to enhance the garden merit and adaptability of *Sarracenia*. Cell suspension culture might be used to select strains that are more salt tolerant. Of course, the promise of strikingly different forms and colors in both leaves and flowers is there. It is an unusual opportunity for lovers of the unusual.

SCROPHULARIACEAE

Figwort family   222 genera, 4450 species

GENERA DISCUSSED   *Antirrhinum • Calceolaria • Castilleja • Hebe •*
Isoplexis • Paulownia • Pedicularis • Veronica

OTHER ORNAMENTAL GENERA   *Digitalis • Penstemon • Verbascum*

The figwort family is a large one. Included among its members is an astonishing variety of annuals, perennials, shrubs, vines, and trees, many of extraordinary beauty and garden importance. The great diversity suggests all sorts of hybrids that might further expand the usefulness of the Scrophulariaceae, but only a few will be considered here.

Antirrhinum Snapdragon
The snapdragon (*Antirrhinum*) is one of the most popular of all bedding plants. Eight-inch (20-cm) dwarfs and 3-ft (0.9-m) giants are found within this genus, as well as all sizes in between. The curiously formed flowers, with the snapping lip that gives the plant its common name, are to be had in white, yellow, orange, red, and violet, as well as bicolored patterns, in singles and doubles. Usually grown as an annual, the snapdragon does have a tendency to reseed even in colder regions, and it shows some perennial leanings on occasion. As a hybridizing partner of some of the other figworts, *Antirrhinum* has a great deal to offer and a great deal to gain.

Calceolaria Pouch Flower
Calceolaria offers some of the most curiously beautiful flowers to be found in the garden—pouched flowers that look a bit like slipper orchids. In *Calceolaria biflora* 'John Innes' the flowers are yellow, spotted purple, and nearly 2 in (5 cm) across, and they are borne from late June through much of July on plants about 4 in (10 cm) tall. Given moist peaty soil in partial shade, this plant will survive in zone 4 to zone 10. In my garden it is a reluctant grower and a reluctant bloomer; maybe this is good in that it accentuates the precious quality of the plant's beauty. But most gardeners who grow it always want more of it. Perhaps a shot of polyploidy would yield more vigor and sturdier, more floriferous plants.

Maybe crossing it with a strong-growing *Penstemon* or *Veronica* would do the job without violating the extraordinary flower shape. Even an approximation is likely to be highly desirable.

Castilleja Indian Paintbrush   PLATE 67
The paintbrushes (*Castilleja*) are among my favorite high-country plants. They are usually found growing as tight clusters of perfectly vertical stems 1.5 to 2 ft (0.45 to 0.6 m) in height. The upper part of each stem sports a cylinder of bracts, much like that borne by the shrimp plant (*Justicia brandegeana*), but it is carried upright and colored scarlet, pink, white, or green depending on the species. Castillejas remain showy for most of the summer. The yellow paintbrush (*Castilleja sulphurea*) has pale greenish yellow bracts and makes an excellent companion to the purple bergamot (*Monarda fistulosa*), a zone 4 perennial herb often found nearby in the wild.

Strikingly singular in appearance, the Indian paintbrushes would be showpieces in any garden. Unfortunately, they are very difficult to obtain from commercial sources. Some say that they are difficult to grow, but other gardeners maintain that that is not the case if the soil is both fast draining and moisture retentive. Castillejas readily form interspecific hybrids, and one has to wonder if all that is needed is the proper selection of wild clones. If not, one might try to cross a paintbrush with other Scrophulariaceae, like a foxglove (*Digitalis*), a penstemon, or a veronica, and hope to get a more garden-amenable plant while retaining some of the unique character of the paintbrush.

Hebe
Hebe is a genus of evergreen shrubs thought to be closely related to *Veronica*, and it is native to New Zealand and Australia. There are a number of species and cultivars ranging from barely 1 ft (0.3 m) to over 5 ft (1.5 m) in height. The hebes' tiny evergreen leaves and their tolerance to shearing make these plants useful as hedges, and their veronicalike inflorescence in white, purple, blue, and near pink recommend their use as specimen shrubs. In North America they are grown mostly on the Pacific coast, where the moderate temperatures seem to suit them perfectly. On the other hand, at least two hebes do perfectly well in zone 5, on dryish sites, in ordinary soil, in full sun or partial shade: *Hebe buchananii*

'Minor' and *H. pinguifolia*. Both of these plants are about 8 in (20 cm) tall. The *H. buchananii* cultivar has green leaves and racemes of blue flowers, and *H. pinguifolia* has silver leaves edged red and white racemes.

What opportunities these hebes present: a new race of broadleaf evergreen shrubs and shrublets for the regions that need them most. Even a new race of broadleaved semievergreens would be enthusiastically welcomed. Bringing about these new treats might best be achieved by hybridizing the hebes with veronicas. In particular, *Veronica pectinata* might allow the retention of leaves, whereas other veronicas, such as 'Sunny Border Blue', might be chosen to increase not only hardiness and adaptability but floriferousness and duration of bloom as well.

Isoplexis

Isoplexis canariensis is a spectacular evergreen subshrub with 4-ft (1.2-m) inflorescences, the last 1 ft (0.3 m) of the spike bearing coppery yellow flowers. Each flower has two prominent lips, giving it the appearance of a banner. The plant's specific name refers to its place of origin, the Canary Islands, and hints at its intolerance to cold below zone 9. But the Scrophulariaceae are a family with many notably hardy members. In particular, a zone 3 veronica like 'White Icicle' might supply hardiness while not sacrificing all the orange color of the *Isoplexis*. Some taxonomists consider *Isoplexis* to be *Digitalis*, and this suggests attempting a cross with a foxglove, say *Digitalis ambigua*, to increase hardiness.

Paulownia Empress Tree

The figwort family does contain a proper tree, the empress tree (*Paulownia tomentosa*), and in bloom it is as spectacular as any in the temperate zone. It grows to 50 ft (15 m) in height and width, and 1-ft (0.3-m) long panicles of 2-in (5-cm) violet flowers borne in spring are the tree's crowning glory. Unfortunately, the empress tree is hardy only into zone 5, and that may be overly optimistic. The flower buds are set in the fall and are prone to frost damage. The tree is notoriously weak-wooded, and it loses significant parts of itself in heavy winds or snowstorms. Moreover, many think that its leaves are too coarse for most landscape designs.

Suppose that we can cross a veronica or a hebe with the empress tree. Would woodiness prevail? Would we get a tree or a shrub? Would the hybrid be less likely to break up in a storm than its tree parent? Would the new creation be hardy in zone 4? The answers might be of interest to many gardeners in regions below zone 5.

Pedicularis Elephantella, Little Elephant Head, Lousewort PLATE 68
I have found elephantella (*Pedicularis groenlandica*) on droughty alpine tundra and on wet meadows of the montane region. Variable in height to about 16 in (41 cm), it bears spikes of 5-in (13-cm) scarlet blossoms, each blossom resembling an elephant's head—complete with big ears and a trunk.

Why elephantella is not among the top ten garden plants in popularity is a mystery to me. Maybe it is difficult to grow away from its high-country habitat. I know of no commercial source for this plant, but it can be seen at the Denver Botanic Gardens, in Denver, Colorado.

Can we salvage *Pedicularis groenlandica*'s glorious color and extraordinarily shaped blossoms on a more adaptable hybrid? Maybe *Penstemon campanulatus* 'Garnet' or *Veronica spicata* 'Red Fox' can provide the vehicle. Of course, what we want is not just the color of the elephantella to be preserved but also the shape of its blossoms, and that may require several generations of breeding.

Veronica Speedwell
The genus *Veronica* has enormous popularity, and new cultivars and hybrids appear every year. I do want to mention in particular, however, the creeping veronica (*Veronica repens*), a zone 4, 3-in (7.5-cm) tall spreader with enormous potential as a groundcover. Its 0.25-in (0.5-cm) evergreen leaves remind one of another groundcover, baby tears (*Soleirolia soleirolii*). For several weeks in midspring, creeping veronica covers itself in a haze of bright blue or white 0.25-in (0.5-cm) flowers. It tolerates heat, cold, moisture, drought, miserable soil, full sun, and considerable shade. It is a spreader, both by stolons and by seed—a vigorous, irrepressible spreader of weedlike tenacity. Creeping veronica competes successfully with bluegrass and will slowly, inexorably replace it. Short of driving a stake through its green heart, *Veronica repens* cannot be eradicated.

Tame this weedy plant, at least a bit, but do not curb all of its spreading tendencies, for creeping veronica is potentially one of the most useful groundcovers, particularly in areas too hot or too droughty for bluegrass. Select dense, short-growing clones of controllable vigor. Maybe polyploidy will make *Veronica repens* stockier, shorter, and more floriferous. Maybe a mutagen will render it sterile. All creeping veronica needs is a bit of domestication.

TAXODIACEAE

Cypress family   10 genera, 14 species

GENERA DISCUSSED   *Metasequoia* • *Sciadopitys* • *Sequoia* •
Sequoiadendron • *Taxodium*

OTHER ORNAMENTAL GENUS   *Cryptomeria*

The Taxodiaceae are a small family containing some very large trees. The tallest of all trees is the coast redwood (*Sequoia sempervirens*) and the most massive tree with a single trunk is the giant redwood (*Sequoiadendron giganteum*), and both are members of the cypress family. The coast redwood reaches a height of 365 ft (111 m) and the giant redwood a girth of 80 ft (24 m), both a bit large for the average garden. Smaller members of the family, on the other hand, do make excellent landscape plants.

Metasequoia Dawn Redwood, *Taxodium* Bald Cypress,
Swamp Cypress

Each of the genera *Metasequoia* and *Taxodium* contains only a single species. The dawn redwood (*Metasequoia glyptostroboides*) and the bald cypress (*Taxodium distichum*) are tall-growing (to 100 ft (30 m) and 70 ft (21 m) respectively), zone 4 hardy deciduous conifers. Both show modest autumn tints of tan, although the bald cypress sometimes colors up in soft yellow or tannish red. New foliage in the spring is particularly lovely on both trees: feathery soft and bright yellow-green. They are both fairly adaptable, and even the swamp cypress can tolerate some dryness in the atmosphere as well as the soil. Neither tree is very popular, however; perhaps, looking like conifers, these trees are expected to behave like conifers and keep their leaves throughout the year.

But suppose the dawn redwood or bald cypress can be crossed with the coast redwood (*Sequoia sempervirens*). Might the result have the incomparable grace of the coast redwood, with some additional hardiness derived from the *Metasequoia* or *Taxodium* as well as from hybrid vigor? If so, millions of gardeners would be able to grow an evergreen redwoodlike tree for the first time.

Sciadopitys Umbrella Pine
  The umbrella pine (*Sciadopitys verticillata*) is the only living member of its ancient genus. This very different evergreen is a zone 4 tree that grows to 30 ft (9 m) in height. Its distinctive leaves are up to 5 in (13 cm) long and 0.2 in (0.5 cm) wide, borne in whorls of twenty-four. It is these whorls of relatively wide and exceptionally long leaves that give the tree its extraordinary appearance—umbrella-like—and its common name. Although it is hardy in zone 4, the umbrella pine requires free-draining acid soil, and it is not happy in windy sites. Were it not for these special requirements, umbrella pines would be seen across the United States. Maybe the dawn redwood (*Metasequoia glyptostroboides*) can be enlisted in a cross to create a more adaptable tree. But if the character of the umbrella pine's foliage is lost, then so is the point of the cross.

Sequoia Coast Redwood, *Sequoiadendron* Giant Redwood   PLATE 69
  The giant redwood or big tree (*Sequoiadendron giganteum*) is hardy into zone 6. Two 8-ft (2.5-m) giant redwoods were grown from seed in the zone 5 vegetable garden of Professor Bill Jones in Boulder, Colorado. After 15 years, however, they began to lose significant bits of themselves to every Boulder winter, until they died. Although fairly attractive, these shorter versions of *Sequoiadendron giganteum* could easily be mistaken for stout junipers, and I see no reason to push their popularity to colder climates except as conversation pieces.
  The coast redwood (*Sequoia sempervirens*), on the other hand, is magnificent at every stage of its development, from sapling to old age. The young ones, at a height of 15 to 20 ft (4.5 to 6 m), are particularly appealing, with an upright grace that makes spruce (*Picea*, in the family Pinaceae) seem crude and hemlock (*Tsuga*) seem sloppy. The tree shows a great deal of variability, but its lack of hardiness beyond zone 7 restricts its use. Nevertheless, two genera in the family Taxodiaceae, *Metasequoia* and *Taxodium*, present a possibility for creating redwoodlike trees for northern climates.

THEACEAE

Tea family   28 genera, 250 species

GENERA DISCUSSED   *Camellia • Franklinia • Stewartia*

The tea family is mostly tropical and subtropical, and it is indeed the family to which the Asiatic shrub that yields the tea of commerce belongs—of no concern to us here, except that the lovers of that genteel brew might want to know. However, a few of the Theaceae are of interest to those of us concerned with the ornamental side of the family—trees and shrubs of renowned beauty that are just out of reach of most of our gardens.

Camellia

The garden-worthy camellias (*Camellia japonica, C. sasanqua,* and many hybrids and cultivars) are large shrubs or small trees (6 to 20 ft (1.8 to 6 m)) with superb evergreen foliage and exquisite blossoms. The flowers, 5 in (13 cm) across, come in a variety of colors from white to pink and red, streaked or plain, casual or formal, single or double. One or two blossoms and a sprig of its own foliage set in a narrow, white vase makes a crisp, clean, elegant statement that will lend grace to any room. The plant itself is rather stiff and formal, however, and the flowers are formal to the point of appearing artificial. Nevertheless, gardeners in zone 8 (maybe 7 for some varieties) through zone 9 adore camellias, and hundreds of varieties are known, grown, and cherished. In general, *Camellia* needs acid soil and an even supply of moisture at the roots. It is bothered a bit by various insects and diseases, but given the temperature and soil restrictions, this plant is fairly dependable.

Franklinia

The genus *Franklinia* has only one member, the Franklin tree (*Franklinia alatamaha*). Benjamin Franklin is the tree's namesake and he grew it on his own estate, but even back in the 18th century the tree was quite rare in its native Georgia, and now it is no longer found in the wild at all.

Sometimes a small tree to 20 ft (6 m), the Franklin tree usually tends to multistemmed shrubbiness considerably shorter than that. Some say it is zone 4 hardy, others say zone 5; some claim it favors acid soil, others say sweet; some say it is easy to grow, others say it is difficult. Whatever the case, far inland this tree is seldom seen.

What, then, makes this species so desirable? Surely, the splendid yellow-orange-scarlet fall color is a factor, and its lengthy summer-to-fall display of 3-in (7.5-cm), yellow-centered white blossoms must be another popular trait. It is a plant to grace any garden fortunate enough to satisfy its requirements.

Stewartia   PLATE 70

Those looking for small- to moderate-sized trees with four-season appeal should consider the stewartias (*Stewartia koreana, S. pseudocamellia, S. monadelpha*, and other species and hybrids). They range in height from 10 to 40 ft (3 to 12 m), show spectacular, scarlet, red, and purple fall color, and bear yellow-centered white flowers over a long season in early summer. The bark, flaking in patches to show jigsawlike patterns in grays, tans, and browns, is one of the most outstanding features of *Stewartia*, particularly striking in *S. koreana* and *S. pseudocamellia*. These trees need soil on the acidic side and demand good drainage. Some list them as hardy in zone 4, but zone 5 is a safer bet, and 6 is safer still.

The three genera of Theaceae discussed here offer such outstanding ornamental properties over such a long season that it is surprising that so little has been done to make them more adaptable and available. Unfortunately, I know of no northern clan members that might contribute some cold hardiness and more soil tolerance to the project, but *in vitro* selection might facilitate the search. Maybe hybridization between *Stewartia* species or between other genera of Theaceae would bring a measure of hybrid vigor which could translate into increased hardiness and adaptability. Although strategies for developing such plants may seem rather limited, the potential benefit for gardeners is enormous, for these are trees of singular beauty.

Map of Hardiness Zones for the United States

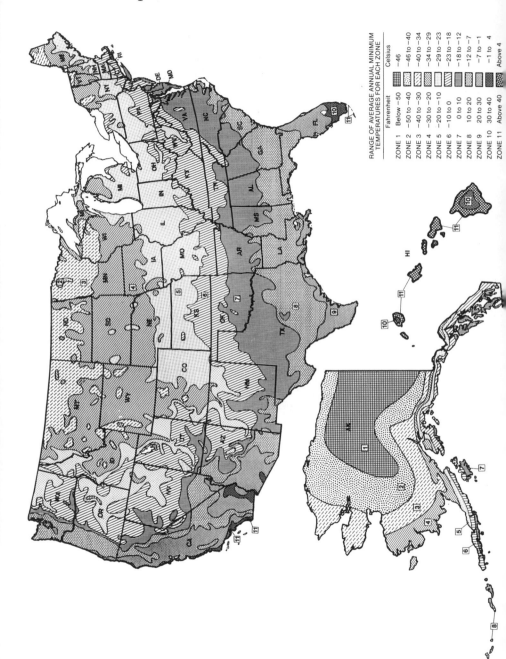

RANGE OF AVERAGE ANNUAL MINIMUM
TEMPERATURES FOR EACH ZONE

	Fahrenheit	Celsius
ZONE 1	Below −50	−46
ZONE 2	−50 to −40	−46 to −40
ZONE 3	−40 to −30	−40 to −34
ZONE 4	−30 to −20	−34 to −29
ZONE 5	−20 to −10	−29 to −23
ZONE 6	−10 to 0	−23 to −18
ZONE 7	0 to 10	−18 to −12
ZONE 8	10 to 20	−12 to −7
ZONE 9	20 to 30	−7 to −1
ZONE 10	30 to 40	−1 to 4
ZONE 11	Above 40	Above 4

Map of Hardiness Zones for Europe

HARDINESS ZONE
TEMPERATURE RANGES

°F	ZONE	°C
below −50	1	below −45
−50 to −40	2	−45 to −40
−40 to −30	3	−40 to −34
−30 to −20	4	−34 to −29
−20 to −10	5	−29 to −23
−10 to 0	6	−23 to −17
0 to 10	7	−17 to −12
10 to 20	8	−12 to −7
20 to 30	9	−7 to −1
30 to 40	10	−1 to 5

Bibliography

The following is a short list of books that I have found particularly helpful. Excluded from the list are the numerous regional guides to flora that were used in the process of compiling the Wishlist; such guides are readily available at many bookstores and nurseries.

Armitage, A. M. 1989. *Herbaceous Perennial Plants*. Varsity Press, distributed by Timber Press.

Bock, G., and J. Marsh, eds. 1988. *Applications of Plant Cell and Tissue Culture*. John Wiley and Sons.

Brockman, F. 1968. *Trees of North America*. Golden Press.

Capon, B. 1990. *Botany for Gardeners*. Timber Press.

Chen, Z., et al., eds. 1990. *Handbook of Plant Cell Culture*. Vol. 6, *Perennial Crops*. McGraw-Hill.

Clark, D. E. 1983. *New Western Garden Book*. Sunset Books.

Clausen, R. R., and N. H. Ekstrom. 1989. *Perennials for American Gardens*. Random House.

Courtright, G. 1988. *Trees and Shrubs for Temperate Climates*. 3rd ed. Timber Press.

De Wolf, G. P., ed. 1987. *Taylor's Guide to Shrubs*. Houghton Mifflin.

————, ed. 1988. *Taylor's Guide to Trees*. Houghton Mifflin.

Dirr, M. A. 1990. *Manual of Woody Landscape Plants*. 4th ed. Stipes.

Graf, A. B. 1981. *Tropica: Color Cyclopedia of Exotic Plants and Trees*. 2nd ed. Roehrs.

Harding, J., et al., eds. 1991. *Genetics and Breeding of Ornamental Species*. Kluwer.

Köhlein, F., and P. Menzel. 1994. *Color Encyclopedia of Garden Plants and Habitats*. Timber Press.

Kung, S., et al., eds. 1989. *Plant Biotechnology*. Butterworth-Heinemann.

Mabberley, D. J. 1990. *The Plant-Book*. Cambridge University Press.

Poor, J. M., ed. 1984. *Plants That Merit Attention*. Vol. 1, *Trees*. Timber Press.

Porter, C. L. 1967. *Taxonomy of Flowering Plants*. 2nd ed. W. H. Freeman.

Scott, G. H. 1982. *Bulbs: How to Select, Grow, and Enjoy*. H P Books.

Snyder, L. C. 1980. *Trees and Shrubs for Northern Gardens*. University of Minnesota Press.

Sowers, A. E., ed. 1987. *Cell Fusion*. Plenum.

Stuessy, T. F. 1990. *Plant Taxonomy*. Columbia University Press.

Tilney-Bassett, R. A. E. 1986. *Plant Chimeras*. Edward Arnold.

Vasil I. K., ed. 1986. *Cell Culture and Somatic Cell Genetics of Plants*. Vol. 3, *Plant Regeneration and Genetic Variability*. Academic Press.

Woodland, D. W. 1991. *Contemporary Plant Systematics*. Prentice Hall.

Wyman, D. 1969. *Shrubs and Vines for American Gardens*. 2nd ed. Macmillan.

————. 1990. *Trees for American Gardens*. 3rd ed. Macmillan.

Index of Plant Names

Numbers in boldface refer to plate numbers.